THE 1994 ELECTIONS TO THE EUROPEAN PARLIAMENT

Edited by Juliet Lodge

Professor of European Politics
and
Director of the Centre for European Studies,
University of Leeds

PINTER

For Keri-Michèle, David, Chris and Annabel

PINTER
A Cassell Imprint
Wellington House, 125 Strand, London WC2R 0BB, England

First published in Great Britain 1996

© Juliet Lodge and Contributors 1996

British Library Cataloguing-in-Publication Data

A CIP catalogue record for this book is available from the British Library.

ISBN 1 85567 280 4 (Hardback)
  1 85567 281 2 (Paperback)

Printed and bound in Great Britain by
Biddles Ltd, Guildford and King's Lynn

Contents

Contents

List of Figures

List of Tables

Abbreviations

A	Austria
AD	Adhérent direct (direct membership of UDF)
AGALEV	Anders Gaan Leven
AN	National Alliance
AOV	Alters Verbond
ARE	Alliance radicale européenne (Radical European Alliance)
B	Belgium
BNG	Bloque Nacionalista Galego
CAP	Common Agricultural Policy
CCD	Christian Democratic Centre (I)
CD	Centruum Democraterne
CDA	Christen Demokratisch Appel
CDS	Centre des Démocrates Sociaux
CDS	Centro Democratico Social
CDS	Centro Democratico y Social (E)
CDU	Christlich Democratische Union
CFSP	Common Foreign and Security Policy
CNJA	Conseil national des jeunes agriculteurs
CSCE	Conference on Security and Cooperation in Europe
CSP	Confederation of Socialist Parties
CSV	Chreschtlech Sozial Vollekspartei
CVP	Christelijke Volkspartij
CiU	Convergència i Unio
D	Germany
D'66	Demokraten 66
DC	Democrazia Cristiana
DG	Dei Greng
DIANA	Centre Right Greek Party
DK	Denmark
DL	Democratic Left
E	Spain
EBRD	European Bank for Reconstruction and Development

EC	European Community
ECOLO	Mouvement 'Ecolo' – 'les verts'
ECSC	European Coal and Steel Community
ECU	European Currency Unit
EDA	European Democratic Alliance
EDN	Europe des Nations
ELDR	European Liberal, Democratic and Reformist Parties
EMS	European Monetary System
EMU	Economic and Monetary Union
EN	Europe of Nations
EP	European Parliament
EPEN	Ethnikí Politikí Énossis
EPP	European People's Party
ERA	European Radical Alliance
ERM	Exchange Rate Mechanism
ETA	Eustkadi ta Askatsuna
EU	European Union
EUL/NGL	Confederal Group of the European United Left – Nordic Green Left
EUT	Draft treaty establishing the European Union (1984)
F	France
FE	Forza Europa
FF	Fianna Fail
FG	Fine Gael
FI	Forza Italia
FIN	Finland
FN	Front National
FYROM	Former Yugoslav Republic of Macedonia
GAP	Greng Alternativ Partei
GB	Great Britain
GE	Génération Ecologie
GLEI	Greng Lëscht fir Ecologesch Initiativ
GLS	Group for Luxembourg Sovereignty
GPV	Gereformeerd Politiek Verbond
GR	Greece
HB	Herri Batasuna
I	Italy
IGC	Inter-Governmental Conference
IMF	International Monetary Fund
Ind	Non-attached MEPs
IRE	Ireland
IU	Isquierda Unida
JHA	Justice and Home Affairs pillar of the TEU
KKE	Kommounistiko Komma tis Elladas
KPL	Kommunistesch Partei Letzëburg

L	Luxembourg
LN	Northern League
LSAP	Letzeburger Sozialistisch Arbechterpartei
MEP	Member of the European Parliament
MPT	Movimento do Partido da Terra
MRG	Mouvement des radicaux de gauche
MRPP	Movimento para a Reconstrução do Partido Proletariado
MUT	Movimento para a Unidade dos Trabalhadores
NATO	North Atlantic Treaty Organization
NB	National Bewegong
ND	New Democracy
NOMP	Independent and Neutral Human Rights Party
NWP	Natuurwetpartij
P	Portugal
PASOK	Panellinio Sosialistiko Kinima
PCF	Parti communiste français
PCI	Partito Communista Italiano
PD	Progressive Democrats
PDS	Party of Democratic Socialists
PDS	Progressive Democrats (I)
PES	Party of European Socialists
PLI	Partito Liberale Italiano
POL.A	Politiki Anoixi
PP	Pardido Popular
PPM	Pardido Popular Monárquico
PR	Parti républicain
PRI	Partito Reppublicano Italiano
PRL	Parti Réformateur Liberal
PS	Parti socialiste
PSC	Parti Social Chrétien
PSD	Pardido Social Democrata
PSD	Parti social démocrate (member of UDF)
PSDI	Partito Socialista Democratico Italiano
PSI	Partito Socialista Italiano
PSOE	Pardido Socialista Obrero Español
PSR	Pardido Socialita Revolucionário
PvDA	Partij van de Arbeid
PVV	Partij voor Vrijheid en Vooruitgang
RDE	Rassemblement des démocrates européens (European Democratic Alliance)
RGB	Rood Groene Beweging
RPF	Reformatorische Politieke Federatie
RPR	Rassemblement pour la République (Gaullists)
S	Sweden
SEA	Single European Act

SGP	Staatkundig Gereformeerde Partij
SNP	Scottish National Party
SP	Socialist Party (Flanders)
SPD	Social Democratic Party (D)
SYN	Synaspismos coalition
TEU	Treaty on European Union (Maastricht Treaty)
UDF	Union pour la démocratie française
UEL	United European Left
UK	United Kingdom
VLD	Vlaamse Liberalen en Demokraten
VU	Volksunie
WEU	Western European Union
WOW	Waardig Ouder Worden

The Contributors

Philip Daniels is a lecturer in Politics at the University of Newcastle upon Tyne. He has published widely on Italian politics and European politics. He is currently co-writing a book on parties, elections and political change in Italy.

Bart van Deelen is Research Associate of the Centre for European Union Studies, University of Hull.

Kevin Featherstone holds the Jean Monnet chair in European Integration Studies at the University of Bradford. His books include: *Socialist Parties and European Integration* (1988); *The US and the EC in the 1990s* (co-author, 1993); *The Successful Manager's Guide to 1992* (1990); *Political Change in Greece* (co-editor, 1987); and *Greece in a Changing Europe* (co-editor, 1995).

John Gaffney is Professor of French and European Politics at Keele University. Among his books are: *The French Left and the Fifth Republic* (1989); *The Language of Political Leadership in Contemporary France* (co-editor, 1995); *Political Parties and European Union* (editor, 1995); and *Presidentialism in France: The Elections of 1995* (co-editor, 1996).

John Gibbons is senior lecturer in Politics at Manchester Metropolitan University. His research interests cover aspects of Spanish and Irish public policy. He has published articles and chapters on regional and agricultural policy issues.

Simon Green is a researcher at the Institute for German Studies, University of Birmingham. He is engaged in a research project on policy towards foreigners in united Germany and has recently written on the 1994 Federal election in Germany and on 'sleaze' in German politics.

Andreas Kintis is Research Assistant at the Centre for European Studies, University of Leeds. He was formerly a teaching assistant in the Centre for European Studies, University of Hull and founding Editor of its newsletter, *Insight*.

Christophe Lécureuil is a European public affairs consultant at Government Policy Consultants, Brussels. A graduate in political science and international relations from Paris X and Reading Universities, he previously worked as a researcher for the Political and Institutional Affairs Division of the European Parliament and published studies on the right of interference and the common foreign and security policy.

Charles Lees is currently researching the processes of coalition formation and maintenance in the German *Länder*. He is a member of the executive committee of the Association for the Study of German Politics and recently co-organized the Association's inaugural graduate conference. He has written on coalition theory, the PDS, the 1994 Euro-elections and environmental politics and policy.

Juliet Lodge is Professor of European Politics, Jean Monnet Professor of European Integration, Director of the Centre for European Studies at the University of Leeds, England; Director of the Jean Monnet Group of Experts on the 1996 IGC on the EU; and formerly Visiting Professor at the Vrije Universitet Brussels. She was European Woman of Europe 1992. Her research focuses on the European Union, EU institutions, transparency and democratic legitimacy, judicial cooperation and foreign affairs. Among her most recent books are: *The EC and the Challenge of the Future* (1993). She is currently working on the social policy, citizenship, external and internal security, and the EU and the IGC.

Jose M Magone is lecturer in European Politics and a member of the Centre for European Union Studies, University of Hull. He was a Robert Schuman scholar at the European Parliament in 1990. Among his recent publications are 'Portugal' in John Loughlin (ed), *Southern European Studies Guide* (1993) and 'Party Factionalism and Democratization in Small New Southern European Democracies: Some Comparative Findings of the Portuguese and Greek Cases (1974–82)' in *Democratization* (1995).

Lee Miles is Senior Lecturer in European Studies at the University of Humberside. He is Chief Editor of the *Occasional Papers in Nordic Studies* and the Editor of *The European Union and the Nordic Countries* (Routledge, 1996).

Edward Moxon-Browne is Jean Monnet Professor in European Integration at the University of Limerick. He was Reader in Politics at Queens University Belfast until December 1992. His main research interests are European citizenship, Irish membership of the EU, and the ethnic roots of political violence. Among his publications are *Nation, Class and Creed in Northern Ireland* (1983) and *Political Change in Spain* (1989).

Hans Jørgen Nielsen is lecturer at the Institute of Political Science, University of Copenhagen. His main field of work is in electoral behaviour and he has published on the Danish Maastricht referendums in 1992 and 1993 in *EF på Valg* (1993). He is also a columnist for the newspaper *Berlingske Tidende*.

Neill Nugent is Professor of Politics at Manchester Metropolitan University. He has written widely on different aspects of European politics and includes among his publications *The Government and Politics of the European Union* (1994). Editor of *The European Union: Annual Review of Activities*, his current research includes work on the EU Commission, a book on which is forthcoming.

Professor William Paterson is Director of the newly-established Institute for German Studies, University of Birmingham. He was formerly Professor of Politics at the University of Warwick before moving to Edinburgh in 1990 as Director of the Europa Institute. He also chaired the University Association for Contemporary European Studies from 1989 to 1994. Professor Paterson has written and edited very many books and articles on German and European themes. He is very active in Anglo–German relations and is a regular participant in the Königswinter Conference.

Susannah Verney completed her PhD on 'Panacea or Plague: Greek Political Parties and Accession to the EC 1974–9' at Kings College, London in 1994. She has authored or co-written several articles on Greek–EU relations and Greek politics. She is Honorary Visiting Research Fellow at the University of Bradford and Visiting Fellow in Mediterranean Politics at the University of Bristol.

Introduction: De-mythologizing the European Parliament

Juliet Lodge

The European Parliament (EP) was never designed or expected by the found-ing fathers of the European Community system to play a momentous role in the promotion of European integration. Originally imbued with very limited powers that were far from making it analogous to a national parliament in any member state, its predecessor was the Common Assembly of the European Coal and Steel Community (ECSC). It was given the task by the Treaty of Paris (1951) setting up the ECSC of drafting proposals for elections by direct universal suffrage in accordance with a uniform electoral procedure (Article 21(3)). The Rome treaties setting up the European Economic Community and European Atomic Energy Community (Euratom) contained similar provisions. The EP has accordingly drafted proposals for an electoral procedure to be used in all member states for Euro-elections which prescribes a degree of common-ality rather than a completely harmonized or single system. From the Dehousse report (1960) to the Seitlinger report (1982) and latterly the De Gucht report (1993), proportional representation (PR) has been advocated as a means of ensuring a reasonably accurate reflection of the proportion of the votes cast for a given candidate of a party and the proportion of seats won by that party in the EP. The system has not yet been adopted, however, because the United Kingdom government has vetoed it in the Council of Ministers which has to approve it. As a result, Euro-elections are conducted according to different national procedures (all a mix of PR except in Great Britain) which produce distortions in the ultimate make-up of the EP (Lodge, 1990; Lodge, 1985; Reif, 1985). This arises primarily because of the British system but also because states using PR have different electoral thresholds which mean that in some states (for example, Italy) it is possible for a candidate to secure election to the EP with less than 2 per cent of the votes cast whereas in others a 5 per cent barrier exists. The effect of the British system has been said to approxi-mate a 15 per cent electoral barrier.

Euro-elections are normally held on a Thursday or Sunday. Results are announced publicly after the last ballot box has closed on the Sunday. MEPs from national contingents form political groups to whom parliamentary rights, obligations, financial provision, privileges and positions are attached (Jacobs and Corbett, 1995). MEPs have their own Rules of Procedure, which they devise and amend themselves and, crucially, through the organization of parliamentary business, they are able to set their own agenda – a right not enjoyed by all national parliaments. The party groups play an information dissemination role in the elections (see Chapter 12) and have secured an increasing share of the EP's budget for this purpose since the first elections.

From the inception of the EP, the level of turnout has been used to justify an increase in the powers afforded the EP. The EP was not given legislative powers by the founding treaties. Its role was strictly advisory and supervisory. However, its members' conceptions as to the appropriate role a putative parliament should play in the evolving supranational organization led them to contest and overstep this limited role definition. The EP's role was and is contentious. Even though its powers were originally limited, there can be no doubt that the EP has had an important impact on the evolution in the EC's structures and policies, and that it has significantly advanced integration in a manner that many would associate with the emergence of a recognizable, decentralized and heterogeneous federal polity.

It is often but erroneously assumed that the Common Assembly was no more than a sop to federalists, an after-thought of little consequence. However, Jean Monnet's first speech to its members indicated that while he expected little interference with the work of the High Authority (predecessor of the Commission) from either the Council of Ministers (added at Dutch behest) or the Common Assembly, his views of the role that parliamentarians might perform in a supranational organization was in line with liberal democratic views concerning representation and control of the executive. He said:

> Within the limits of its jurisdiction your Assembly is sovereign. It is the first European Assembly vested with powers of decision. These responsibilities make you and us the representatives of the entire Community, and together the servants of its Institutions. . . . In the exercise of your mandate you are the representatives of the entire Community.
>   To preserve this sovereign character and the freedom of your decision we have called upon a strictly provisional and entirely independent secretariat, composed of the secretaries-general of the parliaments of our six countries and the clerk of the Consultative Assembly (of the Council of Europe) to prepare this first session. . . . At your January meeting, the High Authority will submit to you a general report on the situation of the Community. This report will be accompanied by a provisional budget which in some way is the first European budget and which includes the obligation to collect corresponding revenues, that is to say the first European tax.

Monnet went on to discuss the financing arrangements, the great importance he attached to ensuring that the High Authority was 'in step with' the Common Assembly, had free discussions with it as work progressed and regular meetings with a standing assembly committee:

> not to debate specific technical problems, but to get accustomed, both of us, to see Community problems in their entirety, and to oblige us, the High Authority, to explain to

you the conduct of policies over which the Treaty has given us control. We would then see, together with your committee, while the organization of the High Authority develops under the impact of its problems, what more complete form our collaboration shall take.[1]

In short, he envisaged a dynamic and pragmatic evolution of mutually beneficial links between the two institutions. The idea that both were involved in a common endeavour – while a great strength to the process of promoting European integration – was also seen by national governments and national parliaments as a potential threat to their autonomy and sovereignty.

The EP has traditionally been seen as a rival to national parliaments for the affection and loyalty of member states' citizens. National parliaments have been seen as the repository of popular sovereignty because the people have elected them directly. Consequently, the provision in the Rome Treaty establishing the European Economic Community which prescribed the direct election of the EP's members (MEPs) was seen by national governments as a direct threat to their sovereignty and was accordingly resisted until after the EC's first enlargement in 1973. Direct elections by universal suffrage in accordance with a common, but not uniform, electoral procedure was agreed in 1976. The first direct elections, originally scheduled for 1978, were postponed for a year because of delays by the member states in introducing national legislation to facilitate Euro-elections according, not to a uniform procedure as required by Article 138 of the Treaty but to different national provisions. The first elections took place in 1979 and have been held every five years since then.

Mobilizing the voters has been difficult for both political and technical reasons deriving from the absence of common electoral provisions. Rules governing eligibility to vote and stand in the elections (ranging from age, residence, nationality and simultaneous political posts criteria), opinion polls, exit polls, official campaign periods, political funding of parties and political advertising have all detracted from the idea of there being one election across the EC/EU to the EP (Lodge and Herman, 1982). Complications have been compounded by the strictly national, territorial distribution of seats which prevents cross-frontier constituency formation and which exacerbates the unequal ratio of voters to seats between the large and small member states.

Villified as impotent, irrelevant and a waste of time and money, the EP continues to receive arguably the worst press of all parliaments (which are often not separated in the public mind from their national government) within the EU. Its negative and poor image has often been seen as one of the main reasons why, over the years, turnout in the Euro-elections has been relatively low (see Table I.1). Indeed, opponents justified their objections to direct elections originally by the invisibility, intangibility and unintelligibility of its unelected predecessor (whose dual-mandated members were appointed from national parliaments by national governments). From the outset, some national parties and governments have contested the legitimacy and viability of the elections often by reference to their supposed pro-integration bias.

Table I.1 Turnout in Euro-elections 1979–94

State	1979	1984	1989	1994	Seats
Belgium	91.4	92.1	90.7	90.7	25[1]
Denmark	47.8	52.3	46.2	52.5	16
France	60.7	56.7	48.7	52.7	87[2]
Germany	65.7	56.8	62.3	60.1	99
Greece	–	77.2	79.9	71.2	25[3]
Ireland	63.6	47.6	68.3	44.0	15
Italy	84.9	83.4	81.5	74.8	87
Luxembourg	88.9	88.8	87.4	86.6	6
Netherlands	57.8	50.6	47.2	35.6	31[4]
Portugal	–	–	51.2	35.6	25[5]
Spain	–	–	54.6	60.0	64[6]
UK	32.3	32.6	36.2	36.4	87[7]
Average 6	74.9	71.4	69.6	66.8	
Average 12				58.5	567

Notes to Table I.1
1. 24 seats in 1989; 14 for Flanders; 10 for Wallonia and 1 for the German speaking region.
2. Like Germany, Italy and the UK, France had 81 seats until 1994.
3. Greece joined the EC in 1981, and first elected MEPs then on a 78.6% turnout with 24 seats until 1994.
4. 25 seats until 1994.
5. 24 seats until 1994. Turnout in the first Euro-elections in 1987 after EC accession in 1986 was 72.4%.
6. 60 seats until 1994. Turnout in the first Euro-elections in 1987 after EC accession in 1986 was 68.9%.
7. Turnout has been consistently higher in Northern Ireland (which uses PR to elect 3 MEPs) compared to Great Britain and was 56.9% in 1979, 64.5% in 1984; 48.8% in 1989 and 48.7% in 1994.

Such allegations have been replaced by a more nefarious suspicion about the EC/EU's objectives which candidates and parties have not always adequately combated or tried to refute. Even those making the EP their primary career target have not always been either assiduous or successful in dispelling disinformation or in impressing their achievements on the electorate. However, there is a cadre of long-serving MEPs who are building a collective memory for the EP. This is advantageous in some respects but it is not a guarantee that ambitions to transform the EP into a bicameral legislative chamber with commensurate powers to that of the Council survive from one legislature to the next: that argument has to be rehearsed and won each time. Nevertheless, increasingly senior and experienced politicians are entering both the Commission and the EP from the member states. This signals an improvement in the status of both institutions. It also means that the pool of political networks within which MEPs operate is wider and better connected. This, too, is likely to be beneficial to the EP providing its members and its parties organize themselves effectively. Indeed, turnover of MEPs at each election need not then be viewed quite so pessimistically. Italy, France and Germany had a relatively high turnover in MEPs with around half being replaced in the EP in 1994.

National governments also feared that if MEPs were directly elected, they would use the mere fact of having been directly elected to justify their claim for greater powers for the EP in terms of the democratic legitimacy they would infer from having been, unlike any other EC institution, directly elected by the people. This anxiety was confirmed but the suspicion that direct elections would spell a zero-sum transfer of popular sovereignty away from member states to the EC was disabused for numerous reasons. However, tension persists between MEPs and national parliaments (some of whom continue to see the EP as a rival for power and influence in the EU) and member governments who are loathe to cede legislative power to the EP. Why?

National governments are represented in the EU's actual legislature: the Council of Ministers. No legislation can be passed in the EU unless it is adopted by the Council of Ministers, normally in closed session. Paradoxically, this body has no public chamber. The EP sees it as the Chamber of the States and itself as the Chamber of the People. It has tried to develop a bi-cameral legislature in the EU accordingly. Therefore, its attempts to change its own powers often directly compromise the supremacy in legislative matters of the Council of Ministers. They directly attack the system of government by executives which has dominated both the EC and the member states. Consequently, all endeavours by MEPs to change their own capacity to influence, modify or amend inter-institutional relations are seen as threatening.

While the member governments were able to argue against the holding of direct elections on the somewhat specious grounds that people would not wish to vote for an invisible, impotent EP devoid of legislative power, even before the first direct elections, MEPs had devised a two-pronged strategy for themselves. This rested on a gradual, minimalist approach to altering procedures internal to the institutions in a quest to enhance the EP's ability to influence legislative outputs. It was combined with a maximalist strategy designed to reform the existing treaties, formally change the EP's powers and develop a written constitution – as opposed to constitutional provisions – for the EC and later for the EU.

Historically the maximalist approach has been the most contentious and overtly federal. The suspicion among member governments that an attempt was being made to construct a federal Europe, in which the member states would be relegated (as member governments saw it) to the status of inferior regions, accounted in part for resistance to such plans. Even though the early attempts did not succeed in full, a good deal of continuity can be detected in the underlying assumptions, procedures, and institutional norms and structures both envisaged in the 1950s and carrying through to the current debate on the future of the EU in the context of the 1996 Inter-Governmental Conference (IGC).

The EP has legislative, budgetary and supervisory powers. It participates in the EU legislative process through four main legislative procedures:

- consultation
- cooperation
- assent
- co-decision

Until 1980, the EP had only a consultative role in the legislative process coupled with budgetary powers. The 1980 Isoglucose ruling of the European Court of Justice reinforced its position and its own innovative interpretation of its own Rules of Procedure which it drafts itself. Through skilful interpretation of its Rules of Procedure, the EP has continued to expand its parliamentary and legislative roles in the EU. It used them to acquire an indirect right to initiate legislative proposals (Article 138b) and to participate in shaping the legislative agenda through the Annual Legislative Programme (prepared by the Commission and submitted to Parliament) and Joint Declarations (first introduced in 1975 when a conciliation procedure was adopted, primarily for budgetary disagreements). Inter-institutional declarations and agreements have been agreed since then on important issues like budgetary discipline (1988 and 1993) and on democracy, transparency and subsidiarity (1993). What MEPs still want − and will press for in the IGC process, however − is the abolition of the distinction between compulsory and non-compulsory spending. That would increase their legislative influence and power immensely.

The inter-institutional declarations and agreements work on the EP's principle that anything that is not expressly forbidden by the treaty is allowed. While they may be designed to improve harmonious working and inter-institutional relations, they − and other informal changes − have significant implications over the longer term for constitutional amendments which enhance the EP's authority, its legislative capacity and its control, scrutiny and supervisory powers designed to ensure democratic accountability over the EU's executive bodies and *vis-à-vis* the Court of Auditors, the Court of Justice, the European Council, the European Monetary Institute, the European Central Bank and Euro-ombudsman.

Changes in the way in which it relates to the Commission, in particular, and the Council of Ministers on operational matters and on a day-to-day basis have helped it significantly to augment its authority, influence and ultimately formal powers. For example, requests for information − questions for oral or written answer, committees of inquiry, petitions − can be and are used politically to enhance openness. In addition, requests to the Commission to explain any refusal to comply with MEPs' opinions or requests that a draft proposal be withdrawn have been used politically to very good effect to expand the scope of EP influence and form the basis of treaty revisions. Informal arrangements have become entrenched in treaty modifications. The kind of arrangements it now seeks are also likely to inform the institutional changes accepted by member governments at the next and subsequent Inter-Governmental Conferences. That is why a number of measures sought by the EP − including the introduction of a single legislative procedure (to avoid the complexities and confusion produced by the co-existence of over eight different legislative procedures coupled with comitology) – are potentially so important to the evolution and shape of the future EU.

The 1987 Single European Act (SEA) introduced the cooperation procedure which applied to only ten articles of the EEC treaty but covered extremely important areas including those central to the realization of the Single Market programme (see Figure I.1). This paved the way for an expansion in the co-operation procedure to 15 new fields following the revisions introduced through the Maastricht treaty on European Union in 1992. In addition, some of the areas previously subject to the cooperation procedure then became subject to the new co-decision procedure.

In essence, the two procedures rest on the dual principle that no legislation should be adopted which does not have the approval of the elected representatives of the EU people and that both the Council and the EP should have a say in the passage of such legislation. Perfect equality between the two bodies of an emergent bicameral legislature has yet to be achieved but significant advances have been made in a relatively short period. The majorities which have to be established in the EP and the Council at various junctures in the first and second readings under the cooperation procedure are designed to ensure that the Council takes notice of MEPs' views. For example, if the EP rejects the Council's common position, the Council has to be unanimous to overrule the EP's decision within a deadline of three months. The overall effect has been to expedite legislation and to engage the Commission, Council and EP in constructive dialogue over legislative details and principles. Between 1987 and April 1993, the Commission accepted 56 per cent of EP amendments at first reading and 47 per cent at second reading; the Council accepted 44 per cent and 25 per cent respectively.

The assent procedure has also been expanded and used politically. The Single European Act provided for the EP's assent to the conclusion of association agreements (Article 238) and for the accession of new member states to the EC (Article 237). These have been used politically by MEPs who have argued against enlargement unless specific institutional changes are introduced to enhance democratic practice, for example. The Maastricht Treaty extended the assent procedure to all important agreements (ie those setting up a specific institutional framework or having important budgetary implications, or requiring the amendment of EC legislation pursuant to the co-decision procedure). Parliament has to be consulted on all other agreements (except trade under Article 113). Nine new articles fall under the assent procedure and include provisions for a uniform Euro-election procedure (Article 138), the powers of the European Central Bank (Article 106(5), freedom of movement (Article 8a) and the objectives of the structural funds (Article 130d). The Council, in effect, cannot adopt a legislative act under the assent procedure unless the EP has approved it.

The co-decision procedure, introduced by the Maastricht treaty, covers 14

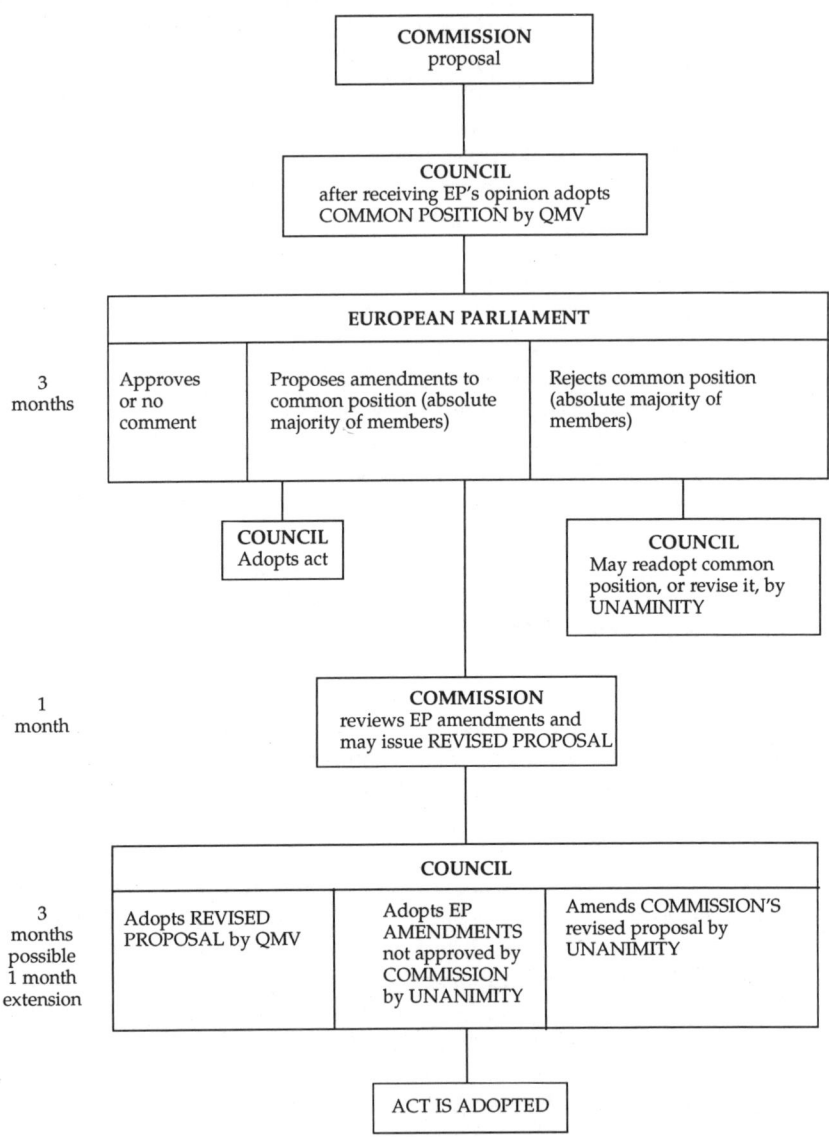

Figure I.1 The cooperation procedure (Article 189c) (simplified presentation)

Source: House of Commons, Foreign Affairs Committee, *Europe after Maastricht*, Vol II, London 1992, p 8.

articles but provides for the expansion of its field of application on the basis of a proposal from the Commission. This is likely to be addressed by the IGC. Co-decision provides for a third reading but is otherwise analogous to the co-operation procedure. Special majorities and a conciliation procedure are built in to promote compromise (see Figure I.2). Among the areas subject to co-decision are: free movement of workers (Article 49), right of establishment (Article 54), mutual recognition of diplomas (Article 57(1), internal market (Article 100b), education (Article 126(4), trans-European networks (Article 129d), consumer protection (Article 129a(2) and environmental programmes (Article 130S(3)).

The EP is not satisfied with the range or scope of its powers and will continue to seek a greater role for itself, as it must, in respect of new areas of competence and responsibility bestowed by the member governments on the EU. The common foreign and security policy and justice and home affairs pillars of the Maastricht treaty do not provide for adequate parliamentary input. These issues will have to be addressed. Continued pressure for a parliamentary role is the inevitable consequence of member governments' reluctance to deal with the central issue of what kind of polity the EU is and what kind of institutions it should have given its stated commitment to the principles of liberal, representative, open, accountable, responsible government.

While Euro-elections have not lived up to the high hopes held for them by people from all walks of life, they have served to transform the nature of the EC from a primarily technocratic organization preoccupied with the management of socio-economic and political processes in a manner compatible with the preservation of peace among states on a constructive basis among former foes to a polity in its own right. The following examination of Euro-elections in each of the EU's member states in June 1994 shows how national issues dominated the agenda; how major European issues were eclipsed; and how turnout fell in most states. It is easy to infer from this a lessening in European awareness and interest. But such an inference would be too easy and potentially misleading. Turnout may have been disappointing but it has not undermined the quest by MEPs (both re-elected MEPs and new MEPs) to transform the EP into a responsible, responsive, democratic and accountable legislative chamber in the EU. If anything, there is renewed vigour for the European enterprise and renewed interest in shaping the EU – and its component member states – along liberal, democratic lines. A participatory Euro-level democracy requires genuine participatory opportunities within the member states themselves. The crisis of legitimacy and political participation affects all levels of government.

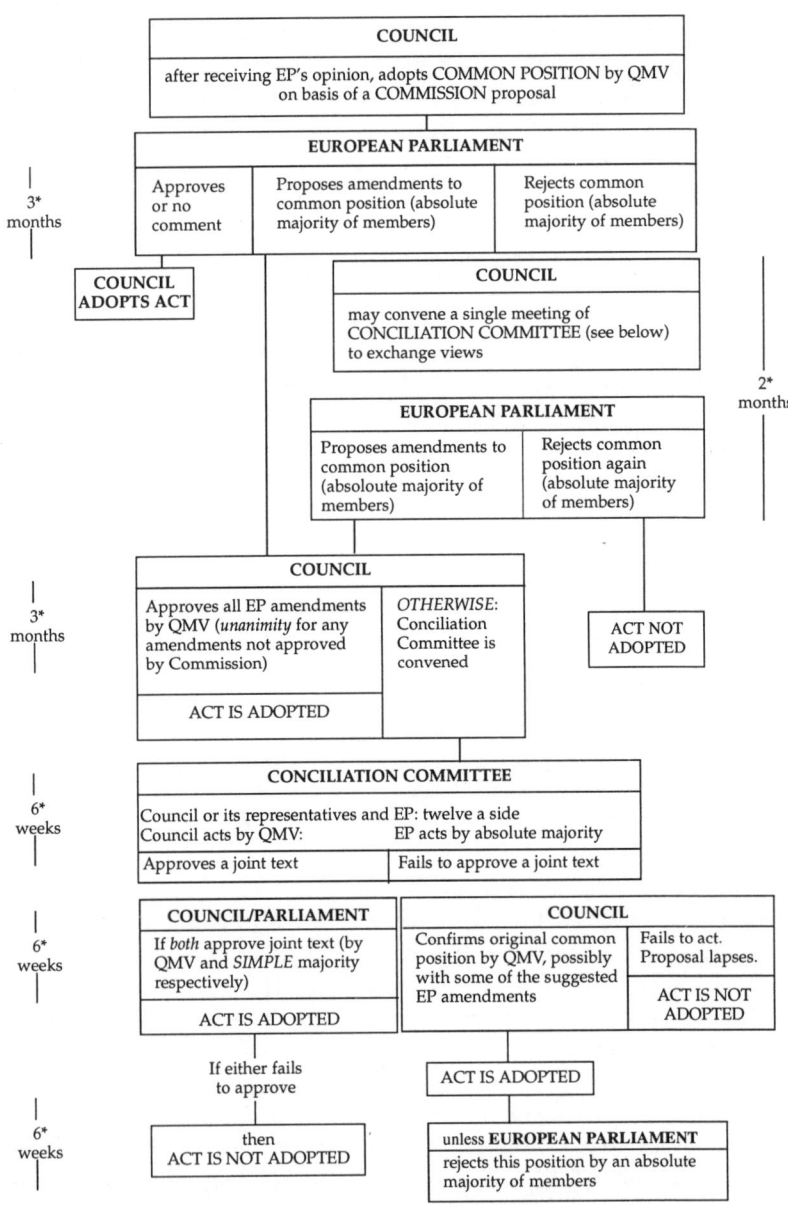

* These periods may be extended by one month or two weeks

Figure I.2 The co–decision procedure (Article 189b) (simplified presentation)

Source: House of Commons, Foreign Affairs Committee, *Europe after Maastricht*, Vol II, London 1992, p 9.

Notes

1. European Coal and Steel Community, *Journal Officiel, Debats de l'Assemblee Commune*, II (1953) p 18 reproduced in H Schmitt, *European Union: From Hitler to de Gaulle*, New York, van Nostrand, 1969.

References

European Parliament (1992) *The European Community in the Historical Context of its Parliament*, 40th Anniversary Proceedings of the Symposium, Strasbourg.
European Parliament (1993) *The Powers of the European Parliament in the European Union*, Working Papers, Political Series E-1.
Jacobs, F and Corbett, R (1995) *The European Parliament*, London, Longman.
Lodge, J (ed) (1985) *Direct Elections to the European Parliament 1984*, London, Macmillan.
Lodge, J (ed) (1990) *The 1989 Election of the European Parliament*, London, Macmillan.
Lodge, J and Herman, V (1982) *Direct Elections to the European Parliament: A Supranational Perspective*, London, Macmillan.
Reif, K-H (ed) (1985) *Ten European Elections – 1979–81 and 1984: Campaigns and Results*, Aldershot, Gower.

1

The European Parliament and Euro-elections: A Quest for Legitimacy and Integration?

Juliet Lodge

The debate over democratic legitimacy in the EC has several features which coincide with different phases in European integration. It is particularly useful to examine them through the history of the European Parliament (EP) because the EP has been instrumental in developing strategies and a set of goals designed to advance democratic practices, democratic accountability and democratic legitimacy at EC level. The different elements have often been conflated with and subsumed in the phase 'democratic legitimacy.' They have all been assumed implicitly to indicate a deepening of European integration along federal lines.

Certainly, any strengthening of the EP's powers and any concomitant intensification of cooperation with the Commission in particular have been interpreted as symptomatic of a qualitative leap from inter-governmental cooperation (in which national governments, notably through the Council of Ministers, remained supreme) to supranational integration presaging a federal future (in which the progressive evolution of a symbiotic relationship between the Commission and the EP impinged on and inhibited Council supremacy, even by the device of developing shared legislative responsibility between the Council and the EP).

Originally, the realization of democratic legitimacy in the EC rested on the attainment of two key objectives: first, expansion of the EP's decision-making powers to enable it to approximate the role traditionally associated with legislatures in Western European democracies; and second, ensuring that the way in which its members were chosen and exercised their powers conformed to accepted democratic practices. In short, this meant that the EP should be elected by direct, universal suffrage. More recently, with the progressive and continuing attainment of earlier goals, the EP has launched into a far broader debate about the *raison d'être* of the EC and its transformation into a European Union. Through a brief survey of key points in the EP's development, it is possible to illustrate just how vital the EP's involvement in pushing forward the parameters of the debate is to realizing a democratic European Union.

Background: the issues – Euro-elections, democracy, the democratic deficit and democratic legitimacy

Democratic legitimacy in the EC has traditionally been seen in limited terms as a problem of securing the election of the EP by direct, universal suffrage. The issue is more complex and multi-faceted. Legitimacy is contested. It is conditional and evolutionary. It is expressed through the dispute over the appropriate balance of power and exercise of authority among the key supranational decision-making institutions and the argument over the issue of decision-making appropriateness, efficiency, transparency and accountability. The continuing problem of democratic legitimacy inheres in the EU's crisis of political authority and identity. The new provisions introduced through the Maastricht process may de-legitimize rather than reinforce legitimacy: they are essential but not sufficient preconditions to remedying the democratic deficit and democratic legitimacy.

Conceptual confusion persists over the term 'democracy' when applied in the EC context. Arguably, until the first Euro-elections in 1979, democracy was conflated first with the quest to secure parliamentary oversight of the EC's newly-acquired own resources in the mid-1960s; and second, and more importantly, with the holding of elections of the European Parliament. Inadequate parliamentary control over the Commission and especially the Council, coupled with the absence of direct elections were seen to make up a *'democratic deficit'* in the EC. By the time of the Edinburgh European Council in December 1992 it had also come to be associated with the idea that the Commission was insufficiently transparent and democratic. In addition, and increasingly in the 1990s, the democratic deficit was seen in terms of an incremental and continuing erosion of national parliaments' powers over EC legislation on a zero-sum basis to the advantage of the EP.

What was and remains ill-understood is the degree to which the EP has not won powers forfeited to national governments by national parliaments: neither can exercise effective control over what national governments do in the EU or what the EU executive does. National governments were responsible for this situation and deliberately engineered a situation whereby national parliaments were denied effective controls over national executives. This made it easier for national governments, working within the Council, to escape national as well as European parliamentary scrutiny and control. Thus, allegations that the EP was engaged in an exercise to increase its powers at national parliaments' expense were based on a false premise: national governments, not the EP, were the beneficiaries of parliamentary weakness at both national and EU level. National parliaments failed to engineer an effective scrutiny, monitoring or controlling role for themselves *vis-à-vis* national ministers and governments. They also failed, until 1990, to engage in constructive dialogue – and more importantly, in continuing, regular communication – with the EP. Given that European Parliamentary scrutiny and control were negligible and deficient, the overall result was to increase the democratic deficit. For a long time, however, electoral preoccupations meant that it was assumed that the democratic deficit would be erased merely by the fact of the EP having been directly elected.

The failure to disaggregate the concept of democracy led to confusion between one aspect of the democratic conduct of politics (the holding of periodic elections in which citizens elect candidates from a variety of parties to represent them in a parliament) with another – that of democratic legitimacy. Moreover, the tendency to equate the holding of direct elections with the EC's transition to a federal polity rather than as a means of enhancing democratic legitimacy muddied the picture still further. Argument raged over the likely impact of direct elections over the longer term on EP–Council relations and on the balance of power between them. It was presumed that ultimately a bicameral legislature would be created in which the Council would represent the states (rather than performing its incompatible dual function as the EC's legislature and the advocate of national interests). In a bicameral system, the EP would become the lower house. Instead of such a development being reviled as federal, it would have been more helpful to recall that bicameral arrangements were far from alien. They were typical of member states' existing polities. They were therefore recognizable features of contemporary political cultures. This might have helped to reinforce a public sense of the EC's growing democratic legitimacy.

Yet democratic legitimacy implies also that government is lawful and that its authority is accepted: something that could not be deduced merely from Euro-elections. The confusion was compounded by the fact that notions of representativeness and accountability are also associated with the conduct of democratic politics in the member states and have been implicitly subsumed in the ways in which the terms democracy, democratic deficit and democratic practice have been applied in the EU setting.

Leo Tindemans was right up to a point when he claimed in 1975 that: 'Direct elections . . . will give this Assembly a new political authority [and] reinforce the democratic legitimacy of the whole European institutional apparatus.'

Euro-elections were expected to perform a dual function. First, to alter the basis of the EC's legitimacy from it being derived to direct; and second, to augment the democratic nature of the EC by providing for public participation (albeit indirectly) in decision-making. It was assumed that by participating in Euro-elections, citizens would assent to the EU's authority structure and so confer direct legitimacy on it. The acquisition of direct legitimacy was seen as important in justifying how political power was exercised, particularly by the EP, and in empowering citizens' representatives to play more than a 'supervisory and advisory' role in the EC. While the elections augmented aspects of democracy in the EC, they did not necessarily lead to concomitant increases in legitimacy (Lodge, 1993). The contrary occurred. Widespread ignorance about the EP and the EC meant that then, as now, voters did not necessarily acquiesce in or actively assent to what MEPs envisaged. Nor is it evident that socialization, familiarization and education processes were at work which instilled in voters a belief in the EC's democratic legitimacy.

The EC's institutions were not, and are not, visible, tangible and intelligible to voters. The one institution traditionally seen as capable of engendering popular belief in its own and the EC/EU's democratic legitimacy, the EP, suffered from the outset from being a marginal player in the system. The mere fact of it having been directly elected was and is not enough to generate the democratic consent needed to give EC authority structures legitimacy (Herman and Lodge, 1978). Yet, legitimacy rests on the capacity to engender and maintain belief in the appropriateness and effectiveness of existing political institutions.

Many observers and practitioners felt that EC institutions were not appropriate in the sense that the exercise of power by certain institutions did not correspond to an ideal type of democracy. The executive and legislature did not function in the same way as they did in the member states: parliament did not determine either the composition or the duration in office of the Commission or of the Council. Nor did the Council (in many ways the EC's actual legislature) operate accountably or publicly at the supranational level. Such failings compromised the vision of the EC engaging popular opinion and support and providing an example of peaceful cooperation worthy of emulation by states around the world.

Internally, the hierarchical ordering of 'direct legitimacy' over 'derived legitimacy' challenged the authority and relative positions of the EP and the Council of Ministers respectively. The Euro-elections were seen to confer 'direct legitimacy' based on the people's sovereignty on both the EP and the EC. This was seen as preferable and superior to the derived legitimacy conferred by member governments' consent: superior because it conferred independence on the EP as a source of political authority. The idea of democratic legitimacy inhering in the one institution that can lay claim to the superior legitimacy has since been superseded by the concept of a dual legitimacy: that expressed through the directly elected and popularly accountable EP, and that expressed through the Council of Ministers whose members may have been directly elected in national elections or who will have been appointed by a government elected by the voters in a member state.

While it is easy to see why the ideas of representativeness, accountability and democracy have become intertwined in the democratic legitimacy debate, Euro-elections have neither closed the democratic deficit completely nor have they caused the Council of Ministers to become daily accountable on a collective basis to any other EU institution. Its accountability is contingent upon the legal base of legislation: only the cooperation and co-decision procedures provide for a form of accountability to the EP. Council members also elude effective and consistent democratic control at national levels. The effect, while unintentional, is to create a double bind: a *double* democratic deficit which inhibits the consolidation of EU claims to democratic legitimacy.

As the scope of EU competence has grown, so has the democratic deficit at supranational and national level. Thus, Euro-elections have not justified the manner in which political power is exercised: they have justified repeated challenges to both the distribution and exercise of political authority in the EC. MEPs sought to rectify failings by asserting their democratic and legitimate claims to exercise genuine influence (bolstered by entrenched expanded legislative competences). They constantly have had to contest how power is distributed since the inception of the Common Assembly and have confronted in often highly innovative ways the problem of altering the distribution of legislative power in particular among the Commission, Parliament and Council.

Contrary to accepted wisdom which cautioned against a frontal assault on institutional and constitutional affairs, it was only when the EP adopted a bolder stance on these matters that real progress began to be made. This coincided with a new institutional/constitutional building phase exemplified by the attempt to set out the parameters of a constitution for European Union from the mid-1980s onwards. However, it is important to note that while the reforms in inter-institutional relations introduced by the Single European Act began to close the democratic deficit through the operation of the cooperation procedure (Lodge, 1986; 1989), improvements at supranational level had the unforeseen and paradoxical effect of re-opening the issue of the EC's and Parliament's democratic legitimacy.

Two factors help to account for this. First, because the EP, through the co-operation procedure, was seen to be able to affect the content of EC legislation in a direct way that national parliaments could not, there were renewed allegations that it was usurping the role of national parliaments in the exercise of rightful control, scrutiny and influencing roles. They were largely excluded from playing such roles in monitoring EC legislation. That their own national governments had, with their concurrence, connived at their exclusion or at providing them with but a minimal role, upon ratification of the Treaty of Rome, was conveniently overlooked. Second, the ratification of the Single Act and the Maastricht Treaty on European Union led to referendums, for instance in Ireland, Denmark and France, which openly contested the very legitimacy of EC processes and the expansion of the scope of the EC's competence into new areas.

Democratic legitimacy and the 1991 Inter-Governmental Conference (IGC)

Democratic legitimacy and the question of redressing the EC's democratic deficit became part of the debate about European Union during the

Inter-Governmental Conference on European Political Union (IGC). The IGC was entrusted with a review of the functioning, efficiency, accountability and democratic nature of the EC's institutions. An underlying assumption was that political action should comply with the rule of law. By the end of December 1991 when the Maastricht Treaty on European Union (TEU) was agreed, it was apparent that the institutional reforms agreed did not match the exponential change in the demands facing the EC with the opening of the Single Market. Not only were additional states clamouring for membership, but the very question of what 'democracy' meant to the EC was being defined and outlined in the treaty. This definition was derived from contemporary liberal democratic practices and assumptions in the member states. It rested on notions of parliamentary pluralism and open, representative government. But its function was not to set out an ideal type of political system to be realized at supranational level. Rather, the crude attempts at definition both symbolized core, shared political values and sent a signal to applicant states, notably in Central and Eastern Europe, as to what the EC meant when it set 'political maturity' as a precondition of EC membership, and when it subsequently argued that enlargement could only proceed if it did not dilute the *acquis communautaire* and if the Community itself was ready for it. This led both to a reappraisal of the question of democratic legitimacy in the EC context and to a reassessment of the question of the durability of existing, and even newly-reformed, legislative practices and institutional arrangements.

The EP and democratic legitimacy: a shared and divided legitimacy?

The EP has been centrally concerned with democratic legitimacy since before the merger of the three Communities (ECSC, EEC and Euratom) in 1967. While democratic legitimacy was largely seen in parliamentary terms and therefore as the EP's preserve, more recently − indeed as recently as 1989−90 − the EC's democratic legitimacy has been conceptualized as divided between the EP on the one hand and the member governments on the other. However, three developments were important in changing the dimensions to the debate.

During the first phase attention focused on the question of what powers the EP should exercise over the EC's 'own resources' (an argument in the mid-1960s which led to de Gaulle's empty chair policy for France) (Camps, 1966). In phase two the concern over powers was supplemented by more vociferous arguments over the 'no taxation without representation' principle. Inspiration was drawn from the earlier constitutional débâcle during the failure of the European Defence and European Political Communities in 1954, from the Parliament's own Dehousse report, and from the practice of liberal democratic, representative forms of federal government. Concern over transforming the 'Assembly' into a 'Parliament' shifted to electoral issues and MEPs (then the dual-mandated appointees from national parliaments) sought to realize

Article 138 of the Rome Treaty. This prescribes the election of the EP by direct, universal suffrage.

Throughout the early 1970s, the desirability of holding elections to a relatively impotent 'Assembly' was repeatedly contested. It was argued that there was no point in trying to mobilize the electorate to vote for a poorly-known institution devoid of power but having parliamentary and legislative pretensions; and that a low turnout would seriously damage the 'Assembly's' claim to democratic legitimacy. It was on this claim that its demand for greater powers rested. The vicious circle of whether or not its powers should be increased before or after direct elections was breached with the first enlargement of the EC to embrace the UK, Denmark and Ireland. It was assumed that the UK (with the 'mother of parliaments') would have a beneficial impact on the 'Assembly's' development and prospects.

Democratization became a leitmotif. But democratization had two faces. On the one hand, it referred to the holding of direct elections, and on the other to making the Council of Ministers accountable to the EP. Both rested on the member governments' unanimous approval: treaty reforms could not enter into force unless ratified in accordance with national provisions. The fact that any such increases would necessarily curb the autonomy of the Council of Ministers (and hence of member governments) did not augur well for MEPs' ambitions. Nevertheless, small advances were made using the financial and budgetary control levers in 1970–73. These paved the way for agreement in 1976 to hold direct elections, first scheduled for 1978 but postponed until 1979 pending the adoption of the necessary enabling legislation in each of the member states. The differing national provisions inevitably meant that the Treaty provision for a uniform electoral procedure would be ignored and that discrepancies would occur in the conduct of the elections. This was seen as a price worth paying in order to get governments to accept direct elections (Lodge and Herman, 1982).

During the third phase, the non-elected MEPs' insistence that direct elections would not induce the elected Parliament to seek greater power, notably at the Council's expense, bedevilled elected MEPs' efforts to transform the EP's authority and to alter its supervisory and advisory functions and transform it into genuine legislative authority. Shortly after the first elections, tension developed between MEPs seeking treaty amendments to meet Parliament's desires and those intent on allaying some governments' anxiety lest an inter-institutional confrontation occur by adopting a strategy of using procedural changes to gradually increase Parliament's influence by exploiting fully existing Treaty provisions. The tension was to prove constructive and productive as MEPs developed a dual-pronged strategy to advance on both fronts simultaneously (Louis, 1985).

This was based on exploiting the minimalist *petits pas* approach advocated by those adept at capitalizing on existing treaty provisions and at revising in an innovative way Parliament's own Rules of Procedure. It owed much to the idea that anything that was not explicitly prohibited by the Treaty was implicitly permissible. This strategy was supplemented by the maximalist approach inspired by Altiero Spinelli and the Crocodile Club (Jacqué, 1983; Spinelli, 1983) of letting political elites and parliaments devise a vision of the future in constitutional terms (Bieber and Schwarze, 1984; Lodge, 1982; 1984). This dual-pronged strategy significantly influenced the evolution of Parliament's position throughout the 1980s. It left its imprint on the history of European integration. Although it is easily encapsulated in the phrase 'the quest for democratic legitimacy', this strategy proved to be a vital legacy to MEPs for the 1990s. Moreover, the déroulement of the IGC on Political Union and the ensuing problems over the ratification of the Maastricht Treaty on European Union showed how essential it remains to learn from and heed its lessons. This strategy needs to be purposefully pursued if democratic legitimacy is to become a reality. It is a necessary but not a sufficient condition of success. But as the Maastricht deliberations showed, without a continual, high profile input from the EP, direction is lost and the fragility of existing democratic legitimacy and equally importantly a sense of common identity and purpose are challenged and shaken. The resulting indecision erodes rather than strengthens democratic legitimacy.

The phrase 'democratic legitimacy' has long been associated with the EP alone. But as the EP has developed, it has become clear that there is a need to inject some clarity into the meaning and application of the concept of democratic legitimacy at EU level. Equally, since the 1991 IGC, a more expansive interpretation of democratic legitimacy has evolved. It has been essentially derived from the obstructiveness and opposition of member governments to remedying the democratic deficit through the expansion of supranational legislative power and authority for the EP. The member governments switched attention to the Commission, arguing – somewhat disingenuously – that the democratic deficit could only be remedied if the allegedly closed and secretive nature of Commission deliberations were made more open and 'transparent': this, from the practitioners of closed and secret decision-making in the Council, the EU's legislature (Lodge, 1994: 343–68).

Combating the democratic deficit: the role of the EP

The EP clearly has played and does play a role in redressing the democratic deficit and addressing the democratic legitimacy problems. Traditionally it has attacked the issue from the vantage point of:

(i) Changing inter-institutional relations, and notably the legislative imbalance between itself and the Council of Ministers. To that end, it engaged in a process of continually revising its own internal organization to enhance its potential effectiveness, bolster incipient coherence and reform its formal powers.

(ii) Changing and adapting decision rules and processes to enable it to enhance its ability to exercise its treaty-given powers effectively and to enable it to acquire genuine legislative authority. To that end, it has developed its budgetary, assent and legislative powers (through the conciliation, cooperation and co-decision procedures), its direct legislative initiative abilities (Article 138b TEU) and indirect legislative initiatives. The latter include own initiative reports, joint declarations (for example, on fundamental rights (1977), the budgetary procedure (1982), racism and xenophobia (1986), budgetary discipline (1988 and 1993) and on democracy, transparency and subsidiarity (1993)). These allow new procedures, not provided for in the treaties to be implemented. They entail legally-binding obligations. Any subsequent legal measures that violate them can be ruled void by the Court of Justice.

Indirect influence is also exercised via the annual legislative programmes prepared by the Commission and submitted to the EP and calling for one-off actions, preparatory studies and so on which opened the door for new items and programmes (such as the food aid programme within the EU's development policy) and its supervisory powers *vis-à-vis* the appointment of the Commission.

(iii) Changing its participation in Euro-elections. To that end, it started in 1978 with a very modest 'information provision' role *vis-à-vis* the national parties that comprised its party groups and through them to the public. This was followed by more overt funding of EP electoral activities and continued pressure for the implementation of a common electoral procedure.

The problem is that these steps have not been sufficient to render the EU's claims to democratic legitimacy sufficiently credible in the eyes of national elites and publics to obviate challenges to them of such magnitude that throw the whole European integration exercise into doubt and by themselves further erode the EU's image of legitimacy.

Moreover, national governments have not responded positively to public opinion polls suggesting public support for greater power to be given to the EP. In spring 1994, *Eurobarometer* found that 44 per cent favoured increased power for MEPs, and 75 per cent against 9 per cent felt that the Commission President and Commissioners should resign unless they enjoyed the majority support of the EP. While the public thinks in terms of 'governments' and 'parliaments', that concept is imperfectly replicated at EU-level. This may help to account for disappointing turnout at Euro-elections and for difficulties in perceiving and accepting the EP's and the EU's democratic legitimacy. Given that there is a crisis of legitimacy, how might this be explained?

Democratic legitimacy: a catalogue of failures?

The democratic legitimacy crisis is most manifest when considering the role of the elected chambers purporting to represent the people and guard them from the abuse of executive power. It is tempting to see in the extent of the democratic legitimacy crisis at EU level, little more than a catalogue of failures. The attempts to rectify the democratic deficit and to enhance democratic legitimacy have addressed a range of related issues which, when listed together, easily lend themselves to being described as a catalogue of failures. They include:

1. Failure to reconcile horizontal institutional rivalry
- imperfect bicameralism;
- imperfect parliamentary supervision and control over ministers;
- imperfect cooperation among the institutions;
- different interpretations of the decision rules that inhibit efficient decision-making and cooperation by the legislative arms;
- imperfect access to information that is essential to optimizing legislative performance by the various institutions.

2. Failure to overcome vertical institutional rivalry
- differential electoral systems;
- weak EP parties;
- failure to establish effective cooperation between national and European parliamentary and representative institutions.

3. Failure of mutual accommodation to enhance the common good
- contradictions in operationalizing the ideal of open government at EU and national levels;
- contradictions in reconciling democratic practice with efficient government;
- failure to advance a European constitution.

4. Failure of mobilization
- failure to mobilize the electorate and promote positive attitudinal change;
- failure on the part of the elected national political elites and leaders themselves to accept and internalize the legitimacy and authority of the system they both construct and work in.

5. Failure of effectiveness
- partial failure to deliver policies/programmes of direct relevance and clearly visible to the electorate;
- imperfect development of parliamentary oversight of and influence on the EMU (from the Central Bank to the EMI and influencing EU economic policy);
- failure to develop a constitutional role with the ECJ.

1. Failure to reconcile horizontal institutional rivalry
Arguably, until the advent of the Single Act and the introduction of the co-operation procedure, inter-institutional competition between the two arms of the EC's legislature – the EP and the Council of Ministers – persisted in part because there was little formal or legal need for them to cooperate. The Council

could, and did, ignore the EP, thereby asserting its supremacy in the legislative process. The cooperation and later the co-decision procedures altered this situation. This change occurred for a number of reasons. First, the EP and the Commission stimulated effective legislative planning and coordination, partly through computerization of the various stages and introducing inter-institutional opaqueness and openness into their internal management of the progress of the legislative programme. Second, the EP successfully challenged the Council over amendments to controversial environmental legislation. Third, the EP used the assent procedure to assert its views against those of the Council and Commission. Fourth, the EP continued to interpret its own Rules of Procedure imaginatively to facilitate an expansion of its role *vis-à-vis* the Council of Ministers and the Commission. Such interpretations paved the way in the 1980s for its augmented legislative influence and the cooperation procedure, and in the 1990s for its currently enhanced position, for example, in respect of the selection and appointment of the incoming Commission. How? First through the vote of investiture (subsequently incorporated into the TEU Article 158:2) and making the terms of office of the Commission and the EP concurrent, and second through its decision to cross-examine those appointed by the member governments prior to their formal assumption of office, and even though MEPs still lack the right to censure individual Commissioners. Will this help enhance democratic legitimacy? Possibly, if it is felt that voters trust MEPs sufficiently to endorse the quasi-leaders of the EU. The absence of effective and meaningful links between the 'government' of the EU and its parliament do imperil the EU's democratic legitimacy given that the publics identify with and more or less trust national leaders more than they do supranational actors.

The overall result has been a procedural reduction in but not the elimination of horizontal institutional rivalry. Commission–EP cooperation has steadily improved: Commission officials attend EP committees and Commissioners often attend part sessions. The amelioration has been less pronounced and more tortuous in respect of the Council and the EP. This is partly because some Council activities take place outside the EC framework altogether: notably those concerning the second and third pillars on the common foreign and security policy and cooperation in justice and home affairs. While symbolic improvements have been made – ministers from the presidency usually attend EP committees in their sphere of responsibility at least twice per presidency, and plenaries – accountability remains weak. The EP continues to work towards the ideal of co-equal legislative power-sharing between itself and the Council: imperfect bicameralism exists; the inter-institutional imbalance to the EP's disadvantage remains; and the onus remains on MEPs to seek, justify and secure changes to the imbalance. The problem in doing so resides partly in the persistence of vertical institutional rivalry and suspicion among national parliaments (see below).

If imperfect bicameralism exists, it follows that parliamentary supervision and control of Ministers neither matches an ideal nor meets the requirements of effective democratic checks on the potential abuse of legislative authority by the Council. It is still the case that the Council may pass legislative proposals that have neither been endorsed by MEPs nor by national MPs. The 'A' points procedure in the Committee of Permanent Representatives (COREPER), for example, while arguably efficient, does not conform to democratic ideals of participation and supervision by the elected representatives of those subject to the resultant law. There has been some improvement in respect of Council secrecy. The Council secretariat press releases may specify the voting (majority or unanimity) on a decision and indicate which member states abstained or opposed the proposal on which it was based. Reasons for voting, however, have to be elicited by MEPs and immediacy and spontaneity is lost at a critical juncture. Some Council sessions are now televised (17 had been by late 1994). MEPs have participated at some Council meetings, a procedure introduced on the initiative of the Kangaroo group of MEPs during the deliberations on the realization of the Single Market in the 1980s. This is neither the norm nor is it accepted as the most appropriate way of engineering supranational parliamentary control over ministers, all of whom, necessarily escape rigorous parliamentary supervision at national level. But this is not sufficient to obscure the fact that Council secrecy has not been eradicated. The absence of a public gallery in the Council's new building suggests that public scrutiny is not wanted.

In short, cooperation between the EU's legislative institutions is imperfect. It develops in an *ad hoc* fashion according to pragmatic principles rather than in line with a known and shared vision of what kind of division of authority among them would be appropriate. This is partly because of continuing uncertainty as to the end-goal. The EU is a polity. It does have a system of governance. But the polity does not yet conform to any existing model of liberal democratic, representative government. It is merely assumed that democratic principles should guide it. Even then, this was not formally entrenched until the TEU.

The picture of incoherence and horizontal inter-institutional rivalry may, of course, be magnified by further inter-institutional rivalries, for example, those between the European Council and the Commission, and those resulting from the introduction of comitology procedures which curtail both the EP's and the Commission's influence and enable the Council to exercise executive powers through management and consultative committees.

This is also exacerbated by the different interpretations of decision rules by the main institutions which may inhibit efficient decision-taking and co-operation among them. This is not to subscribe to notions of a conspiracy theory to explain failings. It is, however, to highlight that both inadvertent and sometimes deliberate differences in the way in which procedures and policy ideas are interpreted and processed may aggravate failings in inter-institutional cooperation. It is, of course, quite usual for the Commission to exercise particular care in the selection of the legal base for legislative proposals. Indeed, the legal base may prescribe or exclude a legislative role for the EP. Exclusion is not compatible with the realization of democratic legislative procedures. But it may better suit the requirement of efficiency, for maintaining the imbalance in power to the Council's advantage over the EP and for highlighting the continuing inferior position of the latter as supplicant.

The EP's inferior position can also be underscored by denying it access to essential information, or by making it difficult for it to acquire current information that may inform its deliberations, possibly to the detriment of Council consensus. The problems are even more acute in respect of the second and third pillars where the EP is either denied any effective oversight, scrutiny or supervisory roles (as in the case of Justice and Home Affairs) or given very limited functions (as in the case of the Common Foreign and Security policy). Under Title VI of the TEU, the EP is to be kept informed and consulted (Article 6). Again, while the Commission is usually cooperative, the Council is less so. When David Martin, MEP, submitted a written Parliamentary question on the publication of the Council's decision, under the Common Foreign and Security Policy (CFSP) on the lifting of EU sanctions on South Africa, he was told that such 'decisions' did not have to be published and if they were, it was a 'courtesy' only (Question no. 95 (H-1082/91)). Moreover, the EP has had to ask the Council to use a legal base to ensure that MEPs may give their views, such as Article 228a (EP, 1994). Beyond that, it may use – and exploit – its budegtary muscle in these two pillars as the administrative and a part of the operational expenditure of both are a charge on the EU budget. Otherwise, the EP must try and influence policies when they are communitized (possibly through the application of Article 100c as in the case of visa policy) or realized through the EU framework.

2.   Failure to surmount vertical institutional rivalry

The democratic deficit is not simply a problem of the horizontal distribution of power among EC-level institutions. The vertical dimension is important and varies significantly from state to state. More recently, concern over the precise meaning of 'subsidiarity' has obfuscated this vertical democratic gap. But if subsidiarity implies that power should be devolved to the most appropriate lowest levels of government, the potency of the vertical deficit is bound to increase. National MPs were remarkably slow in recognizing this. Preoccupied with the alleged (but in actual fact negligible) threat to national parliaments' powers from the EP, they have only recently appreciated how unaccountable national governments have eroded national sovereignty and how, in practice, subsidiarity could further marginalize them. This arises not just because the Maastricht Treaty on European Union established a consultative Committee of the Regions (which has since indicated that it has legislative ambitions), but because of the direct links regional, municipal and local governments have set up with EC bodies, and often in conjunction with the assistance of the relevant MEPs.

The weaknesses in democratic legitimacy are not just a product of unsatisfactory allocation of competence between the EU's legislative bodies. They also inhere in the exclusion of national parliaments from the decision-making processes relating to things EU at the national level as well as the supranational level. While the Single European Act began to close the democratic deficit through the operation of the cooperation procedure, (Lodge, 1986; 1989) improvements at supranational level had the unforeseen and paradoxical effect of re-opening the issue of the EC's and Parliament's democratic legitimacy.

Two factors help to account for this. First, because the EP, through the cooperation procedure, was seen to be able to affect the content of EC legislation in a direct way that national parliaments could not, there were renewed allegations that it was usurping the role of national parliaments in the exercise of rightful control, scrutiny and influencing roles. They were largely excluded from playing such roles in monitoring EC legislation. That their own national governments had, with their concurrence, connived at their exclusion or at providing them with but a minimal role, upon ratification of the Treaty of Rome, was conveniently overlooked. Second, the referendums in Denmark and Ireland on the ratification of the Single Act contested the legitimacy of the expansion of the scope of the EC's competence into new areas. But the problems raised then were not addressed adequately. Consequently, the subsequent referendums on Maastricht also led to a querying of the legitimacy of the distribution of authority among the various institutions, the appropriateness both of the new balance of power among EU bodies and mechanisms for facilitating influence by sub-national actors on supranational legislative processes. The role of national parliaments and regional and local elected bodies was criticized.

The problems caused by imperfect/sub-optimal access to information also inhibit the ability of national parliaments to play a role in influencing the EU's legislative process. Excluded from this role largely by their own governments at the point of accession to the EC, national parliaments have differed widely in their willingness to liaise with MEPs. Too many, for too long, have subscribed to the fatuous view that the EP was their rival and the direct beneficiary of any reduction in their own powers when they should have appreciated the need for parliaments to work together.

National parliamentary parties have often spurned and excluded MEPs though practice varies across the EU. For example, until 1991, when the Labour constitution was amended, Labour MPs failed to use the Euro-expertise of Labour MEPs effectively. Now, five MEPs sit on Labour's policy forum, the National Executive Committee must consult the MEPs over the Euro-manifesto, and MEPs can elect one of their members to regional party executives (Constitutional Amendments, Labour Party 1991). Corbett has shown that elsewhere, in eight of ten socialist parties, MEPs participate *ex officio* with speaking rights in the party congress; in seven of ten MEPs are represented *ex officio* in their party executive or bureau; in five, MEPs attend and speak as of right in national parliamentary party group meetings; in four, a liaison committee exists of the group in the national parliament and MEPs (including the leaders of Landtag party groups in Germany) (Corbett, 1994).

MEPs can also informally influence national parties. But again, this is not always well-appreciated or publicized.

Too often MPs have seen MEPs as rivals for public loyalty and for legislative power. By failing to capitalize on the information and expertise available in the EP, national parliaments have undermined their own ability to supervise their national governments and ministers in the EC. National parliaments have excluded MEPs from relevant deliberations (and even physically from their buildings, as in the case of the House of Commons). The overall effect has been to weaken parliamentary possibilities for holding the EC's executive arms accountable.

National parliamentarians have failed to assist as well as they might in the development of mutually useful links between their parliamentary parties and their respective components in the EP. Again, communication links have often been sub-optimal. This may well have served the MEPs' interests in the exercise of their individual mandate and allowed the supranational party groups to develop their own identities and policies in a relatively unfettered way. However, it had the unintended and unanticipated effect of underlining the sense of vertical institutional competition between the two levels of parliamentary work. Working together, they might have been a good deal more effective in asserting the democratic principles and practices of holding ministers accountable for their actions in the EC and even in influencing policy in ideological directions (inevitably representing a centre-ground compromise).

National parliaments might also have assumed a stronger role in arguing for the introduction of a common electoral procedure for Euro-elections: vested national interests inhibit a few even today from doing this. Yet, the ramifications affect the ideological composition of the EP, undermine the extent to which it can claim to be genuinely representative of the spread of public opinion, and affect citizens and residents in the exercise of a political right (by making it contingent on national rather than European electoral provisions).

National parliaments might also have been more objective in their assessment of the impact of integration on their own oversight powers *vis-à-vis* national governments. As integration has expanded so has the scope of governmental authority which eludes parliamentary oversight. The EP has not recouped such losses. Indeed, following the adoption of the Single European Act, MEPs investigated again the institutional costs of 'non-Europe' (Catherwood, 1988) which informed the Herman report (Official Journal C 190 20 July 1987: 71) on its strategy for European Union (EP Resolution A3-0123/92: 7 April 1992). Particular attention was paid to the democratic deficit (Official Journal C 187 18 July 1988: 229).

Vertical institutional rivalry has not just been apparent among parliaments. Rather, it is even more pronounced where governments are concerned. This inheres in part in persistent confusion over the presumed impact of European integration on national sovereignty, where integration has been seen as having a zero-sum outcome for national sovereignty. It is also clear in governments' reluctance either to accept Commission President Jacques Delors' claim in 1988 that the Single Mareket's realization would mean that around 80 per cent of all legislation enacted in the member states originated at EU level, or take an objective view of the functioning of the EU.

The TEU's pillar approach represented an *ad hoc* and politically expedient response to the need to contemplate further integration as a logical corollary to the removal of internal frontiers in the wake of the creation of the Single Market. But many governments feared that this would lead to further co-operation among national/regional authorities which would further erode their supremacy in practice. By shouting 'foul' and describing new developments as encroachments on national sovereignty to be resisted, they lost an opportunity to clarify the system, preferring instead the resort to the principle of subsidiarity (Commission 1994; Endo 1994; Kapteyn 1991; EPA3-163/90; A3-0267/90). However, vertical institutional rivalry within the member states – for instance among national, regional, local and muncipal governments, where these exist – may re-appear at supranational level as the Committee of the Regions gains a voice and, as a body of elected representatives, seeks a position alongside the EP. Indeed, some Committee members have sought a right of co-decision alongside MEPs within areas of the Committee's competence and others, challenging the legitimacy of MEPs as representatives of the people, want the Committee to become a second chamber of the EP.

There is belated recognition that parliaments must work together to reassert democratic controls over executives at *national* and supranational levels. Because both are popularly elected, both can lay claim to direct legitimacy. Both have a role in lending legitimacy to the exercise of authority. Working together, and with regional bodies, both could serve to justify, legitimize and reinforce the democratic legitimacy of the EU's authority structures.

3.   Failure of mutual accommodation to enhance the common good

Contradictions in operationalizing the ideal of open government at the EU level have revealed weaknesses at the national levels. The TEU provided for the creation of the post of ombudsman (Casini, Forte and Preto, 1994; Millar, 1994), someone to be appointed on the recommendation of the Petitions Committee by the EP and to be responsible for investigating claims of administrative failure by EU institutions. Not only was this post highly controversial but it became linked with two developments exemplifying the problems of vertical and horizontal institutional rivalry. First, the EP's attempt to expand its right of legislative scrutiny and supervision into the judicial, home affairs and common foreign and security policy pillars of the TEU met with a good deal of resistance. This was understandable in terms of the probable sensitive nature of much of the work in that area but was not entirely acceptable in terms of the exercise of democratic principles regarding government/executive accountability. Second, governments tried to evade augmenting the Council of Ministers' (and hence their own) accountability to the EP by insisting that a problem of opacity and a lack of openness existed not within their own ranks, nor in respect of the inter-institutional balance between the EP and the Council of Ministers but instead resided within the ranks of the Commission.

The Birmingham and Edinburgh European Councils sought to enhance 'transparency' in the EU. Attention focused on the allegedly closed nature of Commission decision-making. Rules and guidelines were set out governing the release of documentation to the public, the introduction of green and white consultative papers, processes of consultation with interest groups, lobby bodies and others with a legitimate interest in upcoming Commission legislative proposals. What this exercise revealed was not only that the Commission was probably the most open of all the civil services operating in the EU of Twelve but that several governments operated very restrictive practices and were far from open. Contradictions between the rhetoric and reality became apparent (Lodge, 1994).

Transparency became a vehicle for containing openness. This was clear both in the letter of the guidelines (which prescribed conditions under which the release of information might be refused as prejudicial or because of its financial sensitivity) and in the arguments over the operation of transparency. The Dutch and Swedish parliaments objected that they would not follow the guidelines which conflicted with existing national rules on openness. The ability of the ombudsman to treat objections by citizens of the member states equally (as required by the Rome Treaty) was also challenged since they would not necessarily be equally entitled to information, nor would national ministers or MPs.

The transparency argument magnified the contradictions in reconciling efficient government with democratic government. It is undoubtedly true that secrecy is sometimes essential to the success of negotiations and bargains. But it is less obvious that information open to the public in one member state should be refused to that in another. It is also probable that efficiency gains can be made if parliamentary scrutiny/interference and oversight in policy and decision-making are minimized. Indeed, technocrats might happily dispense with politicians; verbal face-to-face discourse might also be dispensed with on the grounds that efficiency gains and cost savings can be made by communicating as interactive citizens, teleconference fashion, on the information superhighway (DGXIII: 94); and efficiency might also be enhanced if consultation were reduced or eliminated.

While these are extreme examples of the efficiency versus democratic practice dilemma, attention does need to be paid to an appropriate trade-off between the two. More efficient government does not necessarily imply better or even good government. What the pressure to realize greater efficiency does, is to underline the competition for financial resources among policy sectors and their concomitant policy communities which may, of course, include the EU's institutions. As yet, efficient government has to be defined. How would it be recognized? At the very least, it is clear that efficiency gains could be made at the EU level in terms of time-saving, if legislative procedures, practices and inter-institutional interactions were better coordinated and streamlined in pursuit of a common goal.

Such change might be achieved through the elaboration of a document that was recognized and accepted as the constitution of the EU. The series of treaties and treaty amendments, coupled with the ever-changing territorial boundaries of the EU, create an impression of unfinished business. This in turn gives succour to those wishing to inhibit integration, a change in inter-institutional relations and the division and exercise of power and authority in the EU. It also allows the destructive whine of those intent upon measuring every alleged integrative 'gain' against some fanciful ideal of a complete (but illusory) national sovereignty under attack. Once again, the EP — notably since the time of the Crocodile Club — has been instrumental in trying to put a written constitution on the agenda (Martin, 1991).

4.   A failure of mobilization?

Arguably, a written constitution setting out the parameters of the EU and the powers, responsibilities and obligations of its institutions, might stem public uncertainty as to the purpose and scope of the EU and its institutions whose authority is not satisfactorily accepted or regarded as legitimate. In the short term, however, it might have the opposite result and highlight indifference or a grass roots challenge to the EU. In short, the public fails to differentiate between the various components of the EU and to dissociate EU institutions from one another. *Eurobarometer* surveys reveal little discrepancy, for example, between levels of public satisfaction with democracy in the EU and democracy in their own countries: 40 per cent and 43 per cent indicated satisfaction respectively in spring 1994. Intervening national level elections can compound a failure to differentiate between the two arenas. Consequently, any failing in any sphere or institution may easily rebound to the disadvantage of the EU as a whole, casting doubt on its overall legitimacy. This example illustrates a further aspect of the crisis in the EU's democratic legitimacy and its democratic deficit: the EP may see itself as the conscience of the EU, as the voice of its people, as their 'grand forum'. But the people themselves do not identify with it, with its outputs, its parties or its MEPs. The reasons for this are legion. They owe much to:

- the youth of the EP;
- the struggle it has had in securing recognition for itself and in justifying a legislative role for itself through which it could influence the content of policies;
- the fact that the Council has the final word on legislation, the fact that even where MEPs have influenced the shape of legislation that influence may be invisible or masked by subsequent bargaining within the Council of European Council;
- the innumerable problems associated with the Euro-elections and mobilizing the electorate to turn out and vote; and

- the absence of a consolidated socio-psychological community to underpin the EU.

The EP has tried to foster a sense of common purpose and endeavour in the elaboration of a European constitution by closely involving national parliaments in the exercise. The 1990 Rome 'Assizes' were an attempt both to overcome past weaknesses in collaboration between national MPs and MEPs, and to create consensus among the people's elected representatives as to the nature, scope and purpose of democratic institutions for the EU.

The decline in positive attitudinal change towards European integration has many causes outside the scope of this chapter. It reflects a failure of cognition and a failure to mobilize the public, an associated feature of the democratic legitimacy crisis. Just as the democratic deficit could not be entirely remedied merely by increasing the amount of public exposure to information about the EP or by providing for the election of the EP by direct, universal suffrage, so the democratic legitimacy crisis cannot be overcome merely by changing its role in the legislative process and *vis-à-vis* the public. The member governments have aggravated the crisis themselves. They have been seen to fail to internalize the legitimacy and authority of the very system of which they are part and which they are creating simultaneously. If they are not convinced of either its desirability, let alone its legitimacy, they will fail to inculcate a sense of the rightness of the system in the public mind with predictable consequences.

The Maastricht Treaty referendums revealed governments reneging on and denying agreements they had endorsed at the IGC. Indeed, the processes by which the decisions of the IGCs have been ratified have, to some extent, delegitimized the reforms and exacerbated the crisis of democratic legitimacy. It remains to be seen whether the EP can redress the situation through improved links with national parliaments to give its own work greater legitimacy, through more public hearings (which rose from an average of 2 to 20 a year between 1974–79 and 1980–89 respectively) (Corbett, 1994: 178), through continued imaginative or/and obstructive exercises – via Chapter 100 entries, for example – of its budgetary rights and authority to grant or withhold discharge of the budget, or through the elaboration of a draft constitution enjoying their support, or through supporting the Euro-ombudsman and the development of EU citizenship (Meehan 1993).

A European citizenship?

The creation of a European citizenship will not necessarily remedy deficiencies in democratic legitimacy if steps to realize it are misconstrued in a zero-sum way as representing a commensurate loss of national citizenship or as a means to exclude certain groups of people who might have reasonable grounds for believing that they should enjoy parity of treatment with those granted European citizenship. While the concept of European citizenship might in itself be seen as a corrective to negative ideas as to the EU's relevance to 'the ordinary person', its elaboration in terms of an ill-understood and discriminatory set of rights might unintentionally undermine rather than support affective identification with the EU and so widen rather than narrow one aspect of the democratic deficit.

It would be wrong to suppose that the issue of citizenship had not been addressed by the EC before Maastricht (Lodge and Herman, 1977). The Rome Treaty contained the range of measures that have become entrenched in the TEU as citizen rights. These included:

- prohibition of discrimination on grounds of nationality (Article 7);
- freedom of movement for workers within the EC (Article 48);
- adoption of social security measures necessary to ensure the free movement of workers (Article 51);
- freedom of establishment for the nationals of one member state in the territory of another (Articles 52–56);
- the right of citizens of one member state freely to provide services in another member state (Articles 59–66);
- the requirement for equal pay for male and female workers (Article 119).

The October 1972 EC summit (forerunner of the European Councils) on declaring 'European Union' to be an EC goal instigated a debate as to the status of citizens within an EU. In Copenhagen in December 1973, the nine Heads of State and Government adopted a declaration on European identity that stated their determination to 'defend the principles of representative democracy, of the rule of law, of social justice – which is the ultimate goal of economic progress – and of respect for human rights'. These were seen as 'fundamental elements of the European identity' which the Nine felt corresponded with 'the deepest aspirations of their peoples' whom they called on to participate in its realization 'particularly through their elected representatives'.

In July 1975, the EP called for the establishment of a 'Charter of the Rights of the Peoples of the European Community'. In November 1977, it invited the Commission to make proposals for special reciprocal rights. It also listed the kind of civil, political, economic and social rights which it felt should be included. The 1983 Stuttgart Declaration on European Union called for the harmonization of laws to facilitate closer relationships among nationals of the EC's member states.

In 1984, the EP's Draft Treaty establishing the European Union defined Citizenship of the Union as:

> The citizens of the member states shall, *ipso facto*, be citizens of the Union. Citizenship of the Union shall be dependent upon citizenship of a Member State and may not be independently acquired or forfeited. Citizens of the Union shall take part in the political life of the Union in the forms laid down in this Treaty, shall enjoy the rights granted to them by the legal system of the Union and be subject to its laws. (Article 3)

In June 1984, the Fontainebleau European Council stated that it was essential for the EC 'to adopt measures . . . to strengthen and promote the identity of the Community and its image in the minds of its citizens and in the world as a whole'. It set up the Adonnino Committee on A People's Europe whose report and recommendations were approved by the Milan European Council in June 1985. This was followed by the Single European Act and by important reports in the EP by David Martin and Emilio Colombo which outlined the EP's views on citizenship in the EU. The Martin Report of October 1990 accentuated the need for a declaration on Fundamental Rights and Freedoms and on their protection as well as on democracy. The Colombo Report of November 1990 on the Constitutional Basis of European Union included several articles on citizenship which drew on all the preceding ideas. Finally, the TEU entrenched EU citizenship:

1. Every person holding the nationality of a member state shall be a citizen of the Union.
2. Citizens of the Union shall enjoy the rights conferred by this Treaty and shall be subject to the duties imposed thereby.

The TEU also includes a commitment to respect 'fundamental rights, as guaranteed by the European Convention for the Protection of Human Rights and Fundamental Freedoms signed in Rome on 4 November 1950 and as they result from the constitutional traditions common to the Member States, as general principles of Community Law'.

The crisis in democratic legitimacy is often laid at the door of the EP. But this is not altogether appropriate since it obscures a wider crisis of public confidence in the systems of governance encountered at supranational, national and regional level.

The EP may, however, have a special responsibility for challenging and checking the basis of the evolving democracy in the EU. The EU, if it applied to join itself, might find its own democratic credentials a little short of its ideals. However, if public power is derived from the people who invest a directly elected institution with representing their interests, then it follows that the EP must ensure that the other institutions are accountable to it: the EP gives expression not only to the political relationship between citizens (the governed) and the Union (the 'government') but is the vehicle through which democratic legitimacy is conferred on EU laws drafted by authorities who are seen to exercise power in a lawful way. The problem for the EU is not that it acts in an unlawful way, nor even that its interventions are disproportionate in relation to the goals, but that the way in which it acts and the effectiveness of its policies and programmes are either ill-understood, invisible or unconvincing.

5. A failure of effectiveness?

There has been a partial failure on the EP's part to meet the requirement of effectiveness by delivering policies and programmes that are both visible and directly relevant to the electorate. This is a partial failure only because it is primarily one of visibility rather than of competence or commitment. The co-operation procedure augmented the effectiveness of EP influence through the system of two readings whereby the EP's amendments could only be overturned by unanimity in the Council at second reading, and whereby the Council had to adopt its common position by majority rather than unanimity. As a result, 50 per cent of Parliament's amendments were adopted by the Commission and 25 per cent by the Council. This is still too small a proportion but represents progress compared to the situation under the traditional consultation procedure. The relative invisibility of the EP's amendments and the EP's success in securing their adoption means that it is difficult to argue that they have enhanced either public perceptions of the EP's effectiveness or democratic legitimacy.

It is also too early to judge the effectiveness of the EP in exercising its powers of co-decision, notably in the five new spheres of competence in which it has the last word: education, culture, health protection, consumer protection and trans-European networks for transport, telecommunications and energy. According to Commission estimates, these areas – broadly speaking – are likely to account for around half of the future legislative programme of the EU.

It is arguable that the relative invisibility and/or uncertainty as to the origin and identity of the disbursement of EU 'public goods' reduces the possibility for an instrumentally-driven affective link and identification to develop between the EU and the public. The EP has pretensions to being the intermediary between the EU governing bodies and the public. In seeking to redress the democratic deficit by suggesting that the EU is indeed effective, MEPs are limited by several factors: the competing claims of member governments; the public's identification with traditional territorial authorities; the circumscriptions on the EP's powers and ability to deliver high-profile socio-economic packages that might encourage people to identify the EU as the source of 'goodies' and also to identify themselves with the common good they supposedly embody; and the EP's limited impact on expenditure decisions.

The EP has, over the years, managed to alter the distribution of available resources in EU expenditure and redirect a greater proportion to socio-economic welfare programmes by insisting on a cut in expenditure on the Common Agricultural Policy (CAP). The impact and amounts available vary across the member states and are easily masked in national public expenditure programmes except where boards are erected specifically to highlight that a programme (such as industrial renewal of infrastructures) is supported by the EU structural funds. However, enlargement of the EU to Central and Eastern Europe will significantly curtail the availability of such funds to existing impoverished regions in the EU: negative public reaction may ensue and reflect detrimentally on the EP and EU institutions. However, it is unlikely to result in secession bids. Instead, disenchantment with supranational and possibly national actors may encourage a search for alternative means of influencing policy. This development may be encouraged by any appearance of greater fragmentation within the EP if, as a result of further enlargement, party cohesion is undermined by a proliferation of small contingents. The rules affording recognition to groups of MEPs seeking official party status have been repeatedly amended and must be changed again. At present, to qualify for such status, a group must have a minimum of 29 MEPs if from one member state, 23 if from two, 18 if from three and 14 if drawn from four or more member states.

There has been an exponential growth in the lobbying of the EP by private sector and private sector interests which attests to their view of the increasing *importance* of MEPs in the legislative and policy-making processes (EP, Galle report, 16.03.92, doc. PE.200.405). MEPs are useful sources of information and conduits of views as the work progresses in the various committees during the cooperation and co-decision procedures. While the EP's budgetary authority is limited mainly to non-compulsory spending, since Maastricht, an inter-institutional agreement allows it to scrutinize every line of the budget and, in effect, to challenge the legal base of expenditure and assess whether specific lines should follow under headings which make it subject to EP intervention. It has limited powers to amend the draft budget and the final word on the budget overall.

Unless the EP uses opportunities to highlight publicly (or to embarrass) governments over spending plans or failures – as in the case of national governments' apparent acquiescence in agricultural fraud – its activities remain invisible to the public eye. The same is true, except in highly publicized cases, of its use of its assent power. The TEU expanded the right given to it by the Single European Act to give its assent to international agreements, including accession treaties and association agreements. It intervened politically on human rights grounds and refused to vote financial protocols attached to some Association agreements with the EC.

More visible perhaps, was the newly elected EP's attempt to vote against the appointment of Jacques Santer over Jean Luc Dehaene as Commission President. But it is doubtful that this act, which very nearly succeeded, reinforced its democratic credentials and legitimacy in the public mind. The mere exercise of its new rights in respect of the appointment of the Commission is the logical counterpart to its right to dismiss the Commission *en bloc*. Its cross-examination of individual Commissioners prior to their taking up office in January 1995 must be exploited to the full if MEPs genuinely are to influence the content, priorities and orientation of the new Commission's legislative programme. MEPs expect the Commission – as a result of the appointment process – to be more mindful of EP views than previous Commissions. This has yet to be tested fully.

The EP has, however, successfully impressed upon the Commission the need for it to be more responsive to MEPs' views. Even without further treaty amendment some significant advances have been made. Under the new Code of Conduct agreed with the Commission and seen by many MEPs as a working contract between the Commission and the EP, the EP has achieved parity of status with the Council of Ministers in respect of how the Commission treats it regarding the provision and transmission of information and documentation under the co-decision and budgetary procedures. Now, all information is simultaneously to be sent to both the EP and the Council on the basis of assuring parity of treatment. However, whereas in the member states national parliaments could expect a bill to fall if they withheld their support, a proposal rejected by the EP could still, theoretically, be adopted.

The Commission has taken the unprecedented step of agreeing that it will *normally* withdraw any legislative proposals rejected by the EP even if they are based on treaty articles which prescribe decision procedures other than co-decision. If the Commission decides that it nevertheless will not withdraw the proposal, it has agreed to justify its withdrawal at the level of the College of Commissioners and not simply at the level of individual Commissioners. Under the Code of Conduct, the Commission has agreed to: 'take utmost account of amendments adopted by Parliament at second reading of the co-operation and co-decision procedures.' In addition, the Commission has expressly acknowledged the EP's democratic legitimacy and confirmed its intention to respond positively to its views. The Code of Conduct states:

> With a view to contributing to the smooth functioning of the institutions, and having regard to the democratic legitimacy of the elected Parliament, the Commission undertakes to withdraw, where appropriate, any legislative proposal which the European Parliament has rejected. If, for important reasons and after consideration by the College, it decides to retain its proposal, the Commission shall explain the reasons for that decision before Parliament in a declaration.

The symbiotic relationship between the Commission and the EP has been boosted and with it the degree of legitimacy that can be claimed for legislative proposals advanced by the Commission and accepted by the EP. While this does not directly affect the respective powers of the EP and the Council of Ministers, it does affect their relative influence. It also places the onus on the Council of Ministers – and hence the national governments – to justify their positions publicly should they demur from proposals enjoying both Commission and EP support.

The fate of the biotechnology directive, nicknamed the Frankenstein directive by the EP in a bid to attract media attention to it, showed that the Council of Ministers was willing to accommodate the EP. Indeed, this directive fell under the rules governing co-decision. When it became necessary to promote compromise via the conciliation mechanism provided for under co-decision, the Council delegation proved itself highly amenable to changes sought by their counterparts from the EP. While the latter then accepted the amendment proposal by a strong majority, the directive nevertheless fell at the plenary stage in the EP where a simple majority rejected it. This highlighted both a strength and weakness of conciliation. While the aim to reconcile divergence was realized, the outcome was not necessarily seen as acceptable – and hence legitimate – by a larger number of MEPs. This might encourage

Council delegations in conciliation in future to be less accommodating. Alternatively, it may encourage those responsible for examining legislative procedures to propose to the 1996 IGC the introduction of full-blown co-decision and full parity between the Council and the EP.

The final arena in which the EP's effectiveness *vis-à-vis* the public has been tested concerns citizens. Apart from its powers to call the other institutions to account (in committee, in plenary session, by written and oral questions, and through the various stages of the cooperation and co-decision procedures) it can claim to represent voters' interests. It investigates petitions received from them on matters under EU competence; may appoint committees of enquiry to investigate matters of EU concern; appoints the Euro-ombudsman and sets out the rules regarding his/her staff, budget and remit. In short, it has a watch-dog and guardian roles to perform where citizens are concerned. Again, it is doubtful that the public is either aware of this or appreciates its significance. Consequently, while the preparatory groundwork for an accretion in democratic legitimacy has been done, the democratic deficit remains. Nor has the new Committee of the Regions as yet done anything to assist in cutting it.

One way of assessing the public's view of the effectiveness of the EP might be to examine election turnout figures. Turnout can only be one extremely crude measure of democratic legitimacy. But it has been the one indicator which has been used to support or deny the justifiability of the EP's quest for greater power. The lack of correlation between the outcome of the competitive election and the colour of the 'Euro-government' has been used to explain modest turnout figures and the failure, in several states, to mobilize latent support. The overall decline in turnout since 1979 might be interpreted as symptomatic of dissatisfaction with the effectiveness of the EP.

However, it is difficult to disaggregate this from both negative impressions of the EP (whether couched in terms of its peripatetic nature and attendant costliness, the stature of its candidates and outgoing MEPs or its powers) and poor general awareness of what the EP does, or is capable of doing, compared with national parliaments (whose outputs are readily conflated with those of national governments). It is also hard to separate this from the overall problems of increasing turnout which may be attributed to failure of party mobilization, failure of campaigns, weaknesses of national and transnational party organization, perceived absence of candidate and/or party differentials as well as to programmatic failure signalling dissatisfaction with the EU's legislative output and even a lack of conviction that the EP can do much to influence and determine legislative outcomes. If the electorate is not convinced of the utility of voting, improving its awareness of electoral campaigns and opportunities will not significantly increase turnout.

Overall, the unintentional effect of Euro-elections perhaps has been indirectly to heighten scepticism about the EU's democratic legitimacy, effectiveness and the appropriateness of its institutional arrangements. The EP's dynamic role in advancing a European Union endowed with appropriate, democratic institutions and policy-making and legislative procedures has not been sufficiently visible or appreciated by the public to enable it to justify its claim for greater power with reference to its heightened public esteem. Until this happens, it will be difficult for MEPs to redress the democratic deficit in the way originally foreseen. Moreover, if voters are ignorant about or disinterested in European integration, do not distinguish the particular role of the EP in the EU and are at odds with the position that their national governments take on further integration, the legitimacy of the existing EU is likely to be queried. This means that the multifaceted nature of the democratic legitimacy problem has to be addressed from a variety of perspectives. The problem for the EU, however, is deciding how to achieve this and whether there is enough time to do this when new applicants wish to accede to the EU before fundamental difficulties have been overcome. Their competing claims on the EU and their inevitable dissatisfaction and disappointment with EU performance and EU ability to deliver economic goodies as swiftly as might be hoped could seriously further erode the incipient democratic polity.

Furthermore, in an era when the frontiers of political life are no longer contained within the territorial boundaries of the old nation states and when non-elected, non-parliamentary actors, including a range of technocratic and private sector bodies, play an instrumental role in setting, adjusting and influencing the legislative agenda, the issue of defining and rectifying the EU's democratic deficit by reference to the socio-political norms of a bygone age may no longer be entirely appropriate. This observation does not justify abandonment of the exercise. It merely alerts one to the need to take a more imaginative approach to identifying the problem, strategies to ameliorate the situation and approaches to rectifying the democratic deficit in its many guises.

Conclusion

Democracy versus legitimacy: two sides of the same coin?

Legitimacy rests on the capacity to engender and maintain belief in the appropriateness and justness of existing political institutions and their outputs. This means that in the context of the EU, the EP's quest for democratic legitimacy is tied up with more than an attempt to justify its own role and powers in the eyes of the public. Its quest is inextricably linked to the problems of legitimizing European integration. Its position is made more difficult because the arena in which the particular issues must be elaborated shifts. Furthermore, the EP is still in the position of having to challenge inter-institutional arrangements. It does so both to justify its own quest for greater legislative power and to check the potential abuse of power by the chamber which should share power with it and assume an equal, but not superior, voice to it. Gaining public appreciation of the myriad difficulties involved is hard and protracted. However, the EP must continue giving voice to constitutional and policy concerns if it is to be seen as a legitimate player and if citizens are to internalize the EU's legitimacy, identify in some way with it and become active rather than passive subjects in the emergent, integrated polity serving the EU.

References

Bieber, R and Schwarze, J (eds) (1984) *Eine Verfassung für Europa*, Nomos, Baden Baden.
Camps, M (1966) *European Unification in the Sixties*, Oxford University Press, London.
Casini, C, Forte, C and Preto, A (1994) 'A New Champion for Parliament', *European Briefing*, November: 32–24.
Commission Européenne (1994) *Application du Principe de Subsidiarité*, C (94) 1251 fin.
— Report of the High Level Group (1994) 'Europe and the Global Information Society', *I&T Magazine*, DGXIII, autumn: 3–5.
— DGXIII (1994) 'Europe's Way to the Information Society – an Action Plan', *I&T News Review*, autumn: 1–2.
Corbett, R (1994) 'The elected European Parliament and its impact on the process of European integration', unpublished PhD thesis, University of Hull.
Endo, K (1994) 'The Principle of Subsidiarity: From Johannes Althusius to Jacques Delors', *The Hokkaido Law Review*, 1966–2064.
European Parliament working documents:
— (1988) Report on the institutional consequences of the costs of non-Europe, rapporteur Sir Fred Catherwood, A2-39/88.
— (1987) Toussaint report on the democratic deficit, A2-276/87.
— (1990) G D'Estaing reports on subsidiarity, A3-0267/90; A3-163/90/Part B.
— Debates of the EP Session 1991/92, no 412, p 217.
— (1994) *Les Avis Legislatifs du Parlement Européen et leur Impact: Procedures de Consultation, 1: Affaires Etrangères/Securité*, Brussels, May.
Herman V and Lodge, J (1978) *The European Parliament and the European Community*, Macmillan, London and New York.
Jacque, J (1983) 'The European Union Treaty and the Community Treaties', *Crocodile*, 11.
Kapetyn, P (1991) 'Community Law and the Principle of Subsidiarity', *Revue des Affaires Européennes*, 2: 35–43.
Lodge, J (1982) 'The European Parliament After Direct Elections: Talking Shop or Putative Legislature?', *Journal of European Integration*, 5: 259–84.
— (1984) 'European Union and the First Elected European Parliament: the Spinelli Intiative', *Journal of Common Market Studies*, 22: 377–402.
— (1986) 'The Single European Act: Towards a New Euro-dynamism?', *Journal of Common Market Studies*, 24: 47–69.
— (1989) 'The European Parliament – From Assembly to Co-legislature: Changing the Institutional Dynamics', in Lodge, J (ed) *The EC and the Challenge of the Future*, Pinter, London.
— (1993) 'The European Community in the Historical Context of its Parliament', Strasbourg.
— (1994) 'Transparency and Democratic Legitimacy', *Journal of Common Market Studies*, 32: 343–68.
Lodge, J and Herman, V (1977) 'Citizenship, Direct Elections and the European Parliament', *Res Publica*, 19: 579–605.
— (1979) 'Democratic Legitimacy and Direct Elections', *West European Politics*, 2: 226–51.
— (1982) *Direct Elections to the European Parliament: A Community Perspective*, Macmillan, London.
Louis, J-L (ed) (1995) *L'Union Européenne: Le Projet de traité du Parlement Européen après Fontainebleau*, Université Libre de Bruxelles, Brussels

Mackenzie-Stewart, Lord, (1992) 'Subsidiarity – A Busted Flush?' in Curtin, D and O'Keefe, D (eds) *Constitutional Adjudication in European Community and National Law* (Butterworth, Ireland): 19–24.

Martin, D (1991) *Europe: An Ever Closer Union*, Spokesman, Nottingham.

Meehan, E (1993) *Citizenship and the European Community*, Pinter, London.

Millar, D (1994) 'Why a Weak Ombudsman Would Mean a Weaker European Parliament', *European Briefing*, November: 35.

Spinelli, A (1983) 'Die Parlamentarische Initiative zur Europäischen Union', *Europa Archiv*, 38: 739–446.

— (1983a) 'Verso L'Unione Europea', *Il Federalista*, 25: 115–30.

2

The Benelux

Bart van Deelen

Belgium

Background

Since the 1989 European elections Belgium has gone through political turmoil and radical institutional changes. The 1991 national election resulted in an unforeseen number of protest votes and the breakthrough of the extreme right in Flanders. In the aftermath of the elections, the traditional parties in Flanders had started to transform themselves in one way or another. Most important was the transformation of the liberal Partij voor Vrijheid en Vooruitgang (PVV) into the VLD (Vlaamse Liberalen en Demokraten). The party presented itself as the only truly democratic alternative to the ruling Christelijke Volkspartij (CVP) and Socialist Party (Flanders) (SP) which, according to the VLD, represented pressure groups rather than citizens. It managed to attract some Flemish nationalists from the gradually disintegrating Volksunie (VU) and scored consistently higher in the opinion polls than the CVP. An end of CVP hegemony in Flanders which existed since the Second World War would have a radical impact on Belgian politics. In Wallonia, the dominant socialist party, PS, was heavily discredited and more divided than ever as a result of various scandals, which had led to the resignation of several PS ministers from the Wallonian and Belgian government. The goal for the Wallonian opposition parties, particularly the liberal PRL, was to put an end to the Wallonian 'PS state'. On top of the political turmoil, Belgium had been turned effectively into a federal state in July 1993 and the federal government had tried to reduce further the enormous budget deficit with a new far-reaching package of austerity measures, the *Globaal Plan/Plan Global*. The European elections were expected to register the impact of all these events on voters' preferences and attracted a lot of attention from the media.

Towards the elections

Twenty-five MEPs had to be elected in Belgium, one more than in 1989. As a result of the constitutional reforms, 14 MEPs were elected in Flanders, ten in

Wallonia and, for the first time, one in the *Ostkantons*. Eleven parties participated in the elections in Flanders and Wallonia, compared to eight and nine in 1989. Voters elect their MEPs by approving a hierarchical list of candidates which a party presents to them. A 'preference vote' for a particular candidate on the list can be given but the order of the list is rarely reversed.

In Flanders the VLD campaign was led and dominated by Annemie Neyts, former PVV party chairman, and by ex-EC Commissioner Willy de Clercq (who got 230,193 preference votes in 1989). He led the campaign in 1989, and was first on the list. In comparison to most other parties, fewer political heavyweights were put on the VLD list, officially because it was deemed unrespectable to have candidates who would never take up their MEP mandate. In practice, the VLD thought that because of the media attention it had received in the past the name VLD had become more important than the candidates themselves.

The other parties were less ambitious. The CVP hoped to stay ahead of the VLD, with Leo Tindemans and Wilfried Martens as leading candidates. The hope was that the charismatic Tindemans would be able to keep many of his 433,172 preference votes from the 1989 campaign. Former Prime Minister Wilfried Martens, on the other hand, enjoyed increasing popularity since he was continuously portrayed as the CVP's scapegoat for the party's 1991 electoral defeat after having been Prime Minister for 11 years. The successful Belgian EC presidency and the resulting rumours about CVP Prime Minister Jean-Luc Dehaene's possible succession to Jacques Delors as head of the European Commission were extra assets for the CVP's campaign. The party pointed to its European experience and orientation with the slogan 'Europe in good hands'.

The goal of the Flemish socialists (SP) was to keep its three seats in the EP. They took a risk by replacing all their MEPs and putting the federal Minister for Pensions, Freddy Willockx, at the head of their list. Willockx was not unpopular but his European convictions were unclear. Moreover, the numbers two and three of the list, Anne Van Lancker and Steve Stevaert, were newcomers in the party and relatively unknown. The party compensated for this by putting most of its ministers from the federal and Flemish government on the list. The Flemish-nationalist Volksunie's aim was to get its MEP Jaak Vandemeulebroucke re-elected, and the Green Party, AGALEV, was determined not to miss a second seat this time and put MP Magda Aelvoet before MEP Paul Staes. The extreme right Vlaams Blok tried to consolidate its 1991 election victory to win a second seat in the EP.

In Wallonia, the PS tried to limit electoral damage by putting four of its outgoing MEPs again in the first four places. Very few members of the party establishment figured on the PS-list. This proved a great opportunity for popular party rebel and Wallonian nationalist José Happart (308,117 preference votes in 1989) to strengthen his position within the party as leader of the PS campaign. The other parties tried to counter a possible 'Happart' effect by putting their political heavyweights at the head of the list: Jean Gol and

Antoinette Spaak for the PRL-FDF, Gerard Deprez for the Parti Social Chrétien (PSC), and Paul Lannoye for ECOLO. Many smaller parties participated for the first time in the Euro-elections, such as the red-green party Rood Groene Beweging (RGB), the Natuurwetpartij (NWP) and above all Waardig Ouder Worden (WOW), a party for the elderly. In Wallonia, the expectation was that the extreme-right parties AGIR and above all the ultra-Belgicist Front National would perform well.

The composition of the party lists was heavily influenced by the 'national' character of the election. Most parties (except the PS) put more prominent national politicians on the lists to improve the scores than in 1989, though some of them were also prepared to leave for Strasbourg if elected. Thus, experienced and active MEPs such as Karel de Gucht (VLD), Paul Staes (AGALEV), An Hermans (CVP), Lode Van Outrive, Marc Galle and Marijke Van Hemeldonck (SP) had to give way to political heavyweights such as Annemie Neyts (VLD), Magda Aelvoet (AGALEV), Wilfried Martens (CVP) or newcomers (SP). The SP wanted to present a more dynamic profile as a party which would tackle people's daily problems, a profile which it badly needed on the national scene. Against that background, the three outgoing MEPs were considered as 'too intellectual'. The CVP's desire to put Martens on the list meant that because of internal balances in the party outgoing MEP An Hermans was offered the uncertain fifth place on the list. She refused because in 1989 she was in second place. In Wallonia the rotation of candidates was smaller: 10 out of 11 MEPs stood again in the election, compared to 7 out of 13 in Flanders. Finally, only 19,861 out of 469,137 residents in Belgium from EU countries (4.2 per cent) registered to vote for the European elections.

As in the other EU countries, the Belgian Euro-elections took place in a context of Euro-pessimism. Disillusion about the ratification process of the Maastricht Treaty, the EU's shortcomings in Bosnia, and the economic recession with rising unemployment prevailed. Still, there were no real anti-Maastricht parties, although extreme right parties like the Vlaams Blok came close to it. The party's view was that the EP had enough competences and condemned the overregulation by Brussels, but focused its attention on the allegedly 'disastrous' EU immigration and asylum policies, international criminality and the drugs traffic, fraud, the waste of money by an enormous bureaucracy, and the neglect of Flemish interests at the European level.

The 1994 campaign focused less on the future institutional framework of the EU, its enlargement or the future of the Common Foreign and Security Policy (CFSP). Central in the campaign were concrete policy areas in which the EU should act, such as the fight against the economic recession and unemployment. Strengths and weaknesses of the Delors White Paper were often analysed. From time to time, the EU's role in the fight against social dumping, racism, fraud and corruption, drug trafficking and combating crime, or the protection of minority languages were discussed. It was in these more specific discussions of policy areas that differences between parties surfaced. For example, the socialist parties focused heavily on the fight against unemployment but their proposal to cut working time and preserve social rights conflicted with the liberal emphasis on cutting the cost of labour. Liberal and Christian-democratic parties emphasized the importance of the Maastricht criteria as the road to economic recovery. The Green parties, on the other hand, condemned these criteria and the Delors White Paper as short-term actions which did little to switch to more environmentally friendly production processes.

There was less clarity about the framework in which the EU should operate, although in Belgium too, demands were heard for a decentralized, less bureaucratic and more democratic Europe. Only the Christian-democrats Leo Tindemans, Wilfried Martens and Gerard Deprez declared themselves openly as Euro-federalists. The other candidates were vaguer and advocated a 'more integrated' Europe or 'more Europe'.

The most 'European' campaign was run by the Flemish-nationalist Volksunie, though mainly because the party did not want to remind voters of its questionable future on the Belgian political scene. Under the slogan 'for a Europe where Flemish feel at home' it pleaded for a Europe of the Regions, and argued that the Commitee of the Regions, created by the TEU, should become a 'Senate of the Regions'. The VU also wanted to link the right of EU citizens to vote in Flanders to knowledge of the language of the region and paying local taxes. Surprisingly, the VLD had perhaps the most specific European programme. Under its more general philosophy that citizens should have a bigger say in politics and politics should become more transparent, it pleaded for referendums in Belgium on important European issues, the direct election of the EU Commission President and fewer committees in the European Parliament. Still, the VLD campaign was a purely national one heavily directed against the federal government. The VLD used newspaper ads where the word 'Europe' was not even mentioned. This was very different from the 1989 campaign when the PVV focused heavily on the importance of the internal market in an internationalized economy.

The feeling that the population was not interested in the Euro-campaign was reflected in a short campaign of only three weeks. Most electoral meetings attracted few people, with the exception of the tent of 'the two Leos', Leo Tindemans and Defense Minister Leo Delcroix, also on the CVP list. The two Leos held rallies in the tent all over Flanders.

The campaign was more sober than in 1989 because it was affected by a new law on limiting electoral expenses. The law introduced limits on expenditure by the parties, candidates, and on the use of boards and posters. It also prohibited certain practices like the distribution of presents or gadgets. As it turned out, all expenses stayed well within the limits of the law. There were far fewer posters and leaflets than in 1989, and a lot of space on the boards remained unused. The messages on them were vaguer than ever, and the PSC and VLD had no slogans at all. The campaign was also regionally oriented: in Flanders only Leo Tindemans, Wilfried Martens, Annemie Neyts, and Freddy Willockx campaigned everywhere.

Bart van Deelen

Table 2.1   Euro-election results in Belgium

	Seats		Votes %		
Total seats 25 (in 1989: 24)	Number 1994	Gain/ loss	Euro- election 1994	Euro- election 1989	General election 1991
Flanders					
CVP	4	−1	27.4	34.1	27.0
SP	3	0	17.7	20.0	19.2
VLD	3	+1	18.4	17.1	19.2
VU	1	0	7.1	8.7	9.5
AGALEV	1	0	10.7	12.2	7.8
VLAAMS BLOK	2	+1	12.6	6.6	10.6
WOW	0	−	3.4	−	−
Wallonia					
PSC	2	−1	18.8	21.0	20.5
PS	3	−2	30.5	38.5	35.7
PRL/FDF	3	+1	24.2	22.8	25.4
ECOLO	1	−1	13.0	16.5	13.6
FN	1	+1	7.9	−	1.7
Ostkantons					
CSP	1	+1	31.3	41.9	37.3
PFF	0	−	20.1	20.8	23.4
ECOLO	0	−	14.9	21.8	22.8
SP	0	−	12.6	13.0	15.4
PDB	0	−	15.5	−	−

Results

The results of the Euro-election in Flanders (see Table 2.1) were very similar to the 1991 national election results. The CVP remained the largest party with 27.4 per cent of the votes, well ahead of the SP and the VLD. The relative success of the CVP was certainly due to the fact that the numbers one and two on the CVP list were also the two most popular Flemish candidates: Leo Tindemans and Wilfried Martens managed to collect 208,341 and 186,410 preference votes. Compared to the 1989 Euro-elections however, the CVP suffered the greatest loss (down 6.7 per cent), and dropped from five to four seats. The VLD won 1.3 per cent of the vote, enough to win a third seat in the EP, but less than it had hoped for. The *status quo* was a great disappointment. In absolute figures, the real winner of the elections was certainly the Vlaams Blok. The party almost doubled its score from 6.6 per cent to 12.6 per cent and obtained a second seat in the EP. The fact that the party clearly consolidated its breakthrough of 1991 caused less animosity than the breakthough itself in 1991. SP, AGALEV and VU lost lightly but kept their number of seats in the Parliament. This was seen as a success in SP and VU headquarters, although both parties had fallen to a historic low, but not within AGALEV.

In Wallonia, José Happart managed to limit losses to the PS: 5.3 per cent compared to the 1991 election, 8 per cent compared to the 1989 Euro-election. The party fell from five to three seats but one seat would have been lost anyway because there was one MEP less to elect in Wallonia. For Happart, the 265,376 preference votes were a personal success, about 100,000 more than his PRL-challenger Jean Gol. However, PS losses were gains to the extreme right Front National and AGIR, with 7.9 per cent and 1.9 per cent of the votes respectively. The FN even managed to obtain a seat in the EP. Yet, with 30.5 per cent of the votes, the PS remained by far the biggest party. In the Ostkantons, the seat went to the Christian democratic CSP.

Overall, the 25 Belgian MEPs were elected on no less than 12 different party lists, compared to ten in 1989. Seven were Christian democrats, the same number as in 1989. The socialists would send six MEPs (−2), the liberals also six (+2), the extreme right parties three (+2), the Greens two (−1), and the Volksunie one (*status quo*). On balance, there had certainly been a shift to the right of the political spectrum. Eight MEPs were women, compared to six in 1989.

Thirteen out of 24 outgoing MEPs were reelected, but proportionally more in Wallonia (7 out of 11) than in Flanders (6 out of 13). On the Flemish side, seven experienced MEPs were replaced by six MEPs (exception made for Wilfried Martens) who had never shown great interest in European issues before. For three of them it would be their first parliamentary mandate. The average age of the Flemish MEPs was much lower than before. This may at least lead to a temporary loss in expertise and activity, on which points the outgoing MEPs had a good record. On the other hand, Freddy Willockx (SP), Annemie Neyts (VLD), and Magda Aelvoet (AGALEV) have considerable experience in the Belgian Parliament. The expectation was, however, that Annemie Neyts would return to Belgian politics should the VLD be part of the next federal government. The same is true for francophones Jean Gol (PRL) and Antoinette Spaak (FDF): both are chairmen of their respective parties and are unlikely to engage in much activity in the EP. Since almost all other francophone MEPs were reelected, few changes can be expected there.

The impact of the Euro-election on Belgian MEP contributions to augmenting the influence of the European Parliament is probably balanced. Karel de Gucht (VLD) was one of the most active MEPs in this area, but his departure is probably compensated for by the arrival of Wilfried Martens. However, the loss of expertise in the areas of agricultural policy, women's rights, immigration and asylum policies, and cultural policy caused by the departure of Pol Marck, An Hermans, Lode Van Outrive and Marc Galle will probably be harder to replace. Possibly Neyts would take over some of Galle's interests in the cultural and linguistic themes if she stayed long enough in the EP. It is also far from certain whether the new SP and VLD MEPs have the same integrationist view on the future of the EU as their predecessors. More pragmatism may sneak in here.

The Netherlands

Background

The European elections in the Netherlands were held in a very different context than in Belgium. Whereas for the Belgian voters it was the first opportunity to express themselves since the national elections of 1991, Dutch voters were called to the ballot box for the third time in three months. After the municipal elections of 2 March, the 3 May national elections had dealt a severe blow to the CDA/PvdA Christian democratic–socialist coalition partners. Together both parties lost 32 of their 103 seats in Parliament (of a total of 150 seats) and therefore also their parliamentary majority. The CDA alone lost 13 per cent of its vote and 20 seats. Above all, the PvdA overtook the CDA as biggest party. The real winners of the elections, however were the liberal VVD, the centre-left Demokraten 66 (D'66) and Alters Verbond (AOV), a party for the elderly. A 'purple' coalition of socialists, liberals and centre-left seemed to be most in line with the preference of the voters, and eventually the party leaders of these parties formed a new coalition.

Towards the elections

Because it was the third electoral campaign in a row, the Euro-campaign started rather late. Eleven parties took part in the elections, but the AOV did not participate. This was beneficial for the CDA because it was no secret that the CDA had proportionally higher support from the older segments of the population. Also, the CDA has a tendency to score higher in Euro-elections than in national elections. These two factors led the CDA to start campaigning just a week after the national elections. This was well ahead of the other parties which, speculating on 'voter fatigue', only started their campaign on 27 May, ie two weeks before polling day.

The CDA and PvdA lists for the Euro-elections were led by female ministers in the CDA-PvdA government, Ms Hanja Maij-Weggen and Ms Hedy d' Ancona. Both had been MEPs before returning to Dutch national politics, and some observers thought their new Euro-role was an elegant way to replace both ministers in the new government in the making. Piet Dankert, former president of the European Parliament and outgoing 'Staatssecretaris voor Europese Zaken' (Minister for European Affairs), only received the third place on the PvdA list. This was seen as a sanction from the party for the relatively unsuccessful Dutch EC Presidency in the fall of 1991. As in the 1989 campaign, the D'66 list was led by Jan-Willem Bertens, a former diplomat but relatively unknown to the public. The VVD chose for outgoing MEP Givs de Vries to lead the list, whose views were seen as more Euro-integrationist than those of the party establishment. Whereas Mr de Vries openly advocated a federal Europe and more powers for the European Parliament, the official party doctrine emphasized the importance of Economic and Monetary

Union (EMU) more than anything else. Three traditional protestant formations, the Staatkundig Gereformeerde Partij (SGP), the Gereformeerd Poli-
tiek Verbond (GPV), and the Reformatorische Politieke Federatie (RPF)
presented themselves together on a common list.

Perhaps the greatest actor in the Dutch Euro-campaign was outgoing Prime
Minister Ruud Lubbers, who announced his candidacy for the presidency of
the European Commission on the evening of the national elections. The
announcement hardly came as a surprise, and was widely supported across the
political spectrum in the Netherlands. Mr Lubbers became a unifying factor in
the Euro-campaign as most politicians felt a Dutch head of the Commission
would be in the interest of the Netherlands. Moreover, there was a feeling
that the Dutch had a 'right' to the job since the Netherlands was the only one
of the original six EC member states which had not managed yet to get one of
its nationals in the seat of Commission president. And had the Netherlands not
failed to get good candidates appointed for the top jobs in the European Bank
for Reconstruction and Development (EBRD) and International Monetary
Fund (IMF)? Soon speculation about the possible success of the Lubbers campaign across Europe overshadowed the Euro-election campaign in the Netherlands, particularly when Mr Lubbers started campaigning more aggressively
against what was seen by many as a Franco–German 'Diktat' in favour of
Belgian Prime Minister Jean-Luc Dehaene as head of the European Commission.

The Euro-campaign was not only overshadowed by speculation about the
fate of Mr Lubbers, but also about the chances of success of the negotiations
for a national 'purple' coalition government. It was in the interest of the three
parties involved, PvdA, VVD and D'66, to keep a low profile on European
issues for the sake of the negotiation process. Therefore the Dutch Euro-
elections lost much of their relevance for national political life and were generally held in a very serene atmosphere.

All this speculation left little room for debate about the substance of policies
at the European level. If debate did get off the ground, it was usually about
pillars 2 and 3 of the Maastricht Treaty. What would, for example, be the
place of Dutch drugs and immigration policies in a future European approach?
Should the Dutch adapt to the more restrictive European approach or vice
versa? The CDA and VVD approach to get Dutch policies in line with the European approach conflicted with PvdA and D'66 requests for a debate about what
the most effective policy should be to combat drug use and international crime.
Often pleas were made for a more uniform interpretation of the definition of
'political refugee' and a fairer division of numbers of asylum seekers among
EU states. Other states were blamed for not taking up their responsibilities in
this area. Many MEP candidates said they would veto any new European Commission with neo-fascist members. On the Common Foreign and Security
Policy (CFSP), the PvdA distinguished itself from the other traditional parties
by its continuing belief in the Conference on Security and Cooperation in
Europe (CSCE) as the best framework for the CFSP to operate in.

The future of the European architecture was largely absent as a theme, but the few occasions where it did come up showed increasing pragmatism on this point. Leading CDA candidate Maij-Weggen for example opposed a CFSP where the right to veto would be absent. She also criticized the EU for being too bureaucratic, technocratic, and diplomatic instead of being a bulwark of vision and action (*De Volkskrant*, 8.6.94). She was very much in line there with Mr Lubbers who, in his campaign for the Commission presidency, also stressed the need for 'less regulation', and 'to look for the power of the European Union in the countries themselves'. He claimed that from this perspective a social policy at EU level would be difficult to achieve. He was not a federalist if that meant further eroding the nation-states. He was in favour of common action in certain cases, but in other cases an intergovernmental approach was needed, 'within the Europe of the fatherlands'. Enlarging the Union would inevitably lead to more intergovernmentalism anyway (*De Volkskrant*, 28.5.94).

Compared to the lukewarm attitude of the traditional parties towards further European integration smaller parties, like the extreme right Centrumdemokraten (CD), were heavily against it, advocating Dutch independence in a co-operating, non-federal Europe. Groen Links heavily attacked the market-oriented approach of the European Union, the concept of Monetary Union and a European Central Bank – seen as exponents of the Europe of 'big finance' – and the secrecy of European decision-making.

The electoral campaign itself started late and never made the front page of the papers. Most boards which were put up were only partially used. Political parties were each granted a number of five-minute political broadcasts on radio and TV. Citizens also received leaflets on buses, most of them from the CDA as it had the most intensive campaign. The press reflected Euro-fatigue. Many commentators expressed doubts about the ability of the European Parliament to control decision-making. Should it not be replaced by closer cooperation among national Parliaments? Question marks were also put behind the still somewhat integrationist rhetoric of the political elites. Had the turmoil over the ratification of Maastricht not revealed that the general public had doubts about further integration? Some opinion polls had indeed indicated that the Dutch were even less in favour of a federal Europe than the British (the *European*, 13.5.94). Most papers during the Euro-campaign continued to focus heavily on the negotiations for the purple coalition, and less on the substantial differences between the parties, particularly about Europe. Since the negotiations were going well and the Lubbers campaign, on the other hand, seemed to have a life of its own, voters certainly could not get motivated to vote by what the papers had to say.

Results

The results of the Euro-campaign were a surprise in two ways. Compared to the 1989 election results (see Table 2.2), both the CDA and the PvdA lost a substantial number of votes. Their support fell from 34.6 per cent to 30.8 per

Table 2.2   Euro-election results in The Netherlands

Total seats 31 (in 1989: 25)	Seats			Votes %		
	Number 1994	Gain/ loss	Euro-election 1994	Euro-election 1989	General election 1994
CDA	10	0	30.8	34.6	22.2
PvdA	8	0	22.9	30.7	24.0
VVD	6	+3	17.9	13.6	19.9
D'66	4	+3	11.7	5.6	15.5
SGP-GPV-RPF	2	+1	7.8	5.9	4.8
Groen Links	1	−1	3.7	7.0	3.5
AOV	–	–	–	–	3.6
CD	0	–	1.3	–	2.5

cent and from 30.7 per cent to 22.9 per cent of the votes respectively. As in the national elections, the liberal VVD and the social-democratic D'66 each won about 4 to 5 per cent, but the moral winners were the CDA because after the disastrous national election result of 3 May it unexpectedly emerged again as largest party.

Because the number of Dutch MEPs to be elected had gone up from 25 to 31 and the Netherlands is one national constituency for the Euro-elections, the threshold to obtain a seat had gone down from 4 per cent to just over 3 per cent. Thus, both CDA and PvdA managed to keep their number of seats in the new European Parliament at the same level (10 and 8 respectively). The VVD doubled its representatives from three to six and the D'66 representation increased from one to four. Finally, the combined list of the reformed protestants did slightly better than in 1989, but Groen Links dropped from 7 to 3.7 per cent and from two to one seat. The far-right parties failed to get any seats.

The relative success of the CDA was overshadowed by the extremely low turnout of 35.6 per cent, the lowest percentage of the whole EU and considerably lower than the 1989 turnout (47.2 per cent). The comparison with the national election turnout of 78 per cent was painful. The legitimacy of the newly elected MEPs was questionable. Even CDA politicians acknowledged that the good CDA result was more a result of the fact that 57 per cent of those who had voted CDA in the national elections turned out again, compared to only 39 per cent for the VVD, 37 per cent for the PvdA, and 31 per cent for D'66. Also, 63 per cent stayed with the CDA, compared to only 43 per cent for the PvdA, 41 per cent for the VVD and 34 per cent for D'66. The CDA benefited more from the composition of its electorate than from its popularity as a party. A proportionally high share of the elderly and protestant population turned out, categories where the CDA traditionally scored. Protestant voter discipline also explains the good result of the reformed protestant parties.

On the basis of such a low turnout no conclusions could be drawn as to the popularity of the major parties at national level. This suited most parties. The CDA was still analysing its heavy defeat suffered one month earlier, and PvdA, VVD, and D'66 did not receive a clear signal that voters did not approve of a purple coalition, so they could continue to construct one in a 'business as usual' atmosphere. Ms Maij-Weggen claimed the CDA result would strengthen Mr Lubbers' chances for the Commission presidency but most of her colleagues, including Mr Lubbers himself, feared most foreign commentators would rather point to the low turnout in Mr Lubbers' country which, if anything, would rather his bid for the presidency weaken than strengthen it.

As usual, the names of the newly elected Dutch MEPs received little attention because, with a few exceptions, the names are known before the election results. Voters actually decide only the number of seats for each party after the selectorates within the parties have made up the order of the list. Sixteen out of 17 MEPs who stood again were reelected. Ten MEPs were women, compared to seven in 1989.

The extremely dull Dutch Euro-election campaign and the disastrous turnout certainly ended any illusions about a prevailing consensus among political élites and the general public in the Netherlands about the necessity of further European integration towards a federal goal. This led some to argue for the reintroduction of the MP–MEP 'dubbelmandate', for more institutionalized consultation between MEPs and MPs, and for MEPs to make their work 'more visible' to the Dutch public. Others went further, saying that the 'federal Europe had vanished', 'Maastricht is dead', 'Europe will be a confederation at best', and 'the real democratic control has to come from national Parliaments'. These seem overreactions. Thirty-seven per cent of the non-voters were reported to have stayed home because they had 'no interest' in the elections, 11 per cent didn't know whom to vote for and 8 per cent claimed it didn't matter who they voted for. The conclusion was that 'voters only come when there is something to vote for'. This is still not the case, so one could also interpret the low turnout as a signal towards the politicians to ensure there is something to vote for. Moreover, the timing of the Euro-election was bad. It is hardly surprising that voters were not interested in Euro-elections when the PM campaigned for the top job in the European Commission and a new government coalition now being constructed. Since the Euro-elections were perceived to have little effect on both events, the Dutch elections were not 'national' enough, as in Belgium, for example, to create wide interest. However, in the end, the voters were certainly not very enthusiastic about today's Europe. This may lead Dutch leaders and MEPs to be less 'integrationist' than before.

Luxembourg

In Luxembourg, as usual, the European elections were held simultaneously with the national elections. National and European issues are difficult to separate in the Grand Duchy. Because of the service-oriented structure of its economy, Luxembourg is not as vulnerable to economic recession as its neighbouring countries. Thus, since the 1989 Euro-elections the country has had the lowest public debt, the lowest unemployment rate and the highest income per head of the EU. The ruling centre-left CSV/LSAP coalition had introduced some radical tax reforms, a much contested reform of the health care system, and a number of important educational acts but some of the symbols of the luxurious Luxembourgian welfare state, such as generous pension schemes, high wages in the public sector, and the subsidies to study abroad were left untouched.

Under these circumstances, most people expected few changes in the hierarchy between the three traditional political families, the Christian democrats (CSV), the social democrats (LSAP), and the Liberals (DP). The Green Party (Déi Gréng) wanted a drastic change in policies through a blue-red-green coalition government, but the liberals themselves pointed more to the fact that 'new blood' was needed in the government after ten years of CSV/LSAP than a drastic change of course.

Overall, ten parties participated in the national as well as in the Euro-elections. With 12 candidates on each list there were 120 candidates for the six seats in the European Parliament. Candidates stand in alphabetical rather than in a hierarchical order. Many candidates stand in the national as well as in the European elections and the results of the national campaign, followed by the formation of a new cabinet, determines whether newly elected MEPs actually take up their seat or enter the new government. The credibility of a Euro-campaign dominated by candidates who often hope not to end up in the EP has thus far never been an issue in Luxembourg.

In 1989, all the national party leaders also led the party lists in the Euro-elections. This time, in six cases, the people at the head of the party lists in the Euro-campaign were also number one on the national lists. Outgoing Prime Minister Jacques Santer, for example, led his CSV in both elections. Jean-Claude Juncker, party chairman and Finance and Employment Minister, also figured on both lists. On the other hand, only the Euro lists of the socialist LSAP and the liberal DP list were led by Foreign Minister Jacques Poos and Lydie Wurth-Polfer, mayor of Luxembourg, respectively. Mady Delvaux-Stehres, Secretary of State for Public Health, Social Security and Physical Education was the LSAP's second candidate. Among the seven other competing parties two new formations opposed the right to vote for foreigners: the NOMP (Independent and Neutral Human Rights Party), and the GLS (Group for Luxembourgian Sovereignty), next to the National Bewegong (NB), which had already participated in the previous elections. Unlike in 1989, the two Green parties GLEI and GAP had cleared some personal and political differences and had managed to form an alliance (Déi Gréng-GLEI-GAP), which they hoped would finally enable them to obtain a seat in the EP.

Unemployment and crime rates – both high by local standards – turned out to be the most important themes during the campaign which was, as usual,

Bart van Deelen

Table 2.3 Euro-election results in Luxembourg

	Seats		Votes %		
Total seats 6 (unchanged)	Number 1994	Gain/ loss	Euro-election 1994	Euro-election 1989	General election 1989
CSV	2	−1	31.4	34.9	32.4
LSAP	2	0	24.8	25.4	26.2
DP	1	0	18.8	20.0	17.2
Déi Gréng	1	+1	10.9	10.4*	8.6
ADR	0	–	7.0	–	–
KPL	0	–	1.6	4.7	4.4

* The 1989 score is the sum of the two Green parties GLEI and GAP.

very calm. Most parties stressed the necessity of the EMU, a social Europe, a European army and a political union (though the word 'federal' appeared rarely), and also of stronger links between the national parliament and the European Parliament. The need for Luxembourg to keep a Commissioner in any future European Commission and retain the right to hold the EU presidency was seen as vital. In this respect, references were made to the relatively successful last EU presidency held by Luxembourg in 1991. Decision-making by unanimity in tax policies was seen as a must as well.

The traditional parties all lost votes in the Euro-elections (see Table 2.3), ranging from 3 per cent for the Christian democrats to approximately 1 per cent for the liberals. The Green alliance list obtained only 10.9 per cent, less than expected, but enough to win for the first time a seat in the European Parliament. The seat was taken away from the Christian democrats, which dropped from three to two seats. The socialist party and the liberal Democratic Party kept their seats. The pro-pensioner ADR (Action Committee for Democracy and Justice) did rather well, an indication that domestic politics can play a role in Luxembourg. The nationalist parties NB, GLS and NOMP hardly received any support, and the communist party KPL dropped from 4.7 per cent to 1.6 per cent. Remarkably, only 3 per cent of other EU nationals used their right to vote. Turnout was slightly lower in 1994 than in 1989, (86.59 per cent, against 87.4 per cent) but remained very high because voting is compulsory.

Initially elected were Jean-Claude Juncker and Jacques Santer for the CSV, Jacques Poos and Mady Delvaux-Stehres for the LSAP, Jup Weber for the Greens and Lydie Wurth-Polfer for the DP. Juncker (21,999 preference votes) beat Prime Minister Santer (19,702), Lydie Wurth-Polfer (18,093), Astrid Lulling (14,102) and Foreign Minister Jacques Poos (14,090) as most popular candidate. Five of the six outgoing MEPs stood again in the Euro-elections and only Wurth-Polfer was directly re-elected. However, Luxembourg's representation in the EP depended ultimately on the outcome of the formation of the new cabinet. The results of the national elections were more or less similar to the European election results. CSV and LSAP lost and the DP won slightly, but the hierarchy among the three traditional parties was maintained. This underlines the continuity in Luxembourgian politics because after all, the CSV–LSAP coalition was already ten years old. As there had not been a clear demand for another coalition, Prime Minister Jacques Santer was asked to form a government, and he set out to renew the CSV–LSAP coalition since both parties still had a comfortable majority in Parliament of 56 per cent, and 38 seats out of 60. If a new CSV–LSAP government were to be formed, Jacques Santer and the MEPs Juncker, Poos and Delvaux would probably all take up posts in the new cabinet, as they did in 1989, when they were also initially elected as MEPs. In that case, Santer and Juncker would have been replaced by Astrid Lulling and Viviane Reding (CSV), bringing the total of reelected MEPs to three (out of six). Santer became Commission President and was duly replaced.

3

Denmark

Hans Jørgen Nielsen

The Danes are reluctant Europeans. Denmark joined the EC in 1973 but according to opinion polls, it is only in the last decade that a clear majority of Danes has accepted membership (Nielsen, 1993: 19; Worre, 1993: 89). Furthermore the Danes want membership to be as unbinding as possible. Surveys have repeatedly asked Danish voters about their preferred form of European cooperation[1]. In later years, two thirds of Danes have opted for a Europe of nation-states while only 12 to 15 per cent accept more binding forms of cooperation.[2]

Table 3.1   Danish attitudes towards the EU

Which answer is closest to your opinion?

	Denmark should leave EU	In the EU all member states should retain full sovereignty and have the right to veto EU-decisions	The member states should increasingly let EU make decisions and be subordinate to the community	Eventually, the EU should become the United States of Europe	DK, NA
1992	15	65	10	5	5
1993	11	69	6	6	9
1994	16	67	9	5	4

Note: The surveys in 1992 and 1993 were done in the first weeks after the referendums. The 1994 survey was done 10–12 June after the Euro-election on 9 June.

In keeping with this referendum in June 1992 narrowly rejected the original Maastricht treaty on a European Union. A majority accepted the treaty at a new referendum one year later but only after Denmark had won exemptions from unionist goals at the Edinburgh summit. This set the frame for the Euro-elections. There were strong divisions at the referendums and voters defied the advice of their parties to vote 'yes'. At the Euro-election, voters could go against their normal parties again.

The actors

Danish Euro-elections are fairly unpredictable and not simple replications of national elections. First, turnout is lower, around 50 per cent against more than 80 per cent at national elections. Therefore, at Euro-elections much can be won – or lost – by different rates of voter-mobilization. Next, at Euro-elections national political parties are joined by special Euro-sceptic lists. Traditionally the People's Movement against the EC, now the People's Movement against the EC-Union got a fifth of the vote at Euro-elections. The People's Movement wants Denmark to leave the EU. Recently, it was up against the more moderate June Movement, named after the June 1992 referendum. The June Movement accepts membership but opposes further integration. In addition to these two 'movements', all eight parties in parliament took part in the Euro-election. In general, most parties from left to right backed a 'yes-but option' – yes to *status quo* but no to further integration.

Membership	No	Yes	Yes	Yes
Maastricht + Edinburgh	No	No	Yes	Yes
Further integration	No	No	No	Yes
Position in the national political spectrum — Right		Progress Party		
			Conservative Party	Liberal Party
			Christian People's Party	Center Democrats
			Social Liberal Party	
			Social Democrats	
Left			Socialist People's Party	
Non-partisan	People's Movement against the EC union	June Movement		

Figure 3.1 Danish attitudes towards EC/EU integration

Third, the strength of the political parties differed markedly from national elections. The Social Democrats usually got 10 to 12 per cent less at Euro-elections than at national elections, due to the widespread Euro-scepticism among the voters.[3] In 1994, conflicts from the referendums easily spilt over to the Euro-election. Conversely, the small Center Democratic Party traditionally does well at Euro-elections, primarily due to the personality of the party founder, the elderly Erhard Jakobsen, who headed the list in 1989. However, this time Erhard Jakobsen had resigned and domestically the party was in deep trouble. Prospects were sombre. Previously, the Socialist People's Party also faced high risks. The party used to oppose Denmark's membership and in the 1992 referendum advocated a no-vote. However, in 1993 it swung to yes after the Edinburgh exemptions but at the new referendum four-fifths of its voters continued so say no. At the Euro-election, they could easily switch to one of the Euro-sceptic movements.

Outgoing MEPs were at risk too, even if their parties did well at the election. The selection of representatives from each list depends completely on the number of personal votes for each individual candidate.[4] However, being an MEP does not make politicians well-known to the general public. Therefore, many MEPs faced the danger of being eclipsed by senior national politicians that several parties put on the slate.

The Conservatives took the lead in nominating former prime minister (1982–93) Poul Schlüter. It was inevitable that he would be elected. The list was further strengthened by a well-known TV journalist. Similarly, the Liberals nominated three prominent members of national parliament, including the Minister for Education in all Schlüter governments. The Social Liberals probably outdid both by nominating Lone Dybkjær, the fiancee, now wife, of the Social Democratic prime minister. She was both an MP and a former minister but because of her extra-party connection she could now look forward to decades as a second-rank backbencher. However, as a person she was both competent and outspoken. The party got no seats in 1989, but she could threaten members from other parties, not least her husband's Social Democracy.

Finally, the Socialist People's Party nominated Lilly Gyldenkilde as its first candidate to compensate for some of the party's pro-EU changes. The party's MEP, John Iversen, was not well-known to the general public and was associated with the shift towards a more pro-EU stand. By comparison, Lilly Gyldenkilde was well-known, could speak heatedly against EU-bureaucracy and was cherished as a working-class MP in a socialist party manned by the lecturing-classes.

Star candidates were also likely to affect the strength of the different political parties. The two Euro-sceptic movements had no stars and neither had the Social Democrats.[5] Moreover, the star qualities differed. A Gallup poll at the end of May asked whether the respondents knew some of the candidates, and Poul Schlüter, Lone Dybkjær, the Liberal Niels-Anker Kofoed and Lilly Gyldenkilde came out ahead of all others. On the other hand, none of the Social Democratic candidates were mentioned by more than 3 per cent of the voters (Berlingske Toiidende: 20 May 1994).

The issues

There is a long tradition of scepticism towards Euro-federalism in Danish politics (Thomsen, 1993; Ersbøll, 1994). This is probably one of the reasons for Euro-scepticism among the voters: few voters are federalists because few politicians have argued in favour of federalism. Euro-scepticism would make it dangerous for parties to campaign vigorously for strong European institutions. Yet few parties want such a change and on this level there is not much of a difference between voters and politicians. This had a number of consequences. The federalist parties, Center Democrats and Liberals, were in favour of general legislative powers for the EP. However, most parties opposed such a change but with the qualification that the EP should have the right to initiate proposals and not be confined to raise amendments to proposals from the Commission. Further, most parties emphasized the critical role of the EP as a watch-dog *vis-à-vis* the Commission and not the constructive role as an initiator of further cooperation. The watch-dog role was well in line with a Euro-sceptic attitude: the higher the scepticism the greater the need to keep an eye on what is going on. And Poul Schlüter even made the fight against fraud in the EU-system his prime goal and was immediately joined by Social Democrat candidates. With a few exceptions, the strengthening of European institutions was simply not an issue in Danish politics. However, within specific fields there was much more willingness to accept closer cooperation.[6] Even the June Movement argued that it should be possible to decide by a simple majority on EU restrictions on cross-border pollution. Both the Social Liberals and the Social Democrats also favoured concerted action to protect the environment and the Social Democrats also wanted the EU to improve working conditions. On a more specific level, the traditional left-right pattern had its impact. The Left wanted intervention whereas the Right did not. In line with this is also the stand of the Liberals. The party is strongly pro-EU but also strongly opposed to state intervention. Therefore, it demanded *more cooperation but in fewer fields.*

Not only politicians but also voters are more positive towards the EU within specific fields. For example, Eurobarometer-surveys have repeatedly shown the Danes in favour of letting the EU decide on environmental policies, in favour of a common foreign policy towards non-EU countries, and in favour of a common fight against organized crime (for an overview, see Nielsen, 1992: 27–28). However, this is not in order to strengthen EU-institutions but in order to fight pollution and crime. Principal Euro-scepticism is mitigated by considerations of practical expediency.

Apparently, politicians were left with some degree of freedom. They could capitalize on popular Euro-scepticism by warning against the EU but also arguing in favour of cooperation in specific fields. However there was an inherent danger in the latter strategy. In the past, Danish voter opinions about the details of EU-cooperation had turned out to be highly unstable (Nielsen, 1993: 81). Therefore, even where voters accepted closer cooperation, opinions could easily swing if cooperation were depicted as examples of crypto-federalism, leading to stronger institutions.

The Euro-sceptical strategy seemed safer and came to dominate the campaign. The Conservative Party was a case in point. The *style* was clearly

Euro-sceptic. Not only did Poul Schlüter focus on fraud in the EU-system, the party's slogan was also to *work for Europe but fight for Denmark*. This was close to the mark when a leader of the June Movement after the election commented that Poul Schlüter had sounded like a member of the June Movement.

If anything, the campaign had only one heated issue. Namely, whether Denmark should stick to the exemptions it got at the Edinburgh summit and especially whether it should stay outside the Western European Union (WEU). This was a phoney discussion as it was a matter for the Danes and not for the EP. However, the discussion was a way to highlight principal viewpoints on the intensity of EU-cooperation. Both pro-integrationist parties, Liberals and Center Democrats, said no, and were joined by the Conservatives, while other parties – first of all the Social Democrats – opposed. There were two agendas. Euro-scepticism dominated it at a general level but on particular points a number of specific fields for further cooperation were accepted.

The campaign

European politics is a low priority for most voters and is not something people get highly upset about. Further, whereas referendums – on the Single Market in 1986 and the Maastricht treaty in 1992 and 1993 – are issues people can support or oppose, issues were downplayed in the Euro-election. The election campaign became, by almost all standards, utterly dull.

Two of the parties, the Liberals and the Social Democrats, turned the campaign into a general contest between the two party leaders, neither of whom were candidates for the election. This pushed the candidates for the European Parliament into the background. This probably hit the Social Democrats hardest as they had the least well-known candidates. The campaign also became more Americanized than was normal in Danish election campaigns. Candidates took pensioners on duty-free ferry trips on the Baltic, drove in horse-drawn carriages through the city centre, and the Liberal leader rowed his dinghy to a party meeting on a maritime fortress in the Sund. These gimmicks had an important function. At least, voters found out that there was an election. However, the campaign missed the crucial point: what difference would a vote make? The EP has never been taken very seriously either by the public or national politicians. Again, great attention was paid to MEPs salaries and benefits. The Parliament was called a Mickey Mouse Parliament. However, little was said about what was going on and the EP's increased role. Why then bother to vote at all? That was only a small problem for the two Euro-sceptic movements. Belittling the Parliament helped to underline their arguments for Euro-scepticism. The Conservatives, the Social Liberals and the Socialist People's Party could be partly satisfied with the campaign. At least, voters had found out that they had well-known candidates. The rest needed a better campaign to sell their lists to the voters.

Table 3.2 Strength of the parties

	1989	1994	For comparison:	
			National election 1990	Present national political strength†
Liberal Party	16.6	18.9	15.8	26
Conservative Party	13.3	17.7	16.0	14
Social Democrats	23.3	15.8	37.4	32
June Movement	*0.0*	*15.2*	*	*
People's Movement	*18.9*	*10.3*	*	*
Socialist People's Party	9.1	8.6	8.4	11
Social Liberal Party	2.8	8.5	3.5	5
Progress Party	5.3	2.9	6.4	6
Christian People's Party	2.7	1.1	2.3	2
Center Democrats	8.0	0.9	5.1	2
Other national parties	0.0	0.0	4.9	3
Electoral turnout	46.2	52.5	82.4	*

† 'Present national political strength' is calculated on the basis of answers to the question about votes at a national election tomorrow in the post-elections survey.

The results

Electoral turnout went up to 52.5 per cent. However, this was almost the same as at the Euro-election in 1984 and, therefore, the EP's increased role in the EU did not occasion a real increase in popular interest in the election. Interest actually is a key factor. According to a 1994 post-election survey, turnout varied from 80 per cent among those 'highly interested' in European politics, to 68 per cent among those who were just 'somewhat interested', and 43 per cent among those with only a 'small interest' in European politics to 21 per cent among those who were 'not interested' at all. Such variations are also found at the national elections but the post-election survey shows two interesting differences. More voters are highly interested in national politics and turnout at national elections is less sensitive to level of interest. The feeling of citizen duty makes people vote even when they are not very interested in the outcome.[7] By contrast, at Euro-elections there seems to be very little feeling of citizen duty. There is also less feeling of loyalty towards one's normal party. In the 10–12 June survey after the 1994 Euro-election, voters were asked which party they would vote for if a national election were held tomorrow and, according to this information, voters seem to have run away in all possible directions.

This made for dramatic shifts in party strength. Some parties were poor performers. The Progress Party and the Christian People's Party did badly but neither ran much of a campaign. More important was the catastrophic result for the Center Democrats as European cooperation always has been a key issue for the party. Social Democracy also came close to a disaster. According

Table 3.3 Party preferences

	%
Preference for a specific party if a national election were held tomorrow	
Voted for the same party at the Euro-election	28
Voted for another national party	9
Voted for one of the two Euro-sceptic lists (June Movement and People's Movement)	10
Did not vote	36
Do not know which party to vote for if a national election were held tomorrow	
Voted for a national political party at the Euro-election	1
Voted for one of the two Euro-sceptic lists (June Movement and People's Movement)	4
Did not vote	12
	100

N=1093.

to recent polls, the party should have won around 33 per cent at a national election. However, at the Euro-election it came a poor third with only 15.8 per cent – two-thirds of what it got in 1989. Closer analysis shows that the party faced all kinds of problems. At the Euro-election, voters who normally voted Social Democratic at a national election were more likely than average to switch to other lists or, especially, to abstain. At the same time, Social Democracy held very little attraction for voters of the parties at national elections.

The Liberal Party was a more mixed performer. It increased its share of the Euro-vote. However, its national election share was around 27 per cent of the vote, and its 18.9 per cent Euro-election share was less satisfying. A closer analysis of the post-election survey shows that the Liberals also had little appeal for voters of other parties at a national election. On the other hand, both voting for other lists and abstentions were slightly below average among national-election Liberals. The party's federalist message had little appeal to non-liberals but was fine for home consumption.

The Socialist People's Party was a mixed performer, too, but the analysis of the post-election survey shows a completely reversed pattern. The party was a bad performer on the home front. According to the survey 26 per cent of the party's national-election support backed the party at the national election while 32 per cent voted for other lists. Fear that the split over the EU could become dangerous at the Euro-election was fully warranted. On the other hand, almost half of the vote at the Euro-election came from people who would not support the party at a national election. It seemed to have been a wise decision to nominate Lilly Gyldenkilde.

The rest were good performers. The Euro-sceptic movements had a substantial success. The loss of the People's Movement was more than made up by the gain of the June Movement. This bears witness to continuing Euro-scepticism among Danish voters. The Conservatives increased their strength over both the past Euro-election, the last national election and in respect of what it might get

Table 3.4 Euro-election results in Denmark

Seats	1989	1994	Change
Liberal Party	3	4	1
Conservative Party	2	3	1
Social Democrats	4	3	−1
June Movement	*0*	*2*	*2*
People's Movement	*4*	*2*	*−2*
Socialist People's Party	1	1	0
Social Liberal Party	0	1	1
Progress Party	0	0	
Christian People's Party	0	0	
Center Democrats	2	0	−2
Other national parties	0	0	

at a new national election. According to the post-election survey, this was due both to a high level of fidelity among the party's normal voters and a fine appeal to voters from other parties. This was true to an even higher extent for the Social Liberals. Its national voters remained loyal but, above all, voters from other parties flocked to the Social Liberals. Almost two-thirds were voters who would not vote for the Social Liberals at a national election.

In terms of seats, the changes were less dramatic. But this is primarily a result of the electoral system. The Danish seats are distributed proportionally. There is no formal threshold, and parties can form electoral alliances.[8] Yet with only 16 seats to distribute it takes on average a 7 per cent change in share of the total vote to move one seat from one list or alliance to another. Three long-term MEPs lost their seats due to star candidates. In the Socialist People's Party John Iversen was replaced by Lilly Gyldenkilde. Few had expected any other result. More remarkable were the changes among the Liberals and the Conservatives. Both parties got more seats. Despite this, the Liberal Tove Nielsen and the Conservative Marie Jepsen were replaced by candidates better known to the electorate.[9]

The post-election survey asked voters to say why they voted as they did, and the answers point to a fairly clear pattern in gains and losses. Attitudes to the EU were important: the two Euro-sceptic lists' references to the nature of the party or lists can here − but not for normal parties − be counted as EU-related as the only aim of the lists are to fight European integration. It should be noted that very few voters explained their vote by reference to the candidates.

The Euro-sceptic lists did well. Therefore, one way to win is to have a popular message (in this case: Euro-scepticism).

The pattern for the Social Democrats seems strange. The party did badly at the election, and now it even seems that many of those who actually voted for the party was unable to say why they did so. Among those who could, there were very few EU-related answers and very few references to the candidates. The main reason for support appears to be general allegiance to the party.

Table 3.5 Explanation of Danish party choice

	Reasons for party-choice (multiple answers)					
	General references to the nature of party/list*	Own attitude towards the EU	The party's or list's EU policy	Candidates	Specific policy fields	Other answers
June Movement	17	46	50	10	0	9
People's Movement	29	35	50	13	0	16
Social Democracy	73	0	10	15	1	4
Liberal Party	67	4	15	23	1	4
Conservatives	49	2	10	43	4	5
Socialist People's Party	30	8	25	47	9	3
Social Liberal	23	0	0	47	9	0
All voters	43	13	21	26	4	13

* 'Party/List' refers to the party or list at the Euro-election.

Notes: Because there were too few cases (less than 20) figures have been left out for the Center Democrats, Christian People's Party and Progress Party. Voters were asked why they voted as they did. No lists were given and the categories were set up in the later analysis. It was possible to give more than one reason.

This was also the main reason for support of the Liberals but with the crucial difference that many more of those of who supported the Liberals were able to explain their vote. Once again there were few EU-related explanations, bearing witness to the poor appeal of the federalist message. And once again there were few references to the candidates.

The two parties did not attract the support of many new voters. Therefore party allegiance may be helpful to keep the loyalty of national-election voters (the case of the Liberals), but it has little appeal to outsiders and therefore does not suffice to win an election.

Finally there were the three parties who attracted a substantial number of votes from outsiders. Once again, there were few references to EU. Instead, in all three cases, many voters explained their support by the candidates. In the case of the Social Liberals the candidates were almost the sole reason. As almost two-thirds of the support came from voters who would not support the party at a national election, party allegiance did not play any role.

Parties also win owing to popular candidates. This marks a sharp contrast to the success of the Euro-sceptic movements. This is sustained by another question to those who voted differently from how they would vote at a national election. More than half of those who supported another national party explained this by the candidates and far fewer by any kind of references to EU. On the other hand, only 5 per cent of those who deserted to an Euro-sceptic list referred to the candidates. Instead references to EU played the dominant role.

The role of candidates also marks a contrast to national elections. Here, voters seldom explain their vote by giving names of party leaders. Instead, they refer to general policies, social position or party allegiances. Therefore, in addition to the sheer differences in party strengths, the importance of candidates is another indicator that Euro-elections are not strongly integrated in the traditional political pattern.[10]

Conclusion

Direct elections to the European Parliament were initiated to enhance the authority of the parliament. Yet in Denmark the consequences have differed. Each Euro-election becomes a new manifestation of widespread Euro-scepticism. This was also the case in 1994. One may even wonder how long Euro-sceptic movements could have persisted had Euro-elections not − together with referendums − highlighted the EU-issue at regular intervals.

Apart from this, Euro-elections reflect an odd phenomenon in Danish politics. Parties downplay positive European policies. Voters abstain from voting and when they do, voting is often unconnected with national political allegiances and often without much policy content.

Notes

1. For other analyses of Danish EC policies and the Maastricht referendums, see Nielsen 1992 and 1993, Siune et al 1992 and 1994 and the essays in Thomsen 1993.

   This paper draws on three surveys. One after each of the referendums in 1992 and 1993 and the survey after the 1994 Euro-election. The two first surveys were conducted by a group of researchers from Aarhus and Copenhagen universities, including the author, and financed by grants from the Danish Institute of International Affairs and the Danish Social Science Research Council. The 1994 survey was conducted on behalf of the Copenhagen Office of the European Parliament with the author as responsible investigator. Danish Gallup did the fieldwork for all three surveys. The Danish Institute of International Affairs has financed another survey of the Euro-election but the data are still not available.

   All analyses use weights to fit the marginals in the data material to the official results of elections and referendums. The weights in the 1992 survey control the national election in 1990 and the 1992 referendum. The weights in the 1993 survey also control the distribution in the 1993 referendum, while the 1994 weights control the 1990 election, the 1993 referendum and the 1994 Euro-election. Using the 1994 weights results in a minor bias when the marginals in the data file are compared with the official results (the 'yes' vote is 2 per cent too high and the 'no' vote 2 per cent too low).

2. The 12 to 15 per cent figure might be a slight underestimation of the willingness for closer cooperation. For example, in response to another question in a survey in June 1994, 25 per cent were willing to transfer more decisions to the EU while 12 per cent agreed that Denmark should accept decisions by the EU to the same extent as now. However, even here 61 per cent agreed that Denmark should be more wary of EU decisions while 2 per cent had no opinion.

3. At the first Danish referendum in 1992 two-thirds of all social democratic voters voted 'no' despite the party's agitation for a 'yes'. In 1993 the balance shifted to a 'yes' majority, but with a substantial 'no' minority (Nielsen, 1992: 55).

4. All kinds of Danish elections – national, local and European – use proportional representation with the possibility for voters either to put their cross at the name of the list ('party votes') or at the name of a candidate within a list ('personal votes'). This makes no difference with respect to the distribution of seats among lists. At that stage both personal and party votes are counted as given to the party. However, personal votes play a crucial role in the selection of representatives from the list. Before the election, parties can choose between different systems but at the Euro-election all parties have opted for a system where the first seat is given to the candidate with the highest number of personal votes, the second seat to the candidate with the second highest etc.

5. Social Democracy does not allow combinations of posts as mayor, as a member of the national parliament or as a member of the EP. As no one wants to give up a career as a national politician it has been difficult for the party to get prominent politicians on its slates for the EP.

6. This is fully in accordance with a functionalist and pragmatic tradition. For example, a broad range of political parties argued that what became the Maastricht-treaty should include a so-called 'social dimension'.

7. The criterion was the vote at the national election of 1990. Data were weighted to fit the actual turnout level. Whereas turnout fell from 80 to 23 per cent at the Euro-election, it only fell from 89 per cent among voters who were highly interested in national politics to 55 per cent among those who were not interested at all in national politics.

8. In a first step, seats are distributed proportionally among alliances and parties not in any alliance, and in a second step among parties within each alliance. Two parties at

the 3 to 4 per cent level therefore have a fair chance to get one seat, but not one seat each, if they combine.

9. It should be noted that the top candidates often got so large a share of personal votes that relatively few personal votes were left to determine who should have the last seat.

10. It should be noted, however, that the two parties who let the party leaders bear the brunt of the campaign did not do very well. Further, while voters often referred to the candidates by name, almost none referred in any way to the Social Democratic and Liberal leaders. It was not enough to use well-known names in the campaign. They had to be candidates as well.

References

Nielsen, H J (1992) 'Danish voters and the referendum in June 1992 on the Treaty of Maastricht' in Kelstrup, M (ed) *European Integration and Denmark's Participation*, Copenhagen, Copenhagen Political Studies Press.

— (1993) *EF på Valg*, Columbus, Cophenhagen.

Siune, K, Svensson, P and Tonsgaard, O (1992) *Det blev et nej*, Politica, Århus.

— (1994) *Fra Nej til Ja*, Politica, Århus.

Thomsen, B N (ed) (1993) *The Odd Man Out? Denmark and European Integration 1948–1992*, Odense University Press, Odense.

Thomsen, N (1993) 'The EEC in Danish Politics 1972-79', in Thomsen, B N (ed) *The Odd Man Out?* pp 49–68.

Worre, T (1993) 'Denmark and the European Union. Public Opinion in the 1980s and the Referendum of June 1992', in Thomsen, B N (ed) *The Odd Man Out?* pp 87–108.

4

The Federal Republic of Germany[1]

William E Paterson, Charles Lees and Simon Green

Introduction

Even under normal circumstances, European elections in Germany are of importance well beyond its borders. However, for a number of reasons, the 1994 campaign was of special significance, both in terms of its content and outcome. First, the elections were the first of their kind since German unification. The expansion of the Federal Republic to include the former GDR has been reflected in the increase in Germany's allocation of seats in the EP from 81 to 99, as agreed at the 1992 Edinburgh summit. Thus, in a very obvious sense, the outcome of the European election in Germany carried more weight than it did in other member states. Second, the 1994 elections also coincided with a busy year of state and local elections (19 in all), culminating in the national elections to the *Bundestag* in October. The consequence of such a *Superwahljahr* — as it was called in Germany — was to impose upon the European election campaign even more of a domestic agenda than is normally the case in European elections in all member states. Third, there had been a great deal of speculation as to whether German public opinion towards 'Europe' was beginning to display a more sceptical tinge than that of the German political elite (*Frankfurter Allgemeine Zeitung*, 8 June 1994). Central to this speculation were fears that turnout would be low, even by the standards of European elections. Finally, as in other member states, there was a very real fear that the far-right parties — in particular the Republicans (*Republikaner*) — would improve upon their success in the 1989 European elections (in which six *Republikaner* MEPs were dispatched to Strasbourg).

These fears aside, election campaigns in Germany tend not to be the most exciting of affairs, and the 1994 European campaign was no exception. The following characteristics of European elections in Germany can be identified:

- The overall awareness and enthusiasm of the population for the election is normally low, as voting for Strasbourg lacks a 'king-maker function' (Kolinsky, 1990: 68). Consequently, turnout for a European election has always been considerably lower than for federal or state elections; indeed,

European elections are considered to be the least important of all elections, ranking below *Bundestag*, state and even local elections in the eyes of the electorate. Thus, in a very real sense, the European elections in Germany can usually be considered a 'fourth-order' election (Roth, in Niedermayer, 1995: 4).

• There is a remarkable degree of consensus within the political élites of all mainstream parties in favour of European integration (Bulmer and Paterson, 1986: 190–91), which was established through the 1950s and has largely persisted ever since.

• As in other European countries, European elections are dominated by domestic rather than trans- or supra-national actors and issues.

• Because European elections do not involve a serious distribution of power, the electorate uses them as an opportunity to voice discontent with the national government and lodge a protest vote against the parties (Niedermayer, 1995: 5; Kolinsky, 1990). Thus the potential for smaller, extreme parties to make an impact is proportionately greater at the European level.

• In terms of electoral law, the usual two-vote 'additional member' system is replaced by a purely list-based way of selecting MEPs[2]. As this removes the possibility of splitting the votes between two parties – a phenomenon common at federal elections – parties like the FDP with a small core electorate (about 3 per cent in the case of the FDP) find it harder to pass the 5 per cent hurdle necessary for representation. Moreover, as there are no directly-elected MEPs from Germany, many candidates consider the election over once they have secured their place on the list, thereby increasing the tendency of campaigns to be rather lacklustre.

• The reimbursement of campaign costs, for which parties became eligible if they scored 0.5 per cent of the vote or more, has, in the past, benefited smaller parties standing for the European elections. As the parties were paid DM 5.00 per eligible voter, regardless of whether or not the voter actually cast his or her vote, the value of each vote *cast* increased dramatically in lower turnout elections, such as the European elections. As Kolinsky (1990: 67) notes, this, combined with a more lenient recognition procedure for parties than at the national level, made it attractive for smaller parties to contest elections to Strasbourg, which provided a welcome method of replenishing their funds. However, following a ruling by the Federal Constitutional Court in April 1992, the party financing laws were altered in November 1993 to introduce a complex new mechanism for state support of political parties that balances reimbursement for electoral success against matching income from party membership dues. Thus, as well as setting a ceiling on state expenditure on the parties, the new law has had the effect of penalizing parties with a small membership (Rudzio, 1994). These changes have reduced the utility of elections – and of the European elections in particular – for refilling emptied party coffers and have been especially damaging to the FDP and the Greens, which also have a relatively low membership base. Ironically, they are less disadvantageous to the PDS, which still retains a high membership. The new law has already affected the number of parties fielding candidates for this election: although the 1994 European election saw 24 party lists, the highest ever, it was only two more than in 1989. Indeed, when the PDS and *Neues Forum* parties which have appeared as a result of unification, are factored out, the number of parties has actually stayed constant.

The main actors in the campaign

Given the fact that the European election in Germany cannot be divorced from the context of *Superwahljahr* as a whole, the parties entered the campaign with a view to both stabilizing (or even enhancing) their support in the run-up to the October Federal elections, as well as using the European campaign as a platform in order to profile themselves in domestic policy terms before those elections. However, within this general context, they followed their own party-specific agendas.

For the Christian Democratic Union (CDU) and its Bavarian sister party, the Christian Social Union (CSU), the European elections provided the opportunity to reverse over three years of electoral malaise and to reap some tangible benefit from the perceived upturn in the economy. Prior to 1994, the CDU had seen their support dip in *Land* elections in, for instance, Rhineland–Palatinate and Hesse in 1991, Baden-Württemberg in 1992 and Hamburg in 1993. Although one must exercise a degree of caution in inferring a causal relationship between the two, the party's unpopularity coincided with the sharpest recession in the Federal Republic's history. Moreover, data relating to both perceptions of economic well-being and to voting intentions indicate that, from the beginning of 1994, there was a strong correlation between a growing sense of economic optimism and an increase in the level of poll respondents supporting the CDU/CSU. The full data concerning poll respondents' party support and economic expectations are laid out in Figures 4.1 to 4.6.

The resurgence of support for the CDU/CSU was mirrored by a parallel rise in the number of poll respondents expecting another victory for the governing coalition[3] in the Federal elections in October. If one accepts that a correlation does exist between economic expectations and levels of party support, it becomes clear that, from the beginning of the year, the expectation of an end to the recession had begun to filter through in the CDU/CSU's opinion poll ratings. However, as Figures 4.1 and 4.2 demonstrate, it was not until around the time of the European elections that the CDU/CSU opened up a clear lead over their main rivals, the Social Democrats (SPD). Moreover, it was at this time that a fourth consecutive government election victory became the most expected outcome of the October *Bundestag* elections. It is interesting to note that this was a full eight weeks after the net balance of the voters' economic perceptions had shifted towards that of optimism. Therefore, one must conclude that while such optimism was important, it was not in itself decisive in

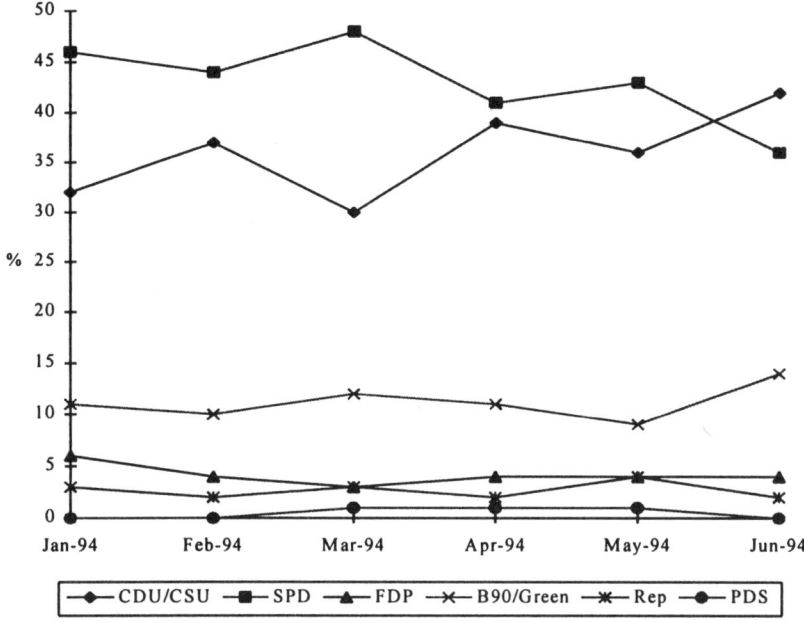

Figure 4.1   Party preference in 'West' Germany: 1994

Source: ZDF Politbarometer.

restoring expectations of a government victory in October. It was necessary for the CDU to campaign well (and to perform at the polls) before it was seen by the voters as likely to win the *Bundestag* elections. Given that, in politics, perceptions are at least as salient as empirical reality, the June 1994 European elections can be interpreted − in the context of *Superwahljahr* − as part of the CDU/CSU's reassertion of itself as still capable of government (*regierungsfähig*).

For the SPD, it was clear that they could no longer rely on the lead in the opinion polls that they had enjoyed since 1991. Thus, if any momentum was to be built upon in the run-up to the October elections, it was crucial that the party make a good showing in the European elections. Like the CDU, the SPD also needed to utilize the European election campaign in order to establish its credibility as a potential government during *Superwahljahr*.

The SPD's need to do this was all the more urgent because of the failure of Rudolf Scharping, the party's candidate for chancellor (*Kanzlerkandidat*), to maintain a convincing lead over Helmut Kohl in the public's perceptions; even in the period when the SPD were still well ahead of the CDU/CSU in the polls. The relative approval ratings of the two *Kanzlerkandidaten* are displayed in Figure 4.7.

Figure 4.7 illustrates how Scharping needed to profile himself in the run-up to the European elections if he were to have a chance of replacing Kohl as

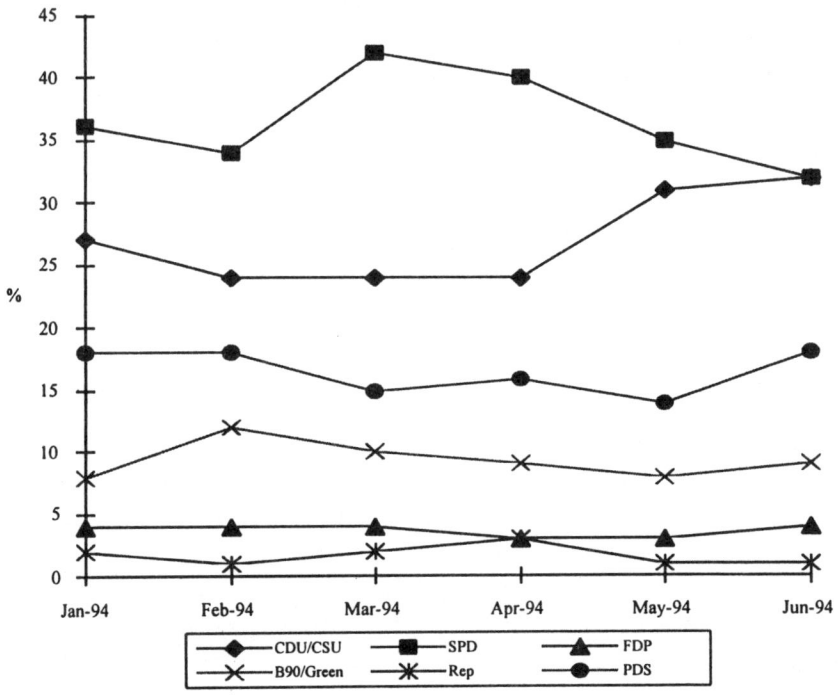

Figure 4.2   Party preference in 'East' Germany: 1994

Source: ZDF Politbarometer.

Chancellor in October. For Kohl, however, there were two reasons why he might feel precedent was on his side. First, no incumbent Chancellor has ever been removed at the ballot box and, second, all the economic indicators and polling responses appeared to be moving in his favour. Moreover, the Chancellor saw European policy as very much his domain and thus the European election campaigns could be seen to be playing to his strengths. Kohl – and, by implication, the CDU in particular – had every reason to be quietly confident.

However, if the CDU could expect to do reasonably well in the European elections, its junior coalition partners were presented with considerable strategic or tactical dilemmas: arising out of both the nature of their respective party organization and support and, also, the specific context of a *European* election.

At the Federal level, the FDP has traditionally made much of its role as the 'pivotal' party in the process of coalition formation (Pappi, 1984; Padgett, 1993). However, since unification, a steady decline in popular support, and consequently its increasing reliance upon the second votes of CDU supporters in *Bundestag* elections, has cast some doubts over its long-term viability within what has become, arguably, a far more fluid party system. Moreover, within the context of the European elections, this vulnerability was accentuated for two reasons. First, the absence of a second vote in European elections means

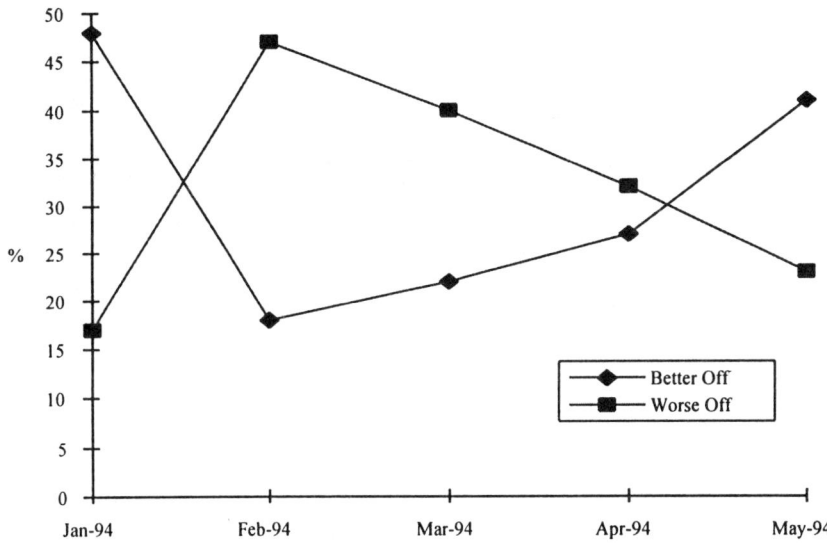

Figure 4.3   Economic expectations in 'West' Germany: 1994

Source: IfD Allensbach.

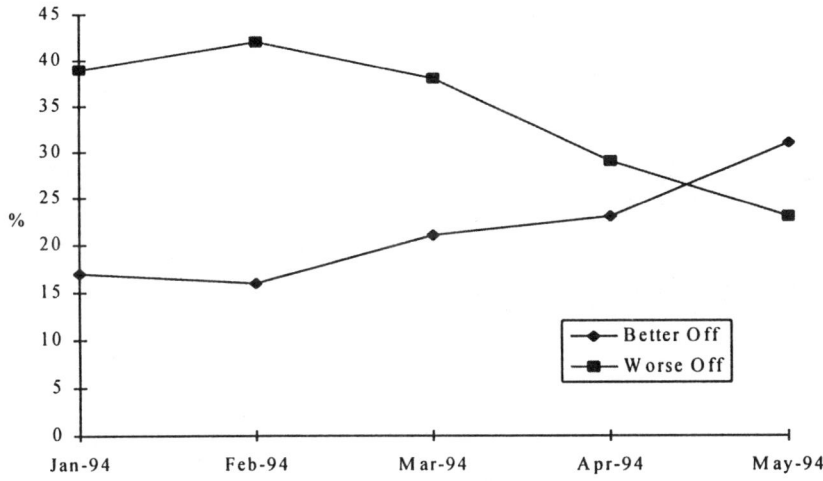

Figure 4.4   Economic expectations in 'East' Germany: 1994

Source: IfD Allensbach.

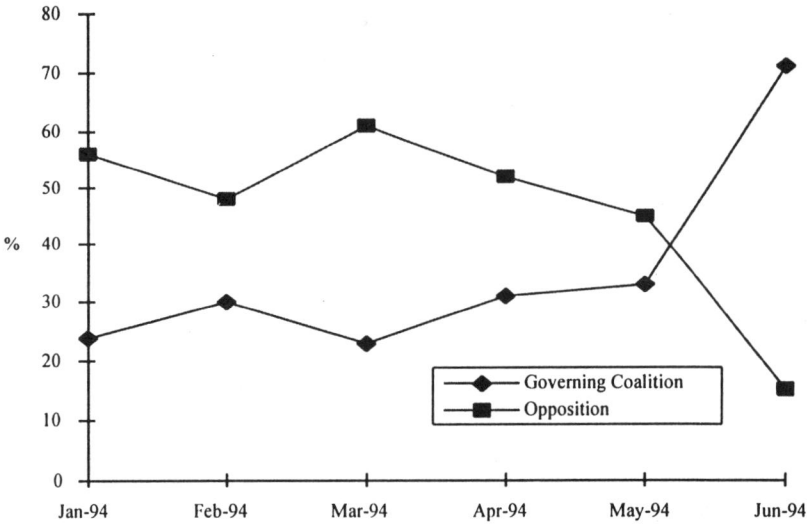

Figure 4.5   Expected winner of October *Bundestag* election (West): 1994

Source: ipos.

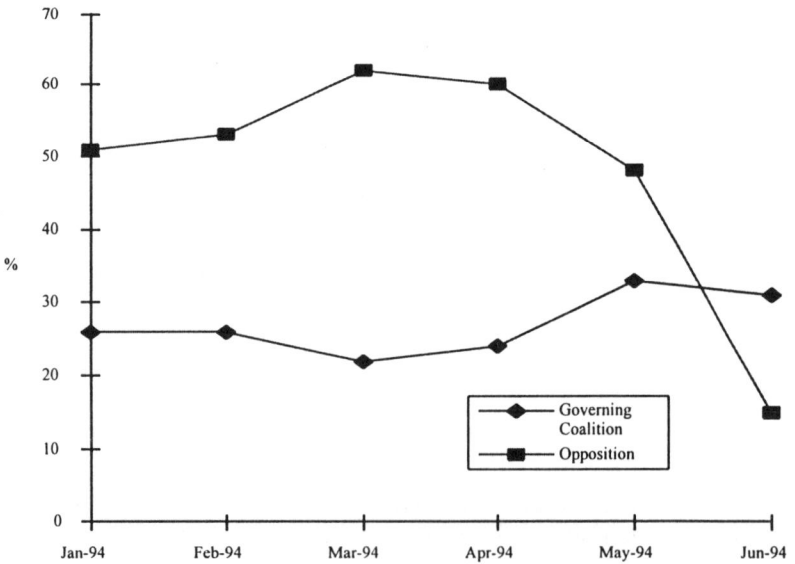

Figure 4.6   Expected winner of October *Bundestag* election (East): 1994

Source: ipos.

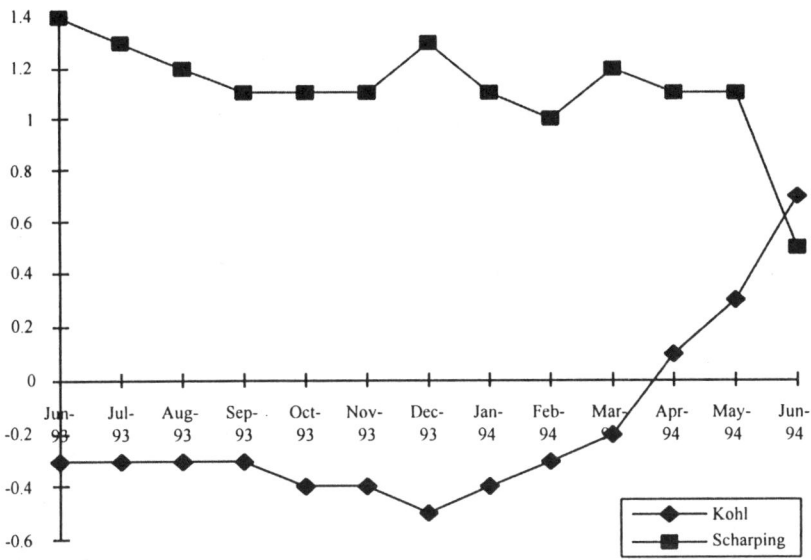

Figure 4.7   Kohl versus Scharping: approval ratings May '93–June '94

Note: Approval ratings are measured on a +5 to −5 scale.

Source: Forschungsgruppe Wahlen.

that the FDP is forced to fall back upon its ever-diminishing core electorate. Second, any coalition-building utility that the FDP may still claim to exercise becomes irrelevant: simply because the sheer scale of the bargaining set within the European Parliament renders it somewhat less than decisive! Moreover, the retirement of long-standing leader Hans-Dietrich Genscher – and his replacement with the comparatively untested Klaus Kinkel – had served to further diminish the party's electoral appeal. As a result, the FDP entered *Superwahljahr* with low expectations, especially with regard to the European elections.

By contrast with the FDP's strategic dilemma, the CSU's problems were essentially of a tactical nature. Whereas the FDP is a national party, with a diminishing social base, forcing it to cast its net wide in order to garner support, the CSU's role has been more ambivalent. Although the CSU has always played a prominent role on the national stage as the sister party to the CDU, its electoral base has been exclusively in Bavaria. Thus, the need to shore up support in that state has always been paramount. Although very much the hegemonic party in Bavaria (it has only once been briefly out of government at *Land* level in the 1950s), the late 1980s and early 1990s saw tentative signs of potential slippage in the CSU's share of the vote. This occurred on two fronts. First, to the SPD in the more urban areas, such as Munich and Nuremberg, and, second, to the right-wing Republican party. Moreover, with the death of Franz Josef Strauss in 1988, the party lost a leader of quite singular charisma. With Strauss gone, the party leadership has become more pluralistic, with Theo Waigel (the party chairman and finance minister in the ruling coalition in Bonn) and Edmund Stoiber (the *Minister-präsident* in Munich) constituting the two main players. In addition, the CSU has declined in relative weight after unification, as the 5 per cent clause which previously had applied only to the western *Länder* now applies in all 16. While the CSU still needs only 38 per cent of the vote in Bavaria to surpass the 5 per cent threshold nationally (a figure it has easily passed for decades), its position becomes precarious as soon as turnout drops. Thus a high profile among its voters and voter mobilization are prime concerns for the CSU in post-unification Germany. It would be vastly overstating the case to imply that the CSU was in any long-term electoral trouble. However, both the tactical need to consolidate the CSU's hold in Bavaria and the as yet unresolved power struggle between Waigel and Stoiber were to have some impact – in terms of the profiling of both issues and personalities – upon the European election campaign. These issues will be returned to later in this chapter.

For Bündnis 90/Die Grünen (hereafter referred to as the Greens), *Superwahljahr* was crucial in re-confirming their status as an established party nationwide, following the failure of the 'western' Greens to pass the 5 per cent electoral hurdle in the 1990 *Bundestag* elections. Given this wider context, the European campaign provided an ideal opportunity to further this process. To this end, the Greens could hope to gain a higher share of the vote, compared with national elections, because of the generally lower turnout at European elections. Thus, compared with the CDU/CSU, SPD and FDP's electorate, the more politicized nature of the Greens' core support made them easier to mobilize and, therefore, could be assumed to ensure their over-representation as a proportion of those who voted (Niedermayer, 1995). Although still firmly placed within the left/post-materialist milieu, the combination of the merger of the 'west' and 'east' Greens, the isolation of the party's fundamentalist wing, as well as the increasing age (and affluence) of the Green electorate, had brought about a more moderate policy profile compared with that of the 1980s.

While the Greens appear to be increasingly acceptable as coalition partners, the stigma that had previously attached to them now seemed to have been transferred to Germany's reform-communists, the PDS. Despite earlier expectations that the PDS' position was untenable, due to their association with the former GDR, they have retained a rump of support in the new *Länder* (see Figure 4.2). However, although the consolidation of their status as the 'eastern' party of protest meant that they might expect to have a chance of entering the *Bundestag* in October through securing three or more direct mandates,[4] the niche that they occupied within the German party system as a whole was not sufficient to support any realistic hopes of election to the European Parliament, despite the European election system's bias in favour of small parties. Thus, even more than the other actors in the campaign, the PDS entered the European elections strategically focused upon October.

Finally, as mentioned in the introduction to this chapter, the fear among the German political élite that the right-wing Republicans may have made some form of electoral breakthrough in *Superwahljahr* had receded by the beginning of the year. The main reason for this was the transient nature of the Republicans' support, bound-up as it was with the asylum issue in Germany (Jung, 1994: 16–19). With the tightening of the criteria for granting asylum in July 1993, the issue lost much of its salience, leaving the Republicans with very little, in policy terms, around which to mobilize. Nevertheless, any degree of success on the part of the *Republikaner* held the potential to provoke alarm both domestically and abroad.

The issues and the campaign

Like others in member states, European elections in the Federal Republic tend to be dominated by domestic issues. Moreover, as discussed earlier, the special circumstances of *Superwahljahr* only served to accentuate this tendency. The absence of supranational issues as a salient factor in the campaign has, in the past, also been a function of the degree of consensus within the political élite with regard to European policy. There have been two reasons for this. First, the semi-sovereign status of the post-war Federal Republic (Katzenstein, 1987) and the need to rehabilitate Germany (and achieve a *rapprochement* with France) following the Second World War made the process of European integration central to (West) German foreign policy. Second, as a result of this centrality, an astonishing congruence has developed between the process of European integration and what could broadly be described as German interests, especially with regard to securing export markets for German manufacturing while protecting the agricultural sector through the Common Agricultural Policy (CAP). As a result, German–European relations, at least prior to unification, resembled a 'virtuous circle' where the one reinforced the other; this resulted not only in a 'European Germany' but also, to the degree that domestic institutional arrangements found an analogue at supranational level, perhaps also to some extent a 'German Europe'. Given this context, European policy has not been as contentious in the Federal Republic as it has been in some other member states (Bulmer and Paterson, 1987; Paterson and Southern, 1991; Markovits and Reich, 1991).

In recent years, however, this consensus has become less seamless. For instance, the rise of the Greens in the 1980s broke the broad consensus between the parties in the Federal Republic. The Greens' emphasis upon grass-roots democracy (*Basisdemokratie*) and suspicion of the established political settlement in 'the West' did not gel with what has essentially been an élite-dominated inter-governmental process. This ambivalence towards the European Union was duly reflected in the Greens' party programme for the European elections, with much emphasis placed on what the party saw as the deleterious effects of the Maastricht Treaty upon the democratic process, the imbalance between economic and environmental policy and the shortcomings of the European Union member states' trade and foreign policy stance, especially with regard to the Third World.

However, with the exception of the Greens, a consensus still remains between the CDU/CSU, FDP and SPD. Yet, even within this consensus, certain nuances can be discerned. There are two main reasons for this. First, with unification and the problems that accompanied it, the degree of congruence between the European agenda and German interests became less self-evident. Second, it is possible to discern a 'cohort effect' within the political elites, *across* parties, that seems to have some bearing on the relative weighting, in strategic terms, of Europe *vis-à-vis* the German national interest. This has been identified as being a division between the older 'Rhineland position', now primarily associated with Helmut Kohl – with an emphasis upon the Franco-German axis and ever-increasing European integration – and the more assertive 'Frankfurt position', with its emphasis upon widening, rather than deepening, the European Union and a greater degree of scepticism towards Economic and Monetary Union (Paterson, forthcoming). Nevertheless, what still amounted to a prevailing general consensus on the desirability of European integration *per se* meant that even when posters referred to Europe, they were vague and uninformative. Thus a CDU poster proclaimed semi-religiously: 'Against War, Violence and Terrorism in Europe: Peace for Everybody!' The SPD, on the other hand, issued posters asserting: 'The Mafia in Europe must be shattered! Security instead of Fear!'

In the face of such an uninspiring approach to the fundamental hurdles facing the EU in the coming decade, it is not surprising, therefore, that overall awareness of European issues was remarkably low. By the last week of the campaign, traditionally the *heiße* (hot) phase, a mere 25 per cent of the population showed any interest in Europe and the forthcoming election. Indeed, only 2 per cent perceived European integration as an important problem facing Germany. When it actually came to the election, two-thirds of the electorate cast their vote according to domestic, rather than supranational issues (Niedermayer, 1995: 2).

However, in one very important respect the 1994 campaign broke new ground: for the first time, a major party (namely the CSU) broke ranks with the overall consensus and (at least unofficially) espoused a 'Frankfurt position' – an attitude to Europe closer to that of the British Conservative Party than the intensely pro-European stance of Helmut Kohl. In a sense, this has a bitter irony to it, as it was the CSU under Strauss in the 1950s which was arguably the most pro-European (Paterson, forthcoming: 11). However, following the establishment of the Grand Coalition in 1966, the CSU adopted a lower profile on European integration, with Strauss during the 1980s becoming gradually more sceptical of the European institutions (Paterson, forthcoming: 13). After Strauss' death in 1988, the German Euro-sceptic mantle was passed on to the Bavarian environment minister, Peter Gauweiler, who has openly criticized the Maastricht Treaty arrangements. However, Gauweiler was forced to resign in Spring 1994 due to irregularities in his financial dealings, and while remaining chairman of the Munich party, has become a pariah in the CSU, not least because he has shared an anti-Europe platform with Manfred Brunner, the break-away chairman of the Bavarian FDP who brought the Maastricht Treaty before the Constitutional Court in Autumn 1993, and with Jörg Haider, the right-wing populist leader of the Austrian Freedom Party (FPÖ). However, the most openly anti-Maastricht stance was taken by the Bund Freie Bürges, founded by Manfred Brunner to contest the Euro-elections in the wake of publicity over his appeal to the Federal Constitutional Court. After an initial surge of interest, the party played little role in the campaign.

The most recent controversy concerning European integration was triggered by the Bavarian Minister-President Edmund Stoiber, who − following his elevation to the top job in Bavaria in Summer 1993 − has placed himself and the CSU firmly on the right of the political spectrum. In an open letter to Helmut Kohl on 3 September 1993, and again in an interview with the *Süddeutsche Zeitung* on 2 November 1993, Stoiber attacked the European Union's institutional structures in the former and then struck a more nationalistic tone in the latter. As Paterson (forthcoming: 18) notes, 'Stoiber did not restrict himself to underlying Bavarian populist resentments however but presented a wider German National alternative to Helmut Kohl which might appeal more widely across the Federal Republic'.

Although, by British standards, Stoiber's stance would probably still seem decidedly 'europhile', his proclamations constitute a major shift away from the political élites' conventional wisdom on European integration. Its relative significance in German Euro-political history merits the question 'Why?', in answer to which four main reasons may be identified. First, the CSU has had a traditionally strong link with agriculture, which is likely to suffer as the CAP is a prime target for cuts in the years to come. Second, as mentioned earlier, the CSU has to exploit its potential in Bavaria more successfully than in the past in order to compensate for its reduced weight within the enlarged Federal Republic. Third, Bavaria was the stepping stone of the extreme-right *Republikaner* in the 1989 European election, where they scored 14.6 per cent, a basis which Stoiber was keen to undermine. Fourth, there may well have been personal reasons in play: Stoiber's ascension to Minister-President of Bavaria was marred by an acrimonious battle with his party chairman Theo Waigel, who also coveted the post. By launching attacks on the future of the European Union, Stoiber directly undermined Waigel's position, who as finance minister is a signatory to the treaty. While Stoiber seems to be an isolated 'Euro-slightly-less-enthusiastic-than-everybody-else' for the moment, his comments illustrate the divisions that exist below the veneer of lip-service to the European ideal. The reason why it was so vehemently decried by other Christian Democrats (Heiner Geißler, a former secretary-general of the CDU even went as far as to call Stoiber a 'traitor') was because its blatant populism was regarded as having potentially struck a note with the electorate. Whereas the German population

Table 4.1 Euro-election results in Germany

	1994 (%)	Seats	1989 (%)	Seats
Turnout	60.1		62.3	
CDU/CSU	38.8	47	37.7	32
CDU	32.0	39	29.5	25
CSU	6.8	8	8.2	7
SPD	32.2	40	37.3	31
FDP	4.1		5.6	4
Greens	10.1	12	8.4	8
Republikaner	3.9		7.1	6
PDS	4.7			
BFB	1.1			

Source: Frankfurter Rundschau, 14 June 1994.

has, in the past, supported the diffuse idea of European integration, it has been notably less enthusiastic about specific proposals. Thus there is widespread unease about the prospect of losing the Deutschmark: as a survey by the *Institut für Demoskopie, Allensbach* shows, only 27 per cent of respondents were in favour of a common currency (*Frankfurter Allgemeine Zeitung*, 8 June 1994).

The results

The results (see Table 4.1) produced a surprise for most observers. The CDU emerged as the largest party, with a better-than-expected 38.8 per cent. However, as was described earlier, this was a predictable result in the light of the improved economic situation which had developed in the spring. Suddenly, Helmut Kohl was back. Indeed, the CDU/CSU managed to become the largest party again, with a full 6.6 percentage points lead over the SPD. Moreover, the CDU/CSU beat the SPD in all federal states except Brandenburg, Bremen, Saarland, Hamburg and Northrhine-Westphalia, a result which would be seen to preview the *Bundestag* elections, where a similar pattern was to occur.

The CSU's result, while an undoubted success, underlines the party's problems in unified Germany. Although its share of the national vote dropped (a not unexpected outcome, given the enlarged all-German electorate), it actually increased its share of the vote in Bavaria, from 45.4 per cent in 1989 to 48.9 per cent in 1994. Yet this illustrates just how susceptible the party is to poor turnout figures: in 1994, only 56.5 per cent of the Bavarian electorate cast its vote in the European election, compared with 61.1 per cent in 1989. As expected, the FDP suffered from its lack of a core electorate. Its failure to enter the parliament was, however, in keeping with its overall electoral performance, on the merits of which it had failed to successfully contest a *Landtag* election since the Schleswig-Holstein and Baden-Württemberg elections of April 1992.

Among the mainstream opposition parties, the SPD's result was disappointing, especially considering its fine performance in 1989. However, as was shown earlier in this chapter, the SPD had already started to lose ground to

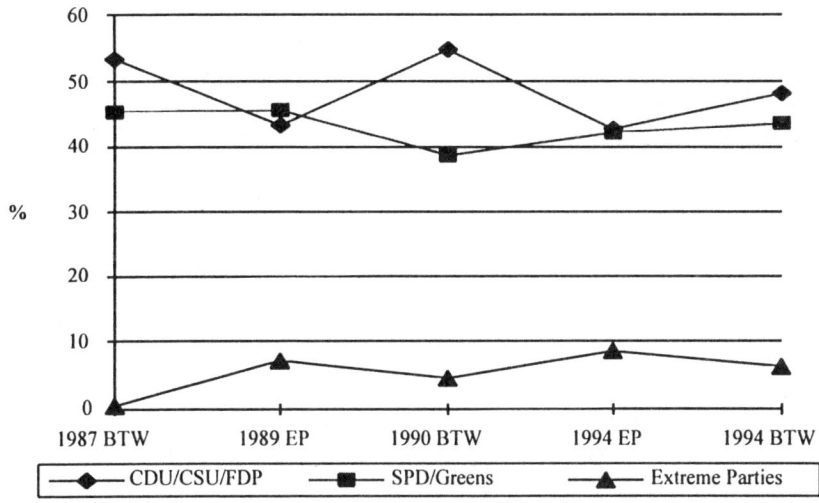

Figure 4.8   German elections at Federal level 1987–94

Note: EP = European Parliament election; BTW = *Bundestag* election; Extreme parties = PDS + Republikaner (NPD for 1987).

Source: *Frankfurter Rundschau*, 14 June 1994; Presse- und Informationsamt der Bundesregierung; von Beyme (1991: 126).

the CDU *before* the European election. By contrast, the Greens polled an unprecedented result at a national election. As previously noted, this was due to their highly motivated and politically active electorate, which could be relied upon to cast their votes on election day. However, Niedermayer (1995: 5–6) argues that European elections, by their very nature of being protest elections and situated between two federal elections, tend to favour the opposition parties. In contrast, the governing parties tend to gain from the incumbency bonus as national election time draws near. Thus Niedermayer has argued that any analysis of the parties' results can only be conducted with reference to the last election at the federal level (ie the 1990 *Bundestag* election). The overall validity of his theory is demonstrated by Figure 4.8, which illustrates that gains made by the opposition parties during the European elections tend to be lost again in subsequent *Bundestag* elections. However, his argument is less applicable in this particular instance, given the proximity of the 1994 European and *Bundestag* elections.

On the far-right of the political spectrum, the *Republikaner* notably failed to re-secure representation at European level, having scored 7.1 per cent in 1989. Moreover, analysis of the *Republikaner* vote at state level shows that it passed the 5 per cent mark in only two Länder (Baden-Württemberg and Bavaria). Nonetheless, its overall score was still 1.8 percentage points above its 1990 *Bundestag* election result, thereby again illustrating the propensity of European

Table 4.2   Turnout in 1994 Euro-elections in Eastern Germany

Land	Turnout (%)
Thuringia	72.9
Saxony	70.6
Saxony-Anhalt	65.9
Mecklenburg-Western Pommerania	64.7
Berlin	53.4
Brandenburg	41.4
Germany	60.1
EU-12	54.0

Source: Frankfurter Rundschau, 14 June 1994.

elections to generate a certain protest vote element. Despite this, as explained earlier, their electoral following has dwindled considerably following the amendment of Article 16 of the Basic Law in July 1993. At the other pole of the left-right axis, the PDS also scored better than in both the 1990 and 1994 *Bundestag* elections, narrowly missing the 5 per cent hurdle. Indeed, its national result masks the considerable share of the vote it obtained in the new *Länder*. As well as coming third in Thuringia, Saxony-Anhalt, Brandenburg and Berlin, it came second in Mecklenburg-Western Pommerania with 22.7 per cent of the vote.

Turnout for the European election was above the European average, but below the 1989 level and below the mathematical average of 61.2 per cent for all four European elections in Germany. However, the turnout figure is, to an extent, falsified by the unusually high levels for the eastern *Länder* (Table 4.2). These should not be interpreted as enthusiasm in the east for European issues, but rather as the fact that the election date coincided with local elections (*Kommunalwahlen*) in all new states except Brandenburg (where the turnout perhaps reflects the true level of attachment of Germany's new citizens to the European ideal). Indeed, Niedermayer (1995: 7) argues that this happy coincidence helped to boost the PDS' result, who were able to rely on a loyal and committed electorate[5]. The poor showing of the Bund Freie Bürges confirmed it as a flash-in-the-pan party.

Conclusion

The outcome of the European election in Germany had a number of significant consequences for the shape of the European Parliament. The failure of the *Republikaner* was a check to those on the extreme right who expected to see the European Parliament act as a Europe-wide focus for extreme-right opinion. Traditionally the SPD is the strongest party in the Socialist group, but although it increased its number of seats from 32 to 40 because of the greater size of the German delegation, it has been overtaken by the British Labour Party, who now provide the leader of the Socialist Group. However, it remains a major force and Klaus Hänsch, its leading candidate and a veteran European Parliamentarian, was elected as President at the new Parliament's first meeting. Hänsch has always taken an advanced position on institutional reform and will argue Parliament's case with some force, taking a position close to that of the Federal government. The CDU/CSU will continue to play a major role in the European People's Party (EPP), given their 47 members. Together with the Spanish Conservatives, they are expected to set the agenda for the EPP. Their position has, however, been slightly weakened by the absence of Egon Klepsch, Hänsch's immediate predecessor as Parliament President, who was dropped from his *Land* list in a much criticized manner to provide a space for a former minister.

Perhaps the most important European implication of the European election in Germany was to confirm Helmut Kohl in his conviction that his views on Europe could still command the support of the electorate. He had strongly resisted plans to drop the 'federal' aspiration in the CDU's Basic Programme and was successful in its retention. He was also encouraged in his pro-European stand by the miserable failure of the Brunner Party. Although he has made some concessions (he claims, for example, to have dropped the creation of a United States of Europe as a party goal), the main contents of his 'Rhineland' policy remain intact and will have a major impact on the 1996 Inter-Governmental Conference. Similarly, Edmund Stoiber, the Bavarian Minister-President, felt that the results also vindicated his less enthusiastic views on Europe and that, following Helmut Kohl's eventual retirement, German European policy will move gradually away from the classic Rhineland position. The FDP, by contrast, is torn in two directions: following its poor electoral performances through 1994 (it was only just returned to the *Bundestag*), the FDP is experiencing pressures from within to adopt a more national-conservative position. Led by the former prosecutor-general, Alexander von Stahl, this group, with a strongly anti-Maastricht agenda, voiced itself at the party congress in Stuttgart in January 1995 and may become stronger if the party fails to perform well in *Land* elections in the immediate future. Above all, Helmut Kohl is faced with the task of reconciling his aim of further integration with an electorate which is growing increasingly wary of ambitious and expensive expansionist moves of the EU.

European elections arguably have limited utility when predicting the outcome of the following *Bundestag* election, because of the different institutional and behavioural characteristics of the two. The 1994 election, however, can be seen as *sui generis*, given the expectations of the media, political parties and electorate. In this context, whoever 'won' the election in terms of gaining the largest share of the vote, with a clear lead over his nearest rival, would be declared as favourite to win the *Bundestag* election in October. When Kohl, therefore, did confound the critics by leading the CDU/CSU to victory, *Die Woche* on 16 June described him as 'Phoenix from the Ashes'. Moreover, the *Süddeutsche Zeitung* of 14 June 1994 judged the SPD to be 'sailing in stormy waters' and needing a 'miracle' to win the October election. As was to become apparent, such a miracle was beyond the SPD's grasp, and Helmut Kohl was duly returned, albeit with a much reduced majority.

To sum up, it is not possible to analyse the 1994 European election in Germany without reference to the wider context of *Superwahljahr*. Given these exceptional circumstances, it must be concluded that it was more akin to a second-order election, rather than — as would normally be the case — a fourth-order election.

Notes

1. The authors would like to record their gratitude to Oskar Niedermayer and Geoffrey Roberts for their help and advice in the writing of this article.
2. As in other countries, non-German EU citizens were allowed to vote for the first time in an election in Germany. However, this seems not to have had any significant effect on the outcome (Niedermayer, 1995: 4).
3. Given the regional appeal of the CSU and the erosion of support for the CDU's other coalition partner, the liberal Free Democrats (FDP), the term 'governing coalition' can, for our purposes, be interpreted as being analogous with the CDU.
4. Due to the party's high concentration of support in East Berlin, where many former regime apparatchiks live and where the PDS was held — correctly as it turned out — to have a good chance of winning up to three directly-contested seats, thus allowing them to circumvent Germany's 5 per cent electoral threshhold.
5   Interestingly, a recent public opinion survey carried out in association with the *Financial Times* (5 December 1994) indicates that there is, in fact, little difference between attitudes towards Europe in the new *Länder* and those in the 'old' FRG.

References

von Beyme, Klaus (1991): *Das politische System der Bundesrepublik Deutschland nach der Vereinigung*, Piper, Munich.

Bulmer, S and Paterson, W (1986) 'The Federal Republic of Germany', in Lodge, J (ed), *Direct elections to the European Parliament 1984*, Macmillan, Basingstoke.

— (1987) *The Federal Republic of Germany and the European Community*, Allen & Unwin, London.

Jung, M (1994) 'Ökonomische Situation und Stabilität der Demokratie: Anmerkungen aus der Perspektive der Meinungsforschung', Paper presented at the Symposium *Demokratie und Wohlstand*, Bayerische Landeszentrale für politische Bildungsarbeit, Munich, 27 January 1994.

Katzenstein, P (1987) *Policy and Politics in West Germany: The Growth of a Semi-sovereign State*, Temple University Press, Philadelphia.

Kolinsky, E (1990) 'The Federal Republic of Germany', in Lodge, Juliet (ed), *The 1989 Election of the European Parliament*, Macmillan, Basingstoke.

Markovits, A and Reich, S (1991) 'Should Europe Fear the Germans?', *German Politics and Society*, 23: 1–20.

Niedermayer, O (1995) 'Die Europawahl im Kontext des Superwahljahrs', *Integration*, 1.

Padgett, S (ed) (1993) *Parties and Party Systems in the New Germany*, Dartmouth, Aldershot.

Pappi, F U (1984) 'The West German Party System', *West European Politics*, 7(4).

Paterson, W (forthcoming) 'The German Christian Democrats and European Integration', in Gaffney, John (ed), *Political Parties and European Integration*, Routledge, London.
Paterson, W and Southern, D (1991) *Governing Germany*, Blackwell, Oxford.
Rudzio, W (1994) 'Das neue Parteienfinanzierungsmodell und seine Auswirkungen', *Zeitschrift für Parlamentsfragen*, 3.

5

France

John Gaffney

Introduction

The European elections of 12 June 1994 in France had three defining characteristics, each related to the other. The first was the relative apathy of the electorate. Turnout was a respectable 53.5 per cent, higher than anticipated.
Abstentionism in all French elections had risen over the previous decade, and
some observers were beginning to talk of a crisis of legitimacy. As is evident
from the voting figures of 12 June, however, the French were still voting (especially when one considers that the European Parliament is seen as having little
relavance). What was changing was difficult to quantify, but involved the *degree*
of interest the French electorate took in election campaigns and in politics in
general. The political classes had been involved in the campaign for months,
and more intensively for weeks. Even during the first week in June, however,
the non-politician would have been forgiven for not realizing a European election was imminent. Only by the middle of the second week, a few days before
voting day, did the elections gain a higher profile with a series of television
debates, radio programmes, party political broadcasts and front-page articles.[1]
The public's awareness was also heightened by the media attention given to
Bernard Tapie, the leader of one of the smaller lists, who in fact distinguished
himself from his rivals on several counts: he was the only main leader to be
resolutely pro-European in a country now questioning its place in Europe; he
was also the only one under investigation for tax fraud, and who had witnessed,
along with the French viewing public, the bailiffs dumping his property into
the street as part of a process of recouping debts owed by the millionaire busi-
nessman-turned-politician. Overall, however, public apathy and ignorance
dominated the elections. This brings us to the second defining characteristic
of the elections, namely the activity of the political class, which was as intense
as the public's attention was slight.

Such activity within the political class itself seems inexplicable when contrasted with the fact that 'out there' no one was listening. A number of factors
suggest reasons for the level of activity. Because of the highly complex nature
of politics in France, where several strong and deep political traditions co-exist,

each with minority constituencies whose organizational expression as political parties necessitates alliances in order to create governing majorities, the European elections – irrespective of their significance for Europe and European issues – are but one moment in an intense cycle of French elections, each of which sees shifts in alliances. In the 1994–5 context, the cycle involved the cantonal elections in March 1994, the European elections in June 1994, the presidential elections in May 1995, and the municipal elections in June 1995. The most significant of these elections in terms of their organizing all the others were the presidential elections of May 1995. A great deal of the context, significance, political activity, and consequences of the European elections of June 1994 can be understood in terms of the influence upon them of the presidential elections of the following year.

Edouard Balladur, the Prime Minister, was an as yet undeclared candidate for the right in the presidential elections of 1995. His disadvantage *vis-à-vis* his rival for the nomination, Jacques Chirac, was that Chirac was the leader of the Gaullists (the RPR, Rally for the Republic), and had been their candidate in both 1981 and 1988. Balladur's advantage was that, although himself a Gaullist, he was supported by many within the Union for French Democracy (UDF), the other partner in the governing coalition. Neither would accept the other's heading the list for the European elections. Besides, even had one or other accepted to do so, any setback in the European elections would reflect badly upon whoever had led the list. The compromise, therefore, was to head a UDF-RPR list with someone who was not a contender for the presidency, and to allow a UDF figure to lead a joint list (on condition that it were not Giscard d'Estaing who might use the campaign to his own presidential advantage).[2] The challenge, therefore, passed to the UDF to find a campaign leader who was acceptable to both parties.

Dominique Baudis became the UDF's choice. As a pro-European he gave the campaign a positive image, although as we shall see, in order to appease the Euro-sceptics within the governing coalition, he conducted his campaign in a less than enthusiastic way. The Baudis list did, however, keep the bulk of the right in line. It also kept the presidential elections out of the debate on Europe. It did not, however, prevent the emergence of a dissident, right-wing and anti-European list, led by Philippe de Villiers. The irony here was that this nationalist element within the right had sprung not from the Gaullists but from within the UDF, de Villiers having been a prominent member of the Republican Party (PR), the UDF's main constitutent element. The de Villiers list had the undeclared sympathy of many within the governing coalition of the UDF and RPR, and allowed the Gaullists to minimize their official support for Baudis in the name of unity itself – the less enthusiasm, the less chance of accentuating division.

Our observations concerning the influence of the presidential elections of 1995 upon the European elections of 1994 have a more general theoretical validity: it is not simply the elections of 1995 but presidentialism itself which in contemporary France drives the political parties forward into treating all political activity from this presidential perspective. We have just discussed the political right, and seen that the European elections were, in fact, controlled by the imperative that no potential national leader must lead the governing majority's campaign. On the left, however, the opposite happened. Michel Rocard, First Secretary of the Socialist Party (PS), made himself head of the party's list in order to assert his control over his party and stop any of his rivals from using the European elections as a springboard to the party leadership or presidential candidacy. This meant, however, that his leadership status and especially his aspirations to be the party's next presidential candidate were implicated in the party's performance at the European elections. A bad showing at the polls would constitute a vote of no confidence in the party's leader. For Rocard, therefore, the decision to lead the party's list was a high-risk strategy.

The European elections also brought other political leaders centre-stage, many to the public's attention and for future reference, if not into the presidential race itself. The most striking example of this was Bernard Tapie, who led the left-of-centre Radical Left Movement's list (MRG). Without dwelling upon Tapie here, it is worth mentioning the startling success of his list (see results); by dominating the media (he was several times daily on television) and doing so brilliantly, he demonstrated the influence of television on public perceptions of politics, and the near-exclusive role played by individuals as proponents of policies. We can make a further theoretical point, which is that the personalization of French politics remained the organizing principle of political and electoral activity even with the national single-round proportional list system used for the European elections (which is not characteristic of French elections at any level). The presidential context and the accompanying personalization of politics had become a major organizing principle of political activity. This brings us to the third defining characteristic of the 1994 European elections.

The elections took place in the middle of a complex process of reconfiguration in French politics. The presidential factor was, as we have seen, crucial. It was not, however, exclusive. In fact, the fortunes and effects of presidentialism were themselves part of a deeper and wider process affecting French political culture. The European elections of 1994 reflected some of these developments as surface phenomena do deeper processes: a relatively high abstention rate; participation itself characterized by a lack of interest; a large number of lists which reflected not only the highly fractured nature of French politics, but also, and paradoxically, a relative indifference to the European elections themselves on the part of politicians; major splits within all the parties, especially over the question of Europe; a strong showing for those opposed to the governing coalition's list, a majority even against *both* of the governing parties of the previous 30 years (see results on pages 99–100); a growing political dealignment of the electorate, especially on the left.

We can say, therefore, that the European elections of 1994 were a revealing reflection of change in French society. Moreover, by virtue of their being inscribed so consequentially into the political process, they were causative of political changes. We can list these changes by simply recapitulating what we have already identified: hyper-activity within the political class; publicly expressed rivalries between presidential hopefuls and their entourages and support; the provision of a forum for political personalities to try and position themselves before the presidentializing machines moved into top gear from the political *rentrée* of September 1994 onwards; the opportunity for *new* alliances to be built between various political groupings; the opportunity for the mainstream political parties to draw consequences from the election broadcasts,[3] rallies and media coverage generally. This was the context of the elections of June 1994 in France. Let us now look at the electoral lists themselves.

The lists

Twenty lists were presented at the European elections. This created real problems for many municipalities lacking this number of hoardings.[4] The number reflected the diversity of opinion and tradition in French political culture; the political frivolity with which the European elections were regarded by some, with very little attempt to resolve differences with proximate political groups; the use of the election by many groups to redefine their relationship to other groups, whether in terms of cooperation or dominance; the use of the proportional system which countered any bi-polarizing or centripetal tendencies within the regime; and the relatively lax attitude in France as regards eligibility for the European elections.[5]

The right

For the government, unity of the governing coalition and parliamentary majority was essential. Disunity in the past had so often been the undoing of the right. Putting forward a unitary list with a single manifesto was to prove difficult, especially as regards the question of Europe itself, European integration being one of the major fault lines between (and within) the generally pro-European UDF and the generally anti-federalist RPR. The RPR had been split in 1992 over the referendum on ratification of the Maastricht Treaty and was still trying to resolve its internal differences over Europe. The list was led by the (slightly) junior partner in the governing coalition, the UDF, a confederation of right-wing political parties extending from the centre across to the extreme right and the blurred line dividing it from the National Front, but which, generally speaking, was pro-European.

The conditions necessary for the list, therefore, were that, even though few of the leading figures were themselves ready to head it, it should be acceptable to all parties of the governing coalition. The front-runner for leader until April had been Jean-François Deniau of the Republican Party who, though pro-

European, had been hesitant on Maastricht, a paradoxical qualification that made him just about acceptable to everyone. However, on 5 April, by 18 votes to 15, with one abstention, the UDF political bureau voted for staunchly pro-European Christian Democrat Dominique Baudis to lead the list. He was a member of the Centre of Social Democrats (CDS) (also a constitutent element of the UDF). Deniau's problem had been that he was supported by François Léotard, another *présidentiable*, and so threatened Giscard d'Estaing's own position and prospects within the UDF. The Republican Party was extremely annoyed by Deniau's defeat and threatened as a result to leave the UDF group in Parliament, although they subsequently withdrew the threat. The RPR then agreed to Baudis.

Early talk was of the need for a real anti-Maastricht number two on the list to allow the list to reflect the coalition's truly diverse nature. Eventually, however, the number 2 position was given to the non-partisan Hélène Carrère d'Encausse, a historian and member of the French Academy, who was herself pro-European (and who had chaired a pro-Maastricht committee in 1992). For form's sake she joined the RPR so the list was nominally balanced. These decisions were expected to generate harmony and a positive, generous, but not too generous, pro-European campaign. In fact, the immediate result was not just dissension within the ranks but outright rebellion, and the setting up by Phillippe de Villiers of a rival anti-European list. This had been threatened since the previous summer and it was assumed that it would be a pin-prick in the government's side. But it won over 12 per cent of the vote, that is, nearly half of the Baudis vote, thereby shifting the centre of political gravity within the governing coalition to the right in the aftermath of the elections.

Perhaps even more significant was the fact that the two pro-Europeans now heading the list and leading all the publicity, appearing on the posters, in interviews, and so on, responded to the situation by saying virtually nothing of any consequence. The logic of the situation was clear: pro-Europeans could lead the list, giving the government an image of smiling unity (Baudis himself was a former television presenter), on condition that they did not push a pro-European line nor upset any of the anti-Europeans in the governing coalition.[6]

The formidable RPR machine itself ran very much in neutral for the duration of the campaign, not wishing to create tension within the party, nor to allow a runaway success for the government which would have strengthened the argument for a single right-wing candidate at the next presidential election, namely Balladur and not Chirac. To this end, figures such as Chirac offered due support to Baudis whenever necessary, lending him his famous artificial smile, embracing him perhaps the better to suffocate him. By the end of the campaign, Baudis appeared forlorn, silenced by the dangerous tensions for which he was the public relations person, and held at amicable arm's length, centre-stage, by all the *présidentiables* of the right, precisely because he was not one of them.

Philippe de Villiers, a Republican Party MP, broke away from the governing majority in opposition to its pro-European stance. Villiers, a hard-line right-winger (often referred to as the Le Pen of the 16th *arrondissement*, a fashionable part of Paris), was financed by the equally right-wing and anti-European Anglo-French financier Jimmy Goldsmith.[7] We shall discuss below the impact and significance of the Villiers campaign; here we can just mention that the list reflected a very real section of opinion both within the country[8] and within and close to the governing coalition; in fact, it had been encouraged with varying degrees of tacit approval by central figures within the governing coalition, in particular Charles Pasqua, the right-wing Gaullist, anti-Maastricht, Interior Minister. The official line was disapproving: de Villiers was considered to have left his Republican Party and betrayed the government. In reality, he had created the conditions for staunching support for Le Pen by offering a more respectable anti-Europe list. Jean-Marie Le Pen on the other hand was beginning to lose his anti-establishment, mould-breaking appeal. With the arrival on the scene of a new generation of politicians, some trying to steal Le Pen's policies (de Villiers), others elements of his style and image (Tapie), Le Pen would have difficulty maintaining the National Front (FN) vote at 10 per cent and certainly difficulty in creating the electoral momentum necessary to increase it. In the 1989 elections, the Front had gained 11.73 per cent, and at the beginning of the 1994 campaign had put forward a target of 15 per cent. Such was the situation with the various Rights. The complexities surrounding the drawing up of the Socialist Party's and the other left-wing lists were no less fascinating.

The left

European elections in France are inscribed into the cycles of national and local elections, which offer challenges, opportunities and threats to the main political parties. This was particularly true of the 1994 Euro-elections and the Socialists who, after having been the main governing party for over a decade (1981–93), had suffered a serious defeat in the legislative elections of 1993. The new leader of the party and presidential hopeful, Michel Rocard, decided (felt compelled, in fact) to use the Euro-elections to enhance both his own authority in the party, and the party's standing in the country. The party had done quite well in the cantonal elections held in March 1994 (23 per cent).

The PS list was made public on 30 March (one or two changes were made to the list a little later). The main consideration for the PS in drawing up its list was fairly to represent the *courants* (organized political factions) on the list. Rocard could have tried to override the *courants* and present a party list which represented a new departure for the party, focused upon Europe and representing an 'opening out' (*ouverture*) to the centrist voters (in this vein, the former Minister for European Affairs, Elisabeth Guigou, had been mooted as a possible leader of the campaign the previous summer). But overiding the *courants* was felt to be too damaging to internal unity, so they, with all the ensuing wrangling, were represented. A degree of *ouverture* was attempted; the main feature of this development was the inclusion of Bernard Kouchner, the non-party, former Minister of Health and Humanitarian Action, as number three on the list (he had suggested earlier that he might present his own list). The smiling faces of the 87 PS candidates on the party's campaign poster belied a party riven with internal problems. If one accepts the principle that the *courants* represent the democratic vectors of opinion within the party, and therefore should take precedence over other considerations, then the list was, more or less, a democratic snapshot of the party. However, if one takes the view that the *courants* had, by 1994, largely become alibis for warring factions organized around presidential and party leader hopefuls, then it was clear that Rocard's new-look Socialist Party was deceptively much the same as before. Added to this was the fact that there were many thirsty ambitions for office, given the legislative hecatomb of 1993 which had removed most former MPs from office; and that forecasts had suggested that the party would not return as many Euro-MPs to the new parliament as were leaving the old one; the scramble for places, therefore, paid little heed to such considerations as the value, still less the feelings, of the sitting MEPs.[9] Even Jean-Pierre Cot, internationally known as an MEP, head of the whole EP Socialist group, and a contender for the presidency of the new Parliament, was nearly bustled off the list, then bustled back in eleventh position. Given the acuteness of the competition for places, the small *courants* within the party led by Louis Mermaz and Jean Poperen were not represented at all. A further element to the drawing up of the list was the decision to have an equal number of men and women alternating on the list. This had been lobbied for within the party, in particular by such figures as Yvette Roudy (who was subsequently not included on the list for her pains), and taken up by Rocard. The notion of male/female parity and the questions raised by this will be discussed in greater detail further on in this chapter.

One of the political ironies of all of these developments was that, over Europe, no one in the PS actually disagreed about policy. This was because the anti-European left-wing tip of the party had gone to set up its stall elsewhere. Jean-Pierre Chevènement, who had been in the party and one of the main leaders of its left-wing since the 1960s, had begun noisily to drift away from the party in the late 1980s. In March 1994 he finally left the PS group in the National Assembly. France's left-wing was awash with personalities and fractions from the Communist Party (PCF), the PS, and other groups criss-crossing one another on the political spectrum. By creating L'Autre Politique, it was Chevènement's hope to harness and federate much of this activity, and to use the European elections to do this; the anti-European strain within the left of the left being one of the few uncontentiously uniting factors, this amplified by Chevènement's bizarre nationalism which would have itself reminiscent of revolutionary 1792, but was, in fact, more so of Boulangist 1889. Chevènement knew that both his movement and the PCF would be chasing the same anti-Maastricht left. If he could do so creditably he would place himself and his movement in a favourable strategic position in terms of future alliances between the PCF and the Socialists. He also hoped to attract the support of Ecologists and the other dispersed left-wing groups (two other ultra-left lists stood, however, one led by David Gluckstein, the other by Arlette Laguiller). The veteran socialist, feminist and respected Gisèle Halimi gave Chevènement's list the wider credibility it would otherwise have lacked.[10] At its 17 April National Council, Chevènement's new Citizen's Movement, like the PS, decided upon male/female parity on its list. Such a move by his Movement (he had, in fact, always represented a (male) authoritarian and sectarian strain within French socialism) was a serious attempt to use the European elections to political purpose. If successful in his undertaking, he would appear as crucial to the re-federation of the left; if unsuccessful, as the presumptuous leader of a self-regarding and ramshackle coalition of the political elite's homeless.

To the left of Chevènement, the Communist Party list, drawn up in February, was led not by the new Party leader, Robert Hue, but by a party MEP of 15 years' standing, Francis Wurtz. Unlike all other political parties and movements under enormous pressure from events and from internal dissent, the PCF had never exploded. Even its implosions were barely perceptible as it surgically removed dissidents at regular intervals in order to maintain a party line. The result, of course, was the dwindling of the party from being the strongest party on the left, holding around a quarter of the national vote after the Second World War, down to its hovering around the 5 per cent threshold of political annihilation. The PCF made attempts in June 1994 to include a range of opinion within the party in order to present a list with a more diverse image, along the lines of Chevènement's. However, with the notable exception of the, by Communist standards, independent-minded party economist, Philippe Herzog, the PCF's list was one which reflected the continuing influence of the former leader Georges Marchais. It is worth noting that ten of the first 20 on the PCF list were women (and more than half of the list overall) although such feminist credentials have always been at least the public hallmark of the PCF (as with the Greens) and in no way reflected the relatively sudden conversion apparent in most of the other parties.[11]

The others

The drawing up of the two French Greens' list prefaced the dramatic and largely self-induced political defeat of both groups. In the 1989 European elections, the Green movement had presented a single list and had gained 10.6 per cent of the vote and eight MEPs. There are, however, many strains in French political ecologism. Of the two dominant ones during the 1980s, one was more willing to collaborate with government; the result, by the end of the 1980s, was Génération Ecologie (GE) led by a former Minister of the Environment, Brice Lalonde. For the other strain, the Verts (Greens), this was indeed collaboration with the enemy (especially given France's nuclear industry and armaments). Antagonism between these two strains was often so intense as to be internecine.

At their conference on 16 and 17 April 1994, the Greens effectively blocked any cooperation with Lalonde's Génération Ecologie (a self-destructive move which was made more internally damaging by the 'minority' opposition inside the party to such a move by figures such as Antoine Waechter who was in favour of a joint list). Lalonde's own subsequent list effectively did the same thing, ie blocked cooperation (with the same internal adverse consequences on internal party unity and activism). The amusing counterpart to this was the inclusion by both sides on their list of members and sympathizers of the other party in order to lay exclusive claim to unity. The two lists began the campaign by ignoring each other, and the very existence of two Green lists called into question the whole ethos and provenance of the movement. Deliberately countering the style of the highly personalized Génération Ecologie's Lalonde, the Greens' list was led by the quite unknown Marie-Anne Isler-Béguin who would have acquitted herself well as the spokesperson for a students' union but whose media performance was not in a league comparable to that of her many adversaries, the most colourful of whom was not Lalonde but Bernard Tapie.

Tapie's heading a list was the result of an enormous gamble taken by the rump of France's oldest party, the Radicals. Since the 1970s, the left-wing Radicals (MRG) had acted as a minor ally to the growing Socialists. Their support for the left had allowed the Socialists to seem 'central' in a left-wing alliance, as offering a point of attraction to centrist voters who wished to keep as far away from the PCF as possible while nevertheless voting for the Union of the Left. Nevertheless, the MRG had really only survived through the goodwill of the Socialists; if the latter had really wished to do so it could have ground the MRG out of electoral existence. As it was, the PS kept away from relative MRG strongholds. In 1994, the proposal that Bernard Tapie should lead the MRG list was tacitly supported by President Mitterrand, but, in fact, opposed by many in the MRG itself who thought the notion of an association with Tapie was to betray Radicalism. The party was seriously divided and throughout April the storm raged in the Radical teacup. Nevertheless, Tapie was voted in as the head of the list, and was to take the party on a trip which was to contrast with its hitherto sobriety of discourse and image to the point where the party simply stood back and let him perform (and ultimately give them more seats in Strasbourg than they could have dreamed of). Tapie's list was, like Rocard's, a mixture of traditional party and media-catching personalities. Personalities on Tapie's list were Catherine Lalumière, a former Socialist Party member and former General Secretary of the Council of Europe (in third place, the second place going to the MRG leader, Jean-François Hory); Christiane Taubira-Delannon, an MP from French Guyana (number four on the list); Noël Mamère, a well-known ecologist; and the feminist Antoinette Fouque, co-founder of the Mouvement de Libération de la Femme. As regards the MRG itself, it is worth pointing out that although the glitz of the 'Tapie show' as it was derogatorily called by its rivals, contrasted with the party it represented, it is nevertheless the case that having a party to represent was of major significance as regards legitimating Tapie. It is highly probable that had he presented a list which had no party backing it would have made no impact at all. Tapie claimed to represent the centre-left tradition of non-socialist republicanism, and did exactly that creditably well. How such a list might affect organized Radicalism in the longer term lies outside the scope of this chapter.

Bernard-Henri Levy, the somewhat media-conscious French philosopher, had recently made a film concerning the plight of the Yugoslavians. On returning to France, he declared that he would put forward a list for the European elections called 'Europe begins at Sarajevo'. The list would be essentially a list of high-profile personalities who would use the European elections to draw attention to the horrors in the former Yugoslavia, and lobby the political parties to do something. As with most ethical issues when faced with political reality, moral questions turned to organizational ones, and these in turn to squabbling. To put it briefly, Levy sanctimoniously withdrew his list at the end of May after having persuaded Rocard to take his ideas on board (ie to go against established PS and presidential policy and entertain the idea of lifting the UN arms embargo on the Bosnian Muslims). As a result, Rocard incurred even more hostility from Mitterrand's close supporters than usual, and looked as if he had been intimidated by the potential threat posed by a Sarajevo list; other members of the list − some of whose anti-Rocard motivations vied with their pro-Sarajevo ones − felt betrayed, and, led by former Minister Léon Schwartzenberg, resolved to soldier on, which they did to the bitter end, leaving the public unsure of whether there was or was not a Sarajevo list at all.

The incident is interesting for the light it sheds on the campaign. First, it demonstrated the easy publicity which could be gained just by threatening to run a list. It also demonstrated how the European elections themselves, even when dealing with an issue as European as the former Yugoslavia, were not really concerned with who was to represent whom in the European Parliament. Third, as much as the European elections came alive at all, it has to be said that the 'Sarajevo' incident did capture the headlines and bring to the fore the elections themselves. By early May the composition of the majority of the lists had been resolved, and the lists presented.[12] They were:

1. **Chasse-Pêche-Nature-Traditions**
   (Hunting, Fishing, Nature, Traditions) (André Goustat)

2. **Rassemblement de l'outre-mer et des minorités**
   (Overseas and Minorities' Rally) (Ernest Moutoussamy)

3. **La Majorité pour l'autre Europe**
   (The Majority for the Other Europe) (Philippe de Villiers)

4. **L'Autre Politique**
   (The Other Politics) (Jean-Pierre Chevènement)

5. **Contre L'Europe de Maastricht, allez la France**
   (Against the Europe of Maastricht, Come on France) (FN) (Jean-Marie
   Le Pen)

6. **Union des écologistes pour L'Europe: Verts**
   (Union of Ecologists for Europe: Greens) (Marie-Anne Isler-Béguin)

7. **Politique de vie pour l'Europe**
   (Politics of Life for Europe) (Christian Cotten)

8. **Démocrates pour les Etats Unis d'Europe**
   (Democrats for the United States of Europe) (Armand Touati)

9. **Lutte ouvrière**
   (Workers' Struggle) (Arlette Laguiller)

10. **Parti Communiste Français**
    (French Communist Party) (Francis Wurtz)

11. **Liste régionaliste et fédéraliste – Regions et Peuples solidaires**
    (Regionalist and Federalist List – Regions and Peoples in Solidarity)
    (Max Siméoni)

12. **L'Emploi d'Abord!**
    (Work first!) (Gérard Touati)

13. **L'Europe commence à Sarajevo**
    (Europe begins at Sarajevo) (Léon Schwartzenburg)

14. **Europe pour tous**
    (Europe for All) (Jean Aillaud)

15. **L'Union UDF-RPR**
    (Governing Coalition) (Dominque Baudis)

16. **Energie Radicale**
    (Radical Energy) (MRG) (Bernard Tapie)

17. **Pour L'Europe des travailleurs et de la démocratie – Parti des
    travailleurs**
    (For a Europe of the Workers and of Democracy – Workers' Party)
    (Daniel Gluckstein)

18. **Parti de la loi naturelle**
    (Natural Law Party) (Benoît Frappé)

19. **L'Europe solidaire**
    (Europe in Solidarity) (PS) (Michel Rocard)

20. **Génération Ecologie pour l'Europe – Les Vrais Ecologistes**
    (Ecology for Europe – The Real Ecologists) (Brice Lalonde)

The campaign and the media

In spite of proportional representation, the classical Fifth Republican party systemic situation was anticipated: the two main governing parties/coalitions in a bipolarity, with lesser parties, movements, and personalities clustered around each of them in varying degrees of alliance, negotiation, and dependency. In fact, the two poles of attraction crumbled to give way, by the time of the election, to a classic Fourth Republican scenario – namely, a range of parties none of which had any determining weight *vis-à-vis* its would-be satellites, and several of which competed with one another for dominance in each camp (and whose dominance was determined no longer by size alone but by position within a spectrum of alliances).

All of the candidates went on provincial tours and held rallies in Paris in the final week. In France, as elsewhere in Europe, these mass meetings are no longer real electoral rallies; the audience – where substantial – is usually made up of local party members dutifully attending or else bussed in. And the audience was not there to learn, the speeches being rarely informative, nor even to commune with their leaders, but to provide a good party showing for the cameras. Most of these rallies were scheduled earlier than formerly so that they might enjoy a clip on the eight o'clock evening news. The other traditional form of campaigning, door-to-door canvassing, was virtually non-existent in France in 1994 (and was only ever in fact extensively practised by the PCF). Even the poster campaign was restricted almost totally to the official hoardings (and most of these were empty); for French elections this was unusual, as postering walls – any flat surface, in fact – has a long tradition, along with defacing rival posters.[13] This meant that the 1994 European elections were perhaps the first characterized by a near-100 per cent television and radio campaign, conducted for the media by the parties, and by the media for the viewing and listening public.[14] When we speak of electoral campaigns we should bear this in mind: all the ideas, all the persuasion, all the jousts and victories took place only on television (and to a lesser extent radio), and the political 'mobilization' of a constituency and electorate meant persuading individuals to remember to vote on their way to mass or their in-laws in the course of Sunday 12 June. A further point of theoretical interest here is that the agency of such persuasion was almost exclusively individual political personalities whose ideas and their expression were irretrievably bound up with one another like never before.[15] Apart from the election broadcasts (which by French tradition are shown one after another so as to be, as any educational psychologist would know, utterly ineffective apart from dubious subliminal effects), the backbone of the election campaign itself was the television debates between various personalities (towards the end of May and the first week in June). Given their importance, let us comment briefly upon the main ones and their significance for the campaign and the political climate more generally.

The Elisabeth Guigou/Philippe de Villiers debate (22 May) demonstrated Guigou's control of her subject, while making de Villiers a nationally known figure. The Baudis/Rocard debate (30 May) demonstrated the near-impossibility of defining a difference in the outlook of the two main blocs, the left demonstrating its equal concern with finances as the right, the right its equal concern with the social dimension of Europe. Rocard was, however, to suffer considerably in a later debate with Giscard d'Estaing (8 June) in which two differing perspectives on Europe were more discernible.[16] Giscard was also on this occasion able to demonstrate his deeper knowledge of the European Union itself and left Rocard looking painfully unaware of some of the basic facts (eg how many votes France had within the Council of Ministers). Chevènement's debate with Hélène Carrère d'Encausse (30 May) was one of the most amicable and left the impression that on the question of Europe there was in fact very little to really argue about. As regards such friendliness, it is perhaps worth mentioning here, although we shall return to the question of women's political style in our conclusion, that debates such as that between Hélène Carrère d'Encausse and Catherine Trautmann (number two on the PS list), and chaired by Christine Ockrent (7 June), although they revealed the lack of fundamental difference between the two and their policy positions, did demonstrate and perhaps inaugurate a new style of political debate in which excessive concern with point-scoring and domination give way to reasonable exchanges and civility. In contrast, and perhaps the most consequential political debate, was that between Tapie and Le Pen on Wednesday 1 June,[17] in which similar types of populist discourse offering differing ideological perspectives clashed. Tapie was the clear winner, Le Pen seeming incapable of countering him, and therefore having to swallow his own rhetorical medicine, and in fact coming across here and elsewhere as something of a tired old man. More significant, however, was the vigour of Tapie and his willingness to 'take on' Le Pen, a willingness declined by so many in the past. The two-hour roundtable debate (9 June), with the heads of each of the main lists (with Kouchner replacing an absent Rocard) was also a relative televisual success[18] where the maximum of points of view were expressed and, with three days to go, the campaign itself driven home to the French viewing electorate. All of these debates were of political significance given that even at the end of May, 43 per cent of those polled were undecided how they would vote.

As regards this question of the public's response to the campaign, it was becoming clearer and clearer to the UDF-RPR list that Baudis' necessary relative silence was being equally matched and countered by de Villiers' volubility, as was evidenced by the latter's rising star in the polls, and the former's proportionate fall. A similar pattern was emerging on the left. By mid-May it was clear that the PS campaign was stagnating. Even the modest 20 per cent barrier hoped for had to be revised downwards, and as the PS position in the polls moved down towards the mid-teens, and the Tapie (though not the Chevènement) polls moved up towards double figures, it looked as if the conditions for a major realignment within the non-Communist left were being created. To counter this, the PS leadership took the debatable decision to duck rather than to hit back, this by minimizing the value of the election campaign itself. Already, at the end of the first week in June, Rocard was calling for a 'New Alliance' for *after* the elections (although this had in fact been planned a week or so in advance of Rocard's speech). The calls for such an alliance were a near admission of defeat, an attempt to pretend that 12 June was unimportant. In fact, the initiative was received by all those on the left very coolly; and the PS sank even further in the polls. In a television interview on *Sept sur Sept* on the same weekend (5 June), Jacques Delors, the outgoing President of the European Commission and Rocard's undeclared rival as the left's presidential candidate, declared a propos of the aftermath of the elections 'I have some ideas in my head, and I'll put them forward'. Rocard, his own presidential hopes tied to the European elections, could only brace himself for the results of 12 June. Such defensive pretence was not confined to the left. On the right too, notably Chirac and Alain Juppé, leading politicians were also saying well before 12 June that what mattered was what came afterwards.

The campaign proposals

The issues which the protagonists debated – unemployment, above all – were cast in domestic terms. Those which had a European dimension but were not of immediate domestic significance – Europe's institutions, above all – were all but ignored by the candidates. There was some reference to cross-national issues such as immigration and drugs, but issues such as competition policy, interest groups, regionalism, and foreign policy were barely mentioned. Bearing in mind this domestic proviso, and the general indistinguishability of the proposals, as well as the marked inattention to the detailing either of policy or of policy differences, let us now look at 'the issues'.

The central point to make, and which we cannot stress sufficiently, is that the similarities of many of the policy proposals of the 20 lists were enough to ensure an overall indistinguishability; the differences, however, were also enough to ensure irreconcilability, so that each list would agree with three or four issues on another list, but not with the rest. Let us schematize the various policy positions in order to demonstrate these points.

The UDF-RPR, PS, MRG, PCF and L'Autre politique (J-P Chevènement) were in favour of Keynesian reflationary measures in varying degrees to undertake major projects of infrastructure and to stimulate employment. In the case of the PS this would be accompanied by an industrial policy; in the case of the MRG, unemployment would itself be declared illegal. These same lists – probably all in fact if all had addressed the issue – were in favour of measures to stop social dumping: the PS and MRG advocated a minimum wage; both the UDF-RPR and the PS (and MRG) advocated a single currency; and all three, although with differing degrees of enthusiasm, the gradual widening of the EU to other countries. L'Autre politique declared it was more in favour of 'la Grande Europe' than of the prevailing institutions, although it was unclear whether this meant widening, deepening (probably not) or abolishing the EU altogether. As regards Europe's institutions, both the UDF-RPR and the PS were in favour of increasing the powers of both the Council of Ministers and the European Parliament. The MRG was more federalist still, advocating the drawing up of a federal constitution. The other parties were all less favourable to giving more power to European institutions.

Some form of European military force was advocated by the UDF-RPR, PS, MRG, and even GE. There was general support for immigration controls (though not always for the Schengen agreements). For the most part, the Chevènement list opposed any moves which would enhance the EU's status, while the National Front and L'Autre Europe (de Villiers), both profoundly anti-European, opposed virtually everything. Having said this, we need to remind ourselves that significant minorities within the political parties behind the lists believed the opposite to their own list's official position, and that pro- and anti-European and pro- and anti-Maastricht elements existed in almost all the lists in differing degrees.

We can make two concluding points on the question of campaign proposals. The first is that many of the differences between proposals could be overlooked because the public were not really interested in them; few voters, for example, seemed at all interested in questions of institutional reform in the EU (and this in spite of the animated Maastricht referendum campaign less than two years before). Second, the one issue which did dominate, and which to a certain extent was the only one discussed, was unemployment. This was because the notion of a Keynsian-style EU-based recovery programme gave the illusion of solving what for two decades had eluded all French governments of both the left and right, in a contest taking place at a time when unemployment was worse than it had ever been in France, with no obvious solutions in sight, and which was now affecting social categories which had traditionally been spectators of the phenomenon.

On the eve of the poll, something that had taken on inordinate consequential significance in French politics, over and above the percentage of the national vote attained, is what we might call the symbolic thresholds attained by candidates, which catapult those who cross them, and damn those who do not. The thresholds are created by a kind of implicit negotiation between the parties' official declarations, the media's own analyses of the current situation, and previous performance. The Socialists had, for example, scored over 20 per cent in the European elections of 1984, and over 23 per cent in those held in 1989. In 1994, the problem for Rocard was to try to create a score in the public's mind which would be exceeded and therefore ensure the security of the leadership's position. By the eve of poll, the thresholds established for each list had been drawn, and would prove as politically fateful as their concomitant significance for the number of MEPs the respective lists would send to the European Parliament. For the UDF-RPR anything below 28 per cent would be considered a major defeat. For the Socialists to fall below 17 per cent would be even more disastrous. In order to be seen to hold his own against the new challenges to his form of anti-establishment politics, Le Pen needed to get past the 10 per cent figure. For Tapie and de Villiers 6 per cent would be seen as a good score, anything higher a major success. For the PCF, it was a question of holding its score at around 6 per cent in order to remain potentially viable politically. As for the small lists, to have any effect, the Sarajevo, Chevènement and two Ecology lists needed to get past the 5 per cent mark (in the case of the former two to affect the reconfiguration of the left; in the case of the latter to halt their own political suicide; and in the case of all four to have their deposits and costs refunded). Let us look at how they performed in relation to these thresholds.

The results

Only six of the lists returned MEPs, the 14 remaining lists gaining scores of relative insignificance.

As is clear from the results, the two main lists combined (UDF-RPR and PS) which between them had been in government over the previous 35 years, had gained only 40 per cent of the vote (in 1989 it had been 61 per cent). In fact, of those eligible to vote only one in four had voted for the main lists. Added to the high abstention rates, the success of what we might call anti-establishment parties suggested a dramatic falling away of support for France's mainstream political parties. The government did badly, the Socialists did disastrously (as did the Ecologists; cf 10.6 per cent in 1989 for the joint list). The Communists continued their slow decline (7.7 per cent in 1989). The National Front vote was interesting in that while it passed the fateful 10 per cent mark, it saw the newcomers, de Villiers and Tapie, streak past it. It is true, however, that the newcomers did not profit at the expense of Le Pen's constituency, their support coming essentially from the two mainstream parties' votes.

The stars of the elections, de Villiers and Tapie, could therefore be expected to play potentially major roles in their respective camps in political developments following the elections, given that, on the right, the dissident de Villiers list had gained half as many votes as the government's list (and was secretly supported by sections within the governing majority), and, on the left, Tapie had come within less than half a million votes of overtaking the Socialists. (Tapie's personal misfortunes, however, placed a question mark over his political fortunes.) Rocard, who lost the leadership of the party as a result of the elections, and the party's nomination as presidential candidate, blamed the divisions within the left. The situation was far worse than this, however, given that even when all the left's lists votes were totalled up, it still gained only 40 per cent of the vote. The results of the vote, therefore, prefaced major changes in French politics.

In terms of developments at the European level, it is worth pointing out that what we might call the pro-Maastricht parties (UDF-RPR, PS, MRG, GE)

Table 5.1 Euro-election results in France*

List headed by	Votes	%	Seats	List headed by	Votes	%	Seats
Baudis	4,985,574	25.58	28	Lalonde	392,291	2.01	–
Rocard	2,824,173	14.49	15	Schwartzenberg	305,633	1.56	–
Villiers	2,404,105	12.33	13	Gérard Touati	125,340	0.64	–
Tapie	2,344,457	12.03	13	Frappé	103,261	0.52	–
Le Pen	2,050,086	10.52	11	Glusckstein	84,513	0.43	–
Wurtz	1,342,222	6.88	7	Simeoni	76,436	0.39	–
Goustat	771,061	3.95	–	Armand Touati	71,814	0.36	–
Isler-Béguin	574,806	2.94	–	Cotten	56,658	0.29	–
Chevènement	494,986	2.54	–	Moutoussamy	37,041	0.19	–
Laguillier	442,723	2.27	–	Aillaud	290	0.00	–

Source: Adapted from *Journal Officiel*, 20 June 1994, No 142

* Eligible to vote: 39,019,797
  Number of voters: 20,566,980
  Valid votes cast: 19,487,470
  Abstentions: 46.53%

only polled 54 per cent of the vote, a majority, but no longer the commanding pro-European one of the 1980s. Calling the UDF-RPR list pro-Maastricht is, in any case, debatable. And the promised unity of the coalition's list evaporated once the election was over. In the European Parliament, the 28 UDF-RPR MEPs split up into three groups: the European People's Party, the European Democratic Alliance, and the Liberals group. The arrival of de Villiers' 13 MEPs and their joining an anti-Maastricht group meant that the MEPs representing France's governing majority were dissipated within four groups. On the left too the divisions were made clear when the MRG, hitherto associated with the Socialist Group, decided to set up an autonomous group. And for the PS, of the reduced number of MEPs going to Strasbourg, only four were from the previous legislature. Neither the French right nor the French left would find it easy to work coherently within the Parliament. Such a fracturing of a national contingent was highly unusual, even for France. The precise breakdown in the European Parliament was as follows:

- The 28 UDF-RPR split into the following groups: 13 UDF (five PR, four CDS, two Clubs Perspectives et Réalités, one PSD, one Adhérent direct) sat with the EPP; one UDF (Yves Galland, Radical) sat with the Group of the Liberal, Democrat and Reform Party; the 14 RPR sat with the European Democratic Alliance (RDE) with Fianna Fail, the Portuguese CDS, and Greek Political Spring;
- the 15 PS sat in the Group of the Party of European Socialists;
- the seven PCF sat with the Confederal Group of the United European Left with the Spanish IU, the Italian Rifondazione, the Portuguese CDU, and both Greek Communist Parties;

Table 5.2 Candidates elected in France – 87 seats (81 in 1989)

UDF-RPR	L'Europe Solidaire	Contre l'Europe de Maastricht, Allez la France!
1. Domique Baudis, Mayor of Toulouse (UDF-CDS)	1. Michel Rocard	
2. Hélène Carrère d'Encausse, member of the French Academy (RPR)	2. Catherine Trautmann,*	1. Jean-Marie Le Pen,*
	3. Bernard Kouchner	2. Bruno Mégret,*
	4. Danièle Darras	3. Bruno Gollnisch,*
3. Yves Galland,* (UDF-Rad)	5. André Laignel	4. Jean-Claude Martinez,*
4. Christian Jacob, former President of the CNJA (RPR)	6. Nicole Pery,*	5. Carl Lang
	7. Jack Lang	6. Marie-France Stirbois
5. Jean-Pierre Raffarin,* (UDF-RPR)	8. Frédérique Bredin	
	9. Pierre Moscovici	7. Bernard Antony,*
6. Armelle Guinebertière (RPR)	10. Elisabeth Guigou	8. Yvan Blot,*
7. Nicole Fontaine,* (UDF-CDS)	11. Jean-Pierre Cot,*	9. Jean-Marie Le Chevallier,*
	12. Pervenche Beres	10. Fernand Le Rachinel
8. Alain Pompidou,* (RPR)	13. François Bernardini	11. Jean-Yves Le Gallou
9. Yves Verwaerde,* (UDF-PR)	14. Michèle Lindeperg	
10. Marie-Thérèse Hermange (RPR)	15. Gérard Caudron,*	**Parti Communiste**
		1. Francis Wurtz,*
11. Jean-Louis Bourlanges,* (UDF-AD)	**L'autre Europe**	2. Sylviane Ainardi,*
	1. Phillipe de Villiers	3. Phillippe Herzog,*
12. Jacques Donnay (RPR)	2. James Goldsmith	4. Gisèle Piquet,*
13. Françoise Grossetête (UDF-PSD)	3. Charles de Gaulle,*	5. René Moreau,*
	4. Thierry Jean-Pierre	6. Mireille Elmalan,*
14. Blaise Aldo (RPR)	5. Philippe Martin	7. Aline Pailler
15. Robert Hersant,* (UDF-Clubs)	6. Françoise Seillier	
	7. Georges Berthu	
16. Anne-Mari Schaffner (RPR)	8. Hervé Fabre-Aubrespy	
17. Francis Decourrière (UDF-PSD)	9. Dominiue Souchet	
	10. Anne-Christine Poisson	
18. Christian Cabrol (RPR)	11. Frédéric Striby	
19. Bernard Stasi (UDF-CDS)	12. Edouard des Places	
20. Jean-Claude Pasty,* (RPR)	13. Marie-France de Rose	
21. André Soulier,* (UDF-PR)		
22. Jean-Pierre Bazin (RPR)	**Energie radicale**	
23. Pierre Bernard-Reymond,* (UDF-CDS)	1. Bernard Tapie	
	2. Jean-François Hory,*	
24. Raymond Chesa,* (RPR)	3. Catherine Lalumière	
25. Georges de Brémond d'Ars,* (UDF-Clubs)	4. Christiane Taubira-Delannon	
	5. Noël Mamère	
26. Jean Baggioni (RPR, ex-UDF-PR)	6. Michel Dary	
	7. André Sainjon,*	
27. Jean-Pierre Bébéar (UDF-PR)	8. Bernard Castagnede	
	9. Odile Verrier	
28. Gérard d'Aboville (RPR)	10. Pierre Pradier	
	11. Christine Barthet-Mayer	
	12. Dominique Saint-Pierre	
	13. Antoinette Fouque	

* outgoing MEP

Source: Adapted from *Le Figaro*, 15 June 1994, official statistics, European Parliament, and *Journal Officiel*, 20 June 1994.

- the 13 Energie Radicale sat with the new Radical European Alliance (ARE) with the Italian Radicals, the Scottish Nationalists, the Belgian VU, and one of the Spanish National Coalition;
- the 13 Majorité pour l'autre Europe sat with the new Group of the Nations of Europe with the two anti-European Danish parties, and the Dutch Calvinist fundamentalists.
- The 11 National Front MEPs sat with the 'non-attached' members, effectively an extreme-right group which includes the Belgian VB and FN, the Allianza Nationale, and a Northern Irish Democratic Unionist.[19]

Let us look at two orders of consequence, the first concerning the short- and medium-term effects of the election (the aftermath), the second the longer term effects and wider implications for French politics (conclusions), given that unlike in previous European elections, the waters did not simply close over the 1994 ones, but, as we have suggested, flowed towards the presidential elections less than one year away.

The aftermath

In the case of the Baudis list, the loser was Baudis himself. It is worth pointing out, however, that had his list done better, Baudis would have become one of the growing number of presidential hopefuls on the right, and given more favourable circumstances he would himself have used his position to political advantage. The eruption on to the political stage of the de Villiers list led the anti-Maastricht and hardening right first out of, then back into the governing majority. This right-wing was strengthened, both relatively and absolutely, as a result of the elections. It had long been the case that unity on the right was seen, in principle, as necessary to its success. De Villiers demonstrated the continuing divisions, yet demonstrated also that division might be propitious in that the combined score of the Baudis and de Villiers list had cast the net as wide as the right could hope for. As a result, de Villiers, and the opinion he represented, became potentially major actors in the political process.

In spite of the poor showing for the government's list, Prime Minister Balladur could draw some comfort from the idea of a more diverse governing majority, as long as the divisions could be managed in such a way as to enhance an overall singularity of purpose Chirac had done himself no damage. Developments on the left would of course be of vital interest in this regard. A Delors candidacy for the left in the presidential campaign would enhance Balladur's position as the most likely person to beat this most promising of left candidates. The PS' long agony of decline so compounded by the European elections therefore comforted some on the right more than others.

Rocard was, of course, seriously wounded by the results. He lost a grip on his party, allowing the rival *courants* to rise against him – though not to improve the overall position of the party – and overnight he ceased to be the party's presidential candidate. Rocard had failed to anticipate the consequences of leading the campaign himself; failed, once again, to measure the effects of Mitterrand's personal hostility towards him and, in this instance, malicious sympathy for Tapie, and had been incapable of reversing (possibly he could have done this through a persuasive personal TV campaign) the leaden popularity of the party to whose fortunes the once darling of the opinion polls was now handcuffed.

On the extreme right, the National Front demonstrated its lasting hold over a section of the electorate, and this despite a desultory campaign by the party and its arguably declining leadership. It is also the case, however, that the National Front thrived best when the left was in power. A right-wing government, particularly one containing hard-line ministers like Charles Pasqua, and with figures such as de Villiers more or less inside the tent, meant that the Front was contained on the, albeit quite substantial, ultra-right.

Le Pen's media counterpart, Tapie, profited from the elections. He saved the left's overall vote from disaster (although arguably contributed to the PS' setback). He also saved the pro-European vote from becoming a minority one (the UDF-RPR, PS and MRG vote combined being 52 per cent; without Tapie, 40 per cent). He also shifted the centre of gravity and of influence on the left towards the centre, making the right's task more difficult. Above all, however, Tapie demonstrated the ever-increasing role of the media in French politics, above all of the television, where he voiced again and again the themes of tolerance, the desirability of a united Europe, and republican virtues and values, and which, because of his characteristic son-of-the-people manner, threw into excruciating contrast the sterile intellectualism of Rocard's now half-hearted Europeanism. Tapie, however, not only showed how the PS should have been presenting its ideas but also to whom they should have been directing them. Tapie's public fearlessness of Le Pen probably had more effect upon denting the FN's image than much of the half-hearted ideological public opposition by the left over the previous decade.

Conclusions

The overriding point to note from our analysis is not only the national-specific character of the European elections in France, but also the disturbing effects of the domestic political system on the elections, and vice-versa.[20] This phenomenon is worth underlining. It is not simply a question, as it is in most member states of the Union, of national politics dominating the European question and the European elections; this has become a truism. In the French case, one aspect of national politics – presidentialism – structures political activity at the national level, especially at particular moments; and when elections such as the European elections fall within, as it were, the strong influence of the presidential campaign's gravitational pull (this was much less the case for the previous three European elections), this becomes even more the case.

Second, change on the left was spectacular with the 'defeat' of Rocard. The question of how the PS was to regenerate itself became, for the first time in nearly 30 years, perhaps more important than the presidential elections themselves. On the left of the PS, the Communists continued to survive within the political system but with little hope of renewal. Tapie's coming to national political prominence marked a possible change in the political élites, particularly as he demonstrated also, along with de Villiers, how the FN had almost become a part of the political establishment, and that they themselves had become the focus of possible new departures.

Another development linked to this question of generations was that of gender. The presence of women was marked – facilitated, of course, by the fact that, because this was not a national election, resistance to them within the political parties was less. The European elections nevertheless indicated something of a sea-change in the significance of women in French politics because their presence was as widespread as it was banal. For many years, certain parties and certain opinion within parties had been practising or campaigning for proper representation for women. In the 1994 elections, from the National Front's inclusion of women in the top slots of its list (three had a chance of election) right across to the politically correct lists on the left, the presence of women was like a social *fait accompli*. The high profile of articulate women (Trautmann (PS), Carrère d'Encausse (UDF-RPR), Gisèle Halimi (*L'Autre politique*) and Guigou (PS) were the most prominent of many examples), the heading of the Greens' and Lutte *ouvrière*'s list by a woman, and the fact that in debate (such as that between Trautmann and Carrère d'Encausse with presenters such as Christine Ockrent) the 'stage' as it were was often exclusively female, shifted the tone and register of debate, and arguably the aims of the debaters, in a direction and style which will inform the other developments we have identified.

Finally, however, in spite of the political consequences we have identified in the domestic arena, we can only observe that Europe as a positive and mobilizing theme – via elections to its Parliament – failed still in 1994 to penetrate the cycles of national politics, even at the moment of the cycle designed specifically for transnational and supranational issues, and that, on balance, it is the converse that is true: the national continues to force its increasingly assertive way through to the levels of transnational political activity in the European Parliament.

Notes

1. The poster campaign itself was restricted to the official hoardings outside polling stations. Most of the 20 panels were empty throughout the campaign, with only the main lists bothering to put up posters.
2. An early suggestion had been Alain Juppé, then Foreign Minister, and a close associate of Chirac. Balladur (who also briefly entertained the idea of leading the list) vetoed the move.

3. The UDF-RPR, PS, and PCF, because they had support from official groups in the French Parliament (National Assembly or Senate), shared equally two hours of television time for their official party election broadcasts; the other lists shared a remaining 30 minutes between them all. A typical election broadcast slot, therefore, would be the following (taken from *Le Monde*, 10 June 1994): On *France 2* after the weather forecast following the one o'clock news and on *France-Inter* after the 8.00pm news – Thursday 9 June: Union UDF-RPR, *Europe solidaire* (PS), PCF (3 minutes each), Lutte ouvrière, Parti de la Loi naturelle (48 seconds each). Friday 10 June: *L'Europe solidaire* (PS), PCF, Union UDF-RPR (3 minutes each).

4. This turned out to be a non-problem as only about half of the hoardings were ever used, many of the lists having no posters. Some of the hoardings were used illegally for other publicity (rock concerts, night clubs).

5. Eligibility was not restricted to political parties. Anyone could present a list for the elections on payment of a deposit of 100,000 francs, reimbursed if the list obtained 5 per cent of the votes (campaign material would also be paid for by the state if the 5 per cent threshold were reached). Estimates of campaign costs for some of the lists were *Génération Écologie* 1.3 million francs, *L'autre Europe* (de Villiers, backed by Jimmy Goldsmith) 27 million francs, *L'Europe solidaire* (PS) 15 million francs, UDF-RPR 20 million francs, *L'Autre politique* (Chevènement) 600,000 francs. Specialists assumed that 2 million francs was necessary to fund a reasonable campaign.

6. In 1984, 43 per cent of the French had agreed that European integration was a priority; in 1994 the figure had fallen to 19 per cent (*Le Figaro*, 25 April 1994).

7. The third person on de Villiers' list, with a high profile initially, was the MEP Charles de Gaulle (grandson of de Gaulle). However, he proved to be a bad public speaker and subsequently played little active part in the campaign.

8. Nationally, the de Villiers campaign drew upon the help of 50,000 supporters.

9. Of the 15 PS MEPs elected in 1989, only four were returned: Catherine Trautmann, Nicole Pery, Jean-Pierre Cot, and Gérard Caudron.

10. The ex-Minister of the Civil Service 1981–84 Anicet le Pors of the Communist Party also joined Chevènement, having left the PCF in March. By supplementing its left-wing nationalism with feminist (and some pro-Mediterranean) themes, the Chevènement camp hoped to offer an attractive political cocktail.

11. It is worth noting here that although the question of women's representation was taken up seriously by the lists, that of ethnic group representation was virtually ignored.

12. The numbering of the lists and therefore of the hoardings at polling stations and ordering of election addresses sent to households was done in the Council of State by drawing lots.

13. It may be of significance that the only defacing in the 1994 elections was of Le Pen's poster; his portrait, on every single NF poster the author saw, was defaced in some way. Nearly all the others were left in pristine condition and utter indifference.

14. It is perhaps interesting to note that the two other events dominating television viewing were the Tennis tournament at Roland Garros, and the 50th anniversary celebrations of the D-Day landings in Normandy.

15. This television coverage of individuals was also taken very seriously by contenders of leadership within parties. One example was the conflict between would-be successors for National Front leadership, Bruno Mégret and Bruno Gollnisch for television coverage.

16. For a good description of these various perspectives see Elisabeth Guigou's article in *Le Monde*, 9 June 1994.

17. This was the debate for which the presenter, Paul Amar, was temporarily suspended from his job for producing boxing gloves at the beginning of the programme and offering them to the candidates (whose irritation was manifest). The viewing figure for the Le Pen–Tapie debate was 44 per cent. Amar subsequently resigned from his post later in the summer.

18. For an informative breakdown of viewing figures for programmes relating to the elections see *Le Figaro*, 10 June 1994.
19. I am grateful to Simon Hix of the European Institute for precisions on the above distribution.
20. The national character of the elections was further suggested by the fact that out of the 700,000 Portuguese, 300,000 Italians, 250,000 Spaniards, and 60,000 Belgians, and several thousand other EU nationals resident in France and eligible to vote, only a few hundred did so.

6

Greece

Susannah Verney and Kevin Featherstone

Introduction

Greece's role in the EU had become somewhat controversial by the time of the 1994 EP elections. The stance of successive Greek governments was said to have exasperated the country's partners; indeed, an unprecedented barrage of foreign press criticism focused on Greece as a liability. But an unusual paradox had emerged: while Greece's partners criticized the country for its continuing economic malaise and for allegedly intransigent positions on Balkan politics, the Greek public had become one of the keenest supporters of European unity (Kazakos and Ioakeimides, 1994). On all major European issues, the Greek position differed markedly from that of the British: while London repeatedly sought to block integration, Athens was part of the European integration mainstream except on isolated issues of great national concern.

The focus on Greece intensified during the first part of 1994, when it took over the EU Council presidency. In December 1993, Theodoros Pangalos, the Deputy Foreign Minister responsible for EU affairs, had caused a storm of protest by attacking Germany's role in the EU. This was an unfortunate distraction, as by common consent Pangalos was seen to be a most able Council operator. Moreover, he was not a novice. A highly intelligent politician, he had held the same post from 1984–9, including during Greece's 1988 presidency. In any case, Pangalos was quickly obliged to retract his outburst. However, the main issue which threatened to disrupt the presidency, while also continuing to sour Greece's relations with the EU in general, was the dispute over the international recognition of the Former Yugoslav Republic of Macedonia (FYROM).

At successive European Council meetings since the dissolution of Yugoslavia, the Greek government had blocked the permanent recognition of FYROM, until the latter adopted a title acceptable to Greece and renounced irredentist claims for a 'Greater Macedonia'. The reactivation of the century-old 'Macedonian question' went to the very core of the Greek sense of *ethnos* (nationhood) and inflamed domestic opinion. From one viewpoint, Greece had a just cause: FYROM maintained provocative articles in its constitution, for example, concerning the possibility of changing international frontiers in the Balkans. But Greek diplomacy appeared ineffective and Greece's stance had made the country highly unpopular internationally. Following the failure of the EU mediation attempt, a number of member states began to contract full diplomatic relations with FYROM. Occurring when the latter had dropped none of its irredentist propaganda, this caused considerable bitterness in Greece; it was described by Prime Minister Andreas Papandreou as 'an example of solidarity which it is difficult for us to forget' (*Eleftherotypia*, 25 April 1994). In February 1994, the PASOK government's imposition of a unilateral trade embargo against FYROM further antagonized the country's partners.

The Commission's subsequent decision to refer Greece to the European Court of Justice had a deep impact on Greek public opinion, aggravating a growing sense of isolation and even nourishing a persecution complex. The effect on attitudes towards the EU was immediate and striking. The Spring 1994 *Eurobarometer* survey recorded a 22 per cent drop in the number of Greek respondents who were satisfied with EU democracy (only 28 per cent satisfied as opposed to 60 per cent unsatisfied). In contrast to the previous survey six months previously, 9 per cent fewer Greeks now thought EU membership was a good thing, while 10 per cent fewer agreed that the country had benefitted from membership (*Eurobarometer* 41, July 1994). More generally, Greece in the 1990s faces a difficult European agenda. There was growing awareness, for example, that progress towards Economic and Monetary Union (EMU) threatens to consign the country to a second tier of EU membership. Thus, in contrast to 1989, when Greece's EC orientation appeared to be the object of growing domestic consensus, the 1994 EP election took place at a time when Greek–EU relations seemed to be coming under strain.

However, this should be kept in perspective. Even with the comparative decline in pro-European sentiment recorded by the *Eurobarometer*, Greek public opinion remained among the most pro-integrationist in the EU.[1] Moreover, despite the FYROM issue, the Greek presidency finally appeared to be a modest success. In a difficult climate for progress within the EU, the presidency had overseen the end of the negotiations on enlargement, initiated a debate on political union prior to the 1996 IGC, and managed the signing of a major new agreement with Russia. As on the two previous occasions when it had held the presidency, the PASOK government made much of its presidential role at home. Thus, in the months before the EP election, the EU received positive as well as negative coverage in Greece.

The actors in the campaign

In terms of domestic politics, the Euro-elections were expected to provide an interim verdict on a party system which had clearly entered a transitional phase. This was the second of four major Greek electoral contests expected to take place within 18 months. It followed a few months after the October 1993 general election, which had seen the fall of the New Democracy (ND) government and the return of PASOK, out of power since 1990. Local government elections were scheduled for October 1994; meanwhile, as in France, attention was already firmly focused on the presidential election due in spring 1995.

According to the Greek Constitution, the president of the republic is elected by parliament. If no candidate can achieve the required two-thirds majority, then general elections must be held, with the new parliament choosing a president by simple majority. As Pasok was ten MPs short of the magic number, all kinds of scenarios were under discussion, with the analysts looking to the EP election to provide some indication of what might happen. It was suggested, for example, that if PASOK scored a clear victory in June 1994, then the other parties would hesitate to risk another electoral defeat in April 1995 and so might support PASOK's candidate for president. On the other hand, a rise in support for the new Politiki Anoixi party (POL.A) could allow it potentially to hold the balance-of-power between the two larger parties and thus have every reason to want new elections ten months later. Much of the media interest in the European election, therefore, had less to do with European issues than with attempting to predict the future of the Greek party system.

Of course, the commentators had been making predictions about the 'post-Papandreou period' ever since the then Prime Minister underwent major heart surgery in 1988. But the possibility of a Papandreou candidacy for the largely ceremonial post of president suggested that a new era was finally imminent. In any case, it was already apparent that the increasingly frail Papandreou no longer maintained his habitual iron control over his party. In its few months in power, PASOK's government image had been damaged by a series of very public policy conflicts between leading ministers, notably the bizarre quarrel between the Interior and Labour Ministers over nightclub opening hours. The party congress in April 1994 had seen a blatant jockeying for position among Papandreou's would-be successors, while the following month, manoeuvring by different inter-party factions had resulted in the exclusion of leading cadres, including Pangalos and former European Commissioner, Vasso Papandreou, from the new Executive Bureau.

Things were little better within the official opposition. During 1990–3, ND's attempt to combine a neoliberal programme of denationalization with its traditional étitist clientelism had resulted in an unconvincing government performance. This had been compounded by the open conflict between Prime Minister, Konstantinos Mitsotakis, and Foreign Minister, Andonis Samaras, over Macedonia. Samaras, a 'hawk' on this issue, was sacked by Mitsotakis in April 1992. The following year he left the party and in June 1993 formed POL.A. When a number of ND MPs defected to POL.A, Mitsotakis was forced to call early elections; following his defeat, former minister and ex-mayor of Athens, Miltiades Evert, was elected as the new leader. The European election was to provide the first test of the Evert leadership. The omens were not promising. Evert had tried to change the party image, and at the party congress in April 1994 dropped Mitsotakis' 'importation' of neoliberalism. But this attempted ideological shift seemed to hold little interest for the electorate, while leading party members publicly attacked the move. Meanwhile, Evert had been fiercely criticized within the party for his mild oppositional style and seemed unable to keep ND's warring barons in line. Speculation in the press was already suggesting that a poor European election result could cut short his career as party leader.

For POL.A, the Euro-elections were to test whether its emergence as third party in October 1993 had simply reflected a passing protest vote or whether it had a real future in Greek politics. Although POL.A had started life as a splinter group from ND, its slogan was *ypervasi* or overcoming the old divisions between right and left. The party combined a hard nationalist line on Greece's foreign policy problems with centrist positions on social and economic issues. At a time when the sense of external threat was rapidly growing in Greece, POL.A's nationalist populism seemed to appeal across the political spectrum, threatening PASOK as well as ND. The emergence of POL.A had also displaced the traditional left from its longstanding position as Greece's third political force.

In fact, the left had suffered a serious decline since 1989, when the Communist Party (KKE), former Eurocommunists and other strands of the broad left had been united in the Synaspismos coalition (SYN). From early on, SYN's problems of internal cohesion were strikingly highlighted within the European Parliament. Of its four MEPs, Michalis Papayannakis from the Elliniki Aristera initially joined the European Unitarian Left and became non-aligned when the group dissolved. The three KKE members joined Left Unity, but within a few months, Dimitris Desyllas became non-aligned after withdrawing from both the KKE and SYN in protest against their participation in a coalition government with ND. In 1991, when the hardliners took over the KKE leadership and withdrew from the Synaspismos, Vassilis Ephremidis stayed with the former while Alekos Alavanos chose the latter. Thus, the two MEPs who were in the same group (Alavanos and Ephremidis) did not belong to the same party; while the two MEPs who stayed in the same party (Alavanos and Papayannakis) did not sit together in the EP.

Both the left parties were hoping that the 'second-order' nature of the European contest would allow some recovery of their electoral fortunes. In 1993, the KKE had seen its habitual 10 per cent of the vote halved to less than 5 per cent. Meanwhile, the Synaspismos, which had transformed itself from a coalition to a unified party in 1992, had polled only 2.94 per cent, a few thousand votes short of the new 3 per cent electoral threshold. Excluded from the national parliament, the SYN was fighting for its political survival. The Euro-elections would also be the first test for its new leader, Nikos Konstandopoulos, elected at the party congress in December 1993.

Also fighting for political survival was DIANA, the centre-right party which had broken away from New Democracy in 1985. In 1989, the party had elected one MEP who subsequently defected to ND. Party leader, Kostis Stephanopoulos, had already announced that he would dissolve DIANA if it did not meet the 3 per cent electoral threshold, now introduced for the European election as well. Of the other 20 minor parties contesting the election, none was electorally significant. There were three extreme right parties, of which the most significant, EPEN, had held an EP seat in 1984–9; two KKE splinter groups, one of them led by MEP, Dimitris Desyllas; and various fringe groupings, like the Greek Hunter's Party. Of the four self-professed ecological groups, the most serious was Politiki Oikologia, the Greek representative of the European Greens. The main green party, the Ecologists-Alternatives, which had one MP in the national parliament in the period 1989–93, had dissolved in some acrimony in 1993. Meanwhile, as in the national election, the 3 per cent threshold had achieved its aim of discouraging independent candidates from the Muslim community in Western Thrace, who held national parliamentary seats in 1989–93.

Greece was the last country to publish its lists of candidates, with all the parties announcing their choice shortly before the late May deadline. The apparent difficulties in compiling the lists were indicative of the internal problems most of the parties faced. Unlike the national elections, in the European contest the whole country is treated as one constituency. There is no preference cross, so candidates are elected in strict order of appearance on their party's single list. This inevitably focused attention on the choice of candidates in electable positions. With Greece's delegation increased from 24 to 25 as a result of the new seat allocation in the EP, these were regarded as the first ten on the PASOK and ND lists and, at most, the first two or three for the other parties. In the case of PASOK, ND and POL.A, candidate selection remained firmly in the hands of their leaders, reflecting the lack of intra-party democracy. In contrast, the Synaspismos balloted all its members, who selected the first seven candidates and placed them in order of preference, with the remaining candidates chosen by the Central Political Committee. The KKE's list was apparently drawn up by the Central Committee from proposals by the party base.

Both the main parties opted for a radical renewal of their EP lists. As in 1989, the high turnover in the PASOK contingent suggested a different conception of the MEP's role, and one which seems less integrated into the party apparatus at home (Featherstone and Verney, 1990). Only two existing MEPs, Christos Papoutsis and Paraskevas Avgherinos, were in electable positions, while Georgios Raftopoulos was placed 14th. Meanwhile, Papandreou's longtime secretary, Angela Kokkola, was placed sixth, and his economic adviser, Georgios Catephores, a former professor at the University of London, was eighth. Heading the list was another professor, constitutional lawyer, Dimitrios Tsatsos, a choice which proved controversial when the opposition resurrected unflattering anti-Papandreou comments he had made 20 years earlier. A surprise inclusion, Konstantinos Klironomos, mayor of Herakleion and a member of the EU's new Committee of the Regions, was rumoured to have been added at the last minute to ensure Cretan representation in PASOK's EP group.[2]

In ND, the high turnover appeared to be the result of an Evert purge of Mitsotakis supporters. Only three current MEPs – Pavlos Sarlis, Panayotis Lambrias and Georgios Anastassopoulos – were included, none placed higher than sixth. Like PASOK, ND included a professor, Antonis Trakatellis, ex-president of Thessaloniki University, who was placed second, while in fourth place was the former President of the Confederation of Greek Industry, Stylianos Argyros. Evert had apparently wanted to head the list with a non-party candidate with popular appeal. His choice of Nana Mouskouri, the popular singer who had been resident abroad for many years, was curious indeed. Ms Mouskouri regularly disavowed any knowledge of or interest in politics; her intentions thus beggared belief. In the end, intense intra-party reaction forced Evert to place her third, while heading the list was a respected party cadre with solid European credentials, Efthimios Christodoulou, a former National Economy Minister and Governor of the Bank of the Greece, who had also served in the EP from 1989-90. National football team coach, Alketas Panagoulias, was sixteenth.

Politiki Anoixi clearly aimed to appeal to the right with its first two choices, Katerina Daskalaki, former editor of the now defunct right-wing newspaper *Mesimvrini*, and ex-ND MP Nikitas Kaklamanis, while former PASOK MEP (1981–5) Kostas Nikolaou only occupied the symbolic 25th position. A high-ranking European Commission official Dimitrios Kourkoulas was placed third. In contrast to the two main parties, the left opted for continuity. The SYN's internal referendum resulted in the party's current MEPs Alavanos and Papayannakis, both regarded as highly successful and particularly active members of the EP, being placed top of the list. Despite rumours that he was to be dropped because of his age (79), KKE MEP Vassilis Ephremidis was retained at the head of the list, with Politburo member and Secretary of the General Confederation of Greek Trade Unions, Yannis Theonas, in second place. Both the KKE and SYN included a member of the Muslim minority in a non-electable position.

In 1989, Greece had been criticized for electing only one woman among its 24 MEPs, the lowest proportion in the EP. In 1994, the parties showed a little more sensitivity. Only Politiki Anoixi, with six women candidates, chose a woman to head its list. PASOK also included six women, two of them among the first ten. ND had eight, but only Nana Mouskouri was likely to be elected. KKE and SYN ran eight and nine women candidates respectively, with the highest placed in fourth and third positions.

A notable feature of the 1994 Euro-election was the distinct lack of European participation. This stood in marked contrast to the EP Socialist Group's remarkable display of solidarity towards PASOK in 1989. Several months before the election, leading Socialist MEPs, including group leader Rudi Arndt and former EP President Piet Dankert, had spoken at PASOK rallies all over Greece in an attempt to restore the image of a party then deeply mired in scandals. In contrast, in 1994 there was no visible involvement by the supranational parties. Moreover, only one Greek party, the very minor European Federal Vision, ran a non-Greek candidate, Gerard Baudson, the French author of a book about ancient Macedonia. Meanwhile, the number of non-Greek EU citizens resident in Greece who took advantage of the new opportunity to vote there provided under the Maastricht Treaty was minimal.[3]

The issues

While the Macedonian issue had resulted in growing scepticism about the meaning and value of Community solidarity, for four of the five main parties the country's place remained unquestionably in the EU. This included POL.A, whose nationalism was essentially a defensive reaction to events in the Balkans, rather than the kind of aggressive xenophobia which was apparently on the rise elsewhere in Europe. While his strong stand on Macedonia did help to nourish anti-EU feeling, Samaras was also the Foreign Minister who had participated in the Maastricht summit, and who subsequently described the TEU as 'the great contract for the coming century' (Debates of the Greek Parliament, 29 July 1992, p 91).

On most major issues concerning the EU's future, PASOK, ND, POL.A, and SYN were roughly in agreement, although with some differences of emphasis. All four parties, for example, called for a federal Union with a European constitution and increased powers for the European Parliament; POL.A, however, also stressed the importance of subsidiarity and the continued right to a national veto in Council. All four also supported the further 'Europeanization' of the CFSP, with the WEU being subordinated to the EU rather than developing as a European pillar for NATO. All maintained that EMU should be based on greater cohesion with more extensive redistributive policies. There were some differences on enlargement. In the EP vote on Austrian and Scandinavian entry, PASOK and ND voted in favour while the SYN abstained. POL.A, which was not represented in the EP, announced that it would vote against the ratification of the accession treaties in the national parliament. With regard to the future, however, all four agreed, first, that the next enlargement must include Cyprus, and second, that it must be preceded by institutional reform.

In contrast, the KKE had readopted its traditional anti-EU stance following its withdrawal from the SYN in 1991. Initially, the party did not openly challenge Greek membership as such, concentrating instead on attacking the new demon of Maastricht. However, with the approach of the Euro-election, the KKE once again came out openly in favour of complete Greek withdrawal. While the other parties called for the strengthening of the institutions, the KKE suggested that national representatives should have no right to take binding decisions without prior approval by the Greek Parliament. It also opposed the CFSP, claiming this would result in Greece being forced to intervene in conflicts against its national interests. For the KKE, cohesion was an illusion, and EU aid the '30 pieces of silver' which would buy Greek acquiescence to the country's transformation into 'a Latin American-type colony'.[4] The party also voted against the Austro–Scandinavian enlargement.

But issues related to the EU by no means monopolized attention. Domestic concerns continued to be central, with much speculation about possible developments within the two big parties. A cabinet reshuffle was expected soon after the elections. The parliamentary investigation into the denationalization of the AGET cement company, regarded by many as PASOK's retaliation for the corruption trials of its own cadres in 1990–1, was already pointing the finger of scandal at Mitsotakis and other former ND ministers. Meanwhile, during the run-up to the elections, both POL.A and the KKE declared that they would not support a Papandreou candidacy for president in 1995.

The campaign

Of the four Greek Euro-elections which have taken place to date, 1994 was probably the occasion on which the greatest discussion of European issues took place.

This was largely related to the nature of the campaign, undoubtedly the most subdued electoral contest to have taken place in Greece since the fall of the military dictatorship in 1974. The usual atmosphere of fiesta was completely absent: walking around Athens a few days before the elections, it was possible to be unaware that elections were about to take place. In this sense, the elections seemed to have become rather 'European'. The apparent indifference and apathy of the electorate indicated a growing disillusion with the political class as a whole which had been increasingly apparent since 1989. It also partly reflected the choice of the two main parties: both were expecting significant electoral losses and so had every reason to play down the importance of the election. Moreover, having just fought a general election, all the parties were short of cash. Despite arrangements for an advance on their annual subsidy from the 1995 budget,[5] their aim, to quote PASOK MEP Christos Papoutsis, was to spend 'as little as possible' (*Eleftherotypia*, 9 May 1994). This was clearly reflected in the relatively small quantity of electoral material produced in comparison to the lavish productions of the past.

Moreover, this was the first Greek campaign since 1974 not to be based around the organization of mass rallies. PASOK's decision not to hold major meetings to be addressed by Papandreou was apparently motivated by concern for the Prime Minister's health; it also helped to distance the party leader from a potentially unfavourable result. PASOK's lead was followed by ND and POL.A, who also decided against major rallies in Athens. Hence, the campaign mainly revolved around smaller, local meetings, and of course, the media. During the 1989 election, access to the two state-controlled TV channels had been a major issue. The following year, private TV channels were licensed for the first time, so the 1994 campaign was characterized by a new pluralism. Indeed, by 1994 political coverage by the plethora of private radio and TV channels had become quite exhaustive.

A few interesting changes in this election indicated some modernization of the political system. First, the parties did not undertake the usual organizational marathon to transport residents of the major urban centres back to the villages.[6] Greeks traditionally vote where they were registered at birth rather than where they live, a hangover of the post-Civil War control system which served to split the progressive vote and facilitate electoral manipulation. Now, for the first time, Greeks could vote in their place of residence without permanently transferring their electoral rights. Almost half a million voters exercised this option, considerably reducing the electoral exodus to the countryside.[7] This was also the first election without the appointment of service ministers to replace the Ministers of Justice, Press and the Interior. This practice provided an apparent reassurance of fairness in a country with a long history of electoral fraud and violence. By 1994, it was clearly an anachronism: there had been no serious accusations of electoral malpractice since the fall of the Junta. Moreover, PASOK argued against making changes during the EU presidency as the service ministers would have to chair Council meetings. Although Evert protested, calling for the opposition to boycott the elections *en masse*, his stance was roundly criticized by the other parties. Another welcome change, probably due to the campaign's generally low-key atmosphere, was the absence of violent incidents such as those which had so marred the 1984 European election.[8]

While the campaign officially began on 16 May, the two left-wing parties in particular began much earlier: the KKE published its election manifesto in January, while the SYN held its first major rally on 13 April. Inevitably, the Macedonian question played a fairly central role. ND even adopted a special flag, featuring the EU's 12 stars surrounding the sun of Vergina (the contested symbol from the tomb of Philip of Macedon, father of Alexander the Great, which FYROM had adopted for its national flag). But interestingly enough, the parties used the Macedonian issue more to score points against each other – either for an alleged lack of patriotism or for generally mishandling the issue – rather than to stir up popular anti-EU sentiment. This was partly because the only openly anti-EU party, the KKE, had a completely different policy on Macedonia. Although it used Greece's referral to the ECJ to attack the EU, the KKE regarded the whole Macedonian issue as a distraction at a time when it believed the Balkans were threatened by an imperialist policy of divide and rule.

Meanwhile the three larger parties essentially appeared to be competing for the title of best defender of Greek interests in the EU, as demonstrated by their remarkably similar election slogans: 'Strong PASOK, strong Greece in Europe'; 'Strong Greece, respected in Europe' (ND); 'Strong Greeks, equal Europeans' (POL.A). In itself, this was indicative of the new climate generated by the Balkan crisis, in which relations with the EU were seen in a more antagonistic light.

In contrast, the KKE focused on its stand as the only anti-EU party, adopting the slogan of 'Five Parties, Two Policies', to claim there was no real difference among the other four. The focus of its campaign, however, was the EU's 1993 'White Paper on Growth, Competitiveness and Unemployment', which was published as a special supplement in *Rizospastis* and also distributed from all party offices. The party gleefully cited the paper's proposals on labour market flexibility as evidence that the EU was dominated by multinationals which threatened to return organized labour to the Middle Ages.

An interesting aspect of the campaign was the emphasis on European organizational links. Both main parties translated their groups' manifestos into Greek and distributed them widely. This was less surprising in the case of New Democracy: having hesitated over which EP group to join for almost a year, ND had decided in favour of the Christian Democrats at the end of 1981 and has been fully integrated into the EPP ever since. It was more interesting in the case of PASOK, which by the early 1990s was stressing its membership of the CSP (Confederation of Socialist Parties) as a means of identifying its own ideological role. This was symptomatic of a long-term shift in attitude away from its old Third Worldist positions of the 1970s (Featherstone, 1988).

PASOK had only joined the CSP in 1989, although its MEPs sat in the Socialist Group immediately after Greek accession in 1981. Both affiliations had indicated a high degree of tolerance on the part of its partners, as hitherto membership of the SI had been a prerequisite. After talking about it for several years, PASOK finally joined the SI at a Council meeting in Cairo in May 1990. Two months later, it became a founder member of the Party of European Socialists (PES). The 1989 election was the first time that PASOK endorsed a Socialist group manifesto; however, it made little use of this text during the subsequent campaign. In contrast, in 1994, the Greek translation of the PES manifesto became the party's main campaign text. Moreover, one of the party's predominant election themes became the confrontation between progressive and reactionary forces at the European level; it called for support for PASOK as the Greek representative of the European Socialists. These developments could be seen as a final acknowledgement of PASOK's redefined role as part of the West European Socialist mainstream (Verney, 1995).

The Synaspismos also stressed its European connections, in this case with the Forum of New Left Forces in Europe, a fairly informal grouping of left-wing forces from existing EU members and candidate states which had been meeting regularly since 1991.[9] In May, the SYN held a press conference with representatives of other member parties to launch the Forum's joint 'Declaration' on the Euro-elections. But given the rather vague nature of this document, which attempted to reconcile the positions of pro- and anti-EU parties, the SYN, unlike PASOK and ND, also produced its own electoral programme.

Meanwhile, the whole question of transnational party membership became controversial when POL.A, claiming its lack of European links[10] allowed it greater independence, accused PASOK and ND of serving the interests of the

PES and EPP. POL.A's advertising campaign centred on giant posters proclaiming the two main parties to be 'for unemployment and against Macedonia', because they had not rejected the White Paper or fought harder for their transnational parties to adopt the Greek position on FYROM.

The results

After the unusually subdued campaign, the turnout (71.1 per cent) was less than in any of the three previous European elections (78.6 per cent in 1981, 77.2 per cent in 1984, and 79.9 per cent in 1989). This was rather low in a country where voting is supposedly compulsory; but it may be partly explained by electoral fatigue, given the number of elections likely to occur during 1993–5. The two largest parties suffered a 'dual shock' (*Eleftherotypia*, 14 June 1994). PASOK's vote fell 9.2 per cent in comparison with the previous October's national election; a massive loss in less than nine months for the governing party. ND's decline in support (6.6 per cent) was also a damning indictment on the main opposition party during a period of austerity. PASOK and ND's combined vote of 70.3 per cent was the lowest seen in any of the European contests to date, stimulating press speculation that after 20 years, the post-dictatorship two–party system was nearing the end of its cycle.

PASOK's result was its second worst in 17 years of national and European contests. Since 1981, its vote has ranged from a high of 48.1 per cent (in the October 1981 national elections) to a low of 36.0 per cent (in the European election of 1989). While Papandreou's lack of active involvement in the campaign meant that the leader was relatively unaffected by the result, it suggested a major blow to his presidential hopes for 1995.

For ND, the result was in many ways worse. This was its poorest result in any nation-wide election since the first European contest in 1981. Not only had its vote fallen from October 1993, but it was also 7.8 per cent down on the previous European election of 1989, the last time it had campaigned against a PASOK government. In both national and European contests, its vote was now at its lowest ebb since 1981. The imminent local government elections probably saved Evert, making it impolitic for his party rivals to launch a new leadership challenge immediately after the Euro–election. But it seemed likely that a new defeat in the near future would severely shake his leadership.

For POL.A, the result was mixed. The party had increased its vote to 8.65 per cent, indicating that its October 1993 result had not simply been the result of an anti-Mitsotakis reaction, and that it did have the potential to grow. However, POL.A failed to reach its aim of 10 per cent, which could have turned it into an arbiter on the national political scene. Indeed, the gain for POL.A. was less than the total loss suffered by ND.

On the Left, the combined vote of 12.54 per cent for the KKE and SYN was the lowest in any European election. This paralleled the October 1993

Table 6.1 Results of Greek Euro-elections 1981, 1984, 1989 and 1994, and national elections 1993

Party	1981 (EP)	1984 (EP)	1989 (EP)	1994 (EP)	1993 (Nat)
PASOK	40.2%	41.6%	36.0%	37.6%	39.3%
ND	31.4%	38.1%	40.4%	32.7%	46.9%
POL.A	–	–	–	8.7%	4.9%
KKE	12.8%	11.6%	14.3%	6.3%	4.5%
Renewal left*	5.3%	3.4%		6.3%	2.9%
DIANA	–	–	1.4%	2.8%	–
Extreme right**	2.0%	2.3%	1.2%	0.8%	0.14%
KODISO	4.2%	0.8%	–	–	–

Table 6.2 Distribution of Greek seats in the EP, 1981–94

Party	1981	1984	1989	1994
PASOK	10	10	9	10
ND	8	9	10	9
POL.A	–	–	–	2
KKE	3	3	4	2
Renewal left*	1	1		2
DIANA	–	–	1	–
Extreme right*	1	1	–	–
Total	24	24	24	25

*   The KKE-Esoterikou in 1981 and 1984, and the SYN in 1989 and 1994.
** The Progressive Party in 1981 and EPEN subsequently.

outcome, when the combined left vote of 7.84 per cent had been the lowest in any of the post-1974 contests. Despite this, these two small parties were regarded as the election's main victors. In contrast to the three main parties, which all failed to meet their electoral targets in terms of both votes and seats, both KKE and SYN exceeded expectations and fulfilled their ambitions of electing two MEPs each. There was also an interesting shift in the internal balance within the left, with just 0.04 per cent separating the two parties, suggesting that for the first time since the Communist Party's 1968 historic split, the dogmatic KKE was no longer the clear majority.

In all, of the 25 parties contesting the elections, seven obtained more than 1 per cent of the national vote, representing a slightly greater fragmentation than in previous European contests. However, as a result of the 3 per cent threshold, only the first five won seats. Ironically, DIANA lost its one seat, even though its 2.8 per cent vote was double its 1989 result. The significant rise in support for this small party, which had essentially been inactive since 1990, tended to confirm suggestions in the press that some of ND's internal dissidents may have encouraged tactical voting against Evert. Consistent with his pre-election promise, Stephanopoulos formally declared DIANA's dissolution.

Indicative of the spirit of the election, some 1.2 per cent of voters gave their support to the maverick party of Vassilis Levendis (Enosi Kendroon). Levendis, a regular 'no-hope' candidate in Greek elections, now has his own TV talk show and his politics are an odd populist mixture: he damns all politicians, an increasingly detectable trend among the electorate. The extreme right fared badly: in 1981, the Progressive Party had won a seat on 2.0 per cent of the vote and in 1984, EPEN took the seat with 2.3 per cent; but in 1994, EPEN obtained just 0.8 per cent, down on its 1989 result of 1.2 per cent. The elections contained a pessimistic message for the Green movement, with Politiki Oikologia gaining 0.26 per cent – less than half the 0.6 per cent polled by the Greek Hunters Party.

Given the composition of the party lists, it was not surprising that there was a high turnover among Greece's MEPs. Only eight, less than one-third, were re-elected. As in the past, the greatest continuity was apparent on the Left, where the KKE's Ephremidis and the SYN's Alavanos were the only Greek members to have served consistently since 1981. As elsewhere in the EU, there was a notable increase in the number of women: there were now four, the highest number ever (there had been two between 1981–9).[11] As in 1989, two Greeks, Georgios Anastassopoulos from the EPP and Paraskevas Avgherinos from the PES were elected as Vice-Presidents of the EP. No Greek MEP was chosen to chair an EP committee, although there were six Greek vice-chairs.[12] In addition, Nana Mouskouri was chosen as one of the vice-chairs of the ACP/ EU Assembly.

While PASOK and ND continued their active participation in the EPP and PES, the group affiliation of the other Greek MEPs proved more complicated. POL.A, which had declared during the election that it would not join any group, was apparently approached by Berlusconi's Forza Europa and Bernard Tapie's Radical Alliance before joining the Gaullists, Fianna Fail, and three Portuguese centrists in the European Democratic Alliance (*Eleftherotypia*, 11 July 1994). Meanwhile, SYN sounded out the possibility of joining the Greens or forming a group with other parties from the Forum of New Left Forces before finally re-founding the European Unitarian Left with the Spanish Izquiera Unida and the Italian Refondazione Communista. Immediately afterwards, the group accepted membership applications from the French, Greek and Portuguese Communist Parties. The KKE's decision to co-operate with the SYN in the EP, at a time when party Secretary General, Aleka Paparriga, was refusing to even meet SYN President, Konstandopoulos, caused quite a few raised eyebrows.

Conclusions

The main impact of the European election results is likely to be on domestic politics, encouraging centrifugal tendencies within the two main parties and opening new prospects for the smaller parties. As in the previous European elections, there was little change in terms of seat distribution in the EP. In

1981, 1984 and 1989, the two main parties shared 18–19 seats, the left won four, while a further one to two seats were held by minor parties. The same pattern was repeated in 1994 (see Table 6.2).

Aleka Paparriga has already explained that within the EP, the KKE's MEPs 'will denounce, will shout, will prove that there is an alternative voice' (*Rizospastis*, 10 June 1994). This suggests the CP will continue the same strategy it has pursued for most of the period since 1981: voting against any further development of integration and keeping up a barrage of oral questions designed to emphasize negative aspects of the EU. In contrast, the other 23 Greek MEPs are likely to be generally pro-integrationist, although in POL.A's case, this will probably be combined with an apparently contradictory attempt to emphasize the rights of nation-states.

In theory, the four pro-EU parties are all firmly in favour of increasing the powers and influence of the EP, although their selection of candidates does raise some questions. With the exception of the left, which chose well-established party cadres, a striking characteristic of the new Greek MEPs is the relative minority of professional politicians; it remains to be seen whether this will affect their performance in the EP. On most major issues, the two major parties will probably continue to adopt positions close to the policies of the EPP and PES. On the other hand, there is likely to be a fairly broad national consensus on issues such as cohesion and hindering moves towards a multi-speed Europe. Greek MEPs are also likely to display a special interest in questions of regional concern, such as Cypriot accession and the development of a more effective EU Balkan policy.

Finally, the election result confirmed that in spite of the Macedonian issue, support for European integration remains high. In 1981, the then anti-EC parties, PASOK and the KKE, were in the majority with 53 per cent. In contrast, in 1994, the anti-EU vote, represented by the KKE, had fallen to 6.3 per cent. A rise in Greek anti-European sentiment, with a possible impact on the attitudes of the country's MEPs, cannot be excluded in the future. But for the time being, it looks as if the Greek members will generally remain in the mainstream.

Notes

1. 64 per cent of Greek respondents still regarded EU membership as a good thing, 69 per cent felt Greece had benefited from membership, and 70 per cent declared that Europe should be advancing rapidly towards unification (*Eurobarometer* 41, July 1994).
2. Crete consistently displays the highest level of PASOK support in the country. The party returns the compliment: PASOK governments almost invariably include at least one Cretan minister.
3. 682, consisting of 217 British, 160 Germans, 81 Italians, 50 Belgians, 47 French, 42 Dutch, ten Danes, five Irish, five Spanish, three Portuguese and two Luxembourgers. Similarly, the majority of Greeks resident in other EU countries opted to vote for

Greek parties (59,309), while only 10,500 (8,500 of them in Germany) chose to vote for parties in their country of residence (*Eleftherotypia*, 10 June 1994).

4. See the party Central Committee's 'Declaration' on the Euro-elections of January 1994 and the speech by Secretary General, Aleka Paparriga, printed in *Rizospastis*, 10 June 1994.
5. The advance of 1 billion drachmas (from the 4 billion drachma subvention to the parties in the 1995 budget) was roughly divided as follows: 2,238m drachmas for PASOK; 1,892m for ND; 320m for POL.A; 305m for KKE; 72m each for SYN and DIANA; plus 27m drachmas to be distributed retroactively among any other parties which gained 0.15 per cent of the vote.
6. In previous elections, all available seats on aeroplanes, trains and boats were taken over by the main parties and allocated among their supporters.
7. 475,964 *eterodimotes* registered to vote in their place of residence, as opposed to some 800,000 who did not (out of a total electorate of 8,459,636) (*Kathimerini*, 10 June 1994).
8. Also in 1993, POL.A leader, Samaras, had been injured by a screw thrown by a New Democracy supporter.
9. Besides SYN, the Forum's members were Izquierda Unida/the Initiative for Catalonia from Spain, the Dutch Greens, the Danish People's Socialist Party, the Swedish Left Party, the Norwegian Left Socialist Party, the Finnish Left Alliance, and the Citizens' Movement from France.
10. Just a few months before the election, POL.A MP Nikitas Venizelos resigned from the European Liberal Federation, of which he was a long-term member, when the latter passed a vote against the Greek position on Macedonia.
11. This is likely increase to five in 1996, as SYN placed trade unionist, Foteini Sianou, third on its list, and decided that its MEPs should alternate after two years.
12. Four from PASOK: Georgios Catephores (Committee on Economic and Monetary Affairs), Konstantinos Klironomos (Regional Affairs), Irene Lambraki (Rules of Procedure), and Georgios Dimitrakopoulos (Petitions); one from the KKE: Yannis Theonas (Economic and Monetary Affairs); and one from POL.A: Nikitas Kaklamanis (Transport and Tourism).

References

Featherstone, K (1988) *Socialist Parties and European Integration: A Comparative History*, Manchester, Manchester University Press.

Featherstone, K and Verney, S (1990) 'Greece', in Lodge, J (ed) *The 1989 Election of the European Parliament*, London, Macmillan, 90–106.

Kazakos, P and Ioakeimides, P (1994) *Greece and EC Membership Evaluated*, London, Pinter.

Verney, S (1995) 'The Greek Socialists', in Gaffney, J (ed) *Political Parties and the European Community*, Manchester University Press, forthcoming.

7

Republic of Ireland[1]

Edward Moxon-Browne

Introduction

It has become customary to regard European Parliament (EP) elections as 'second order' elections in the sense that their function is to provide an indication of the relative popularity of political parties and individual politicians between general elections. In Ireland, EP elections are taken very seriously by the political parties since they are normally fought on domestic issues and the results may have serious implications for the political parties themselves.

Voters, on the other hand, appear to view EP elections rather differently. First, the turnout in EP elections in Ireland is much lower than for general elections. For example, the general election in 1992 attracted a 68 per cent turnout while the 1994 EP election persuaded only 44 per cent of the electorate to go to the polls. In fact, on all previous occasions, EP elections in Ireland had been held simultaneously with some other test of public opinion: local elections in 1979; a referendum in 1984; and a general election in 1989. This apparent apathy may be partly a reflection of the fact that European issues still remain somewhat distant from the daily concerns of many voters but probably, more importantly, a reflection of the fact that all the main parties are in agreement over the issues that are important to Ireland: agriculture, the structural funds, neutrality and institutional reform. To the extent that Irish voters do participate in EP elections, this participation appears to have much more to do with domestic politics and, and as we shall see later, even with intra-party rivalaries than it has with genuine differences in policy over attitudes towards the EU.

The function of EP elections in Ireland appears to be to provide a political stage on which both the parties and individual politicians can compete for approbation. The European 'language' of the campaign has to be seen, therefore, as a convenient alibi behind which the real issues of personality and political preference, are played out. The voters and the candidates collude in this rhetorical charade. Speeches on monetary union and neutrality, beef premia and regional policy are made, and listened to, with tacit acknowledgement on both sides that the words are merely the currency of political exchange but that the real issues on which people will vote, or abstain, lie elsewhere and are seldom articulated.

This is not to say, however, that parties do not express differing views on EU issues in these campaigns. Party manifestos put forward diverging and sometimes conflicting solutions to broadly perceived problems such as the democratic deficit or the disbursement of EU cohesion funds. The influence of these policy differences on the campaign is minimal.

Another currently accepted axiom of EP elections in Ireland, as elsewhere, is that they allow voters to 'punish' the government without actually changing its political complexion. Looking back at EP elections in 1979, 1984 and 1989 we can see that the percentage of the vote received by the government of the day was substantially lower that that received in the previous (or in the case of 1989 simultaneous) general election. The corollary of this phenomonen is that small parties usually do better than in the analogous general elections since voters are apparently prepared to 'take a risk' with their 'European' ballot paper in a way that is not true with their general election choice. For this reason, among others, EP election results are not a reliable indicator of general election performance. Even in 1989, when the general election and EP election were held on the same day nearly half the voters are estimated to have voted for different parties in the two elections.

If domestic issues predominate, what issues are likely to have dominated the campaign in the weeks leading up to 9 June ? The answer is very few. The most publicized controversy, and one intended to discredit the senior of the two parties (Fianna Fail) in government was the notorious 'passports for investment' scandal, of which more later. The government attempted to dampen down any domestic issues that might jeopoardize its future in the election with the result that the campaign was fought rather like a phoney war − using 'European' issues as a camouflage to conceal serious underlying tensions between, and especially within, political parties.

The actors in the campaign

For the purposes of the EP elections of 1994, the Republic of Ireland was divided into four constituencies − Connacht-Ulster (three seats); Dublin (four seats); Leinster (four seats); and Munster (4 seats). This distribution of Ireland's 15 seats had changed slightly since the 1989 election to reflect a demographic shift to the eastern side of the country: Munster in the west now has four seats instead of five, and Leinster has four seats instead of three. In population terms the constituencies range from 496,352 electors in Connacht-Ulster to 755,486 in Dublin meaning, incidentally, that the smallest constituency in terms of area has the largest electorate, and vice-versa. In all, 53 candidates put themselves forward for election. Of these nine were MEPs in the previous parliament.

Dublin as the biggest constituency in terms of electors, proved to be the

most difficult to monitor during the campaign due to its high density population and dramatic contrasts between poverty and wealth. Fifteen candidates
were chasing fours seats: three for Fianna Fail (FF), two for Fine Gael (FG),
two for Labour, one for the Progressive Democrats (PDs), one for Democratic
Left (DL), one for Workers Party (WP), one for the Green Party, one for Sinn
Fein and a miscellaneous three candidates. Fianna Fail aimed to run two candidates in the hope of securing two seats but, in addition to Niall Andrews, an
outgoing MEP, the selection convention chose the relatively unknown John
Stafford over the veteran TD Ben Briscoe. Then in an attempt to woo the
liberal (and female) vote, Olive Braiden was drafted onto the ticket because of
her previous work in the Rape Crisis Centre. In the Labour Party, the sitting
MEP Bernie Malone was considered too lack lustre to carry the party's banner
in the constituency so a well-known RTE journalist, Orla Guerin, was added to
the ballot paper. The split in the Labour Party over its EP candidate was
expected to harm the party's chances of even securing one seat in Dublin and
great efforts were made during the campaign to cement relations between the
two candidates so that vote transfers could be maximized and the party's
chances of representation increased. The addition of Orla Guerin to the
Labour slate in Dublin led to accusations of 'parachuting' – an issue that
rumbled in the background during the campaign but came to be seen as the
price that had to be paid if effective personalities were to represent parties at
Strasbourg in an 'ambassadorial' role. Two other left-wing parties, Democratic Left and the Workers Party, each fielded one candidate with the result
that the left was distinctly over-represented on the ballot paper in Dublin.
Issues that concern voters in Dublin have always contrasted strongly with
issues that attract voters in the rest of the country. The typically urban concerns of pollution, crime, transport, property tax, and unemployment all loom
large in the minds of Dublin voters.

Fifteen candidates were pursuing four seats in Munster which is mainly
agricultural but which contains Ireland's second and third cities, Cork and
Limerick. From being a fairly routine campaign, the fight in Munster became
one of national importance and national interest. Pat Cox, a former member of
the PDs, decided to enter the election late and run against his erstwhile leader
Des O'Malley. Other candidates were well-known national figures: G Collins
(FF), a former Foreign Minister, and G Cushnahan (FG), a former party
leader in Northern Ireland and a sitting MEP. In addition, the reduction of
the constituency's seats from five to four made predictions based on previous
elections harder to make. The constituency also revealed fascinating cross-
cutting pressures on voters. For example, Raftery (FG) from Cork campaigned on the slogan an 'MEP for Cork' thus implicitly weakening his fellow
FG candidate J Cushnahan. Farmers' votes were also reckoned to be divided
between P Lane (an outgoing MEP) based in Clare and Raftery (FG) based in
Cork. Would party or regional ties prove to be more important this time when,
previously, the farming vote had gone to an independent, T J Maher? Maher's
support for an 'independent' seemed, moreover, to favour neither Lane or

Raftery but Mr Cox (PD). Women's issues were well-represented among the candidates with Kathleen Lynch and Nora Bennis representing different but complementary conceptions of a woman's role in Irish society.

Connacht-Ulster, like Munster, was shaken by unexpected news. If Cox's decision to run in Munster had set fire to that campaign, Blaney's decision *not* to run in Connacht-Ulster ignited the interest of voters in the north-west of Ireland. The 71-year-old Blaney, a sitting independent MEP, but representing a political position to the right of FF, had always been a massive vote-puller in Donegal. His potential 50,000 votes were now to fall to other candidates by his decision not to run because of illness. Nine candidates and three seats: which candidates would benefit most by the absence of Blaney? The accepted wisdom was that Fianna Fail, represented by Killilea (MEP) and Pat Gallagher, would attract most of these. But the PD candidate Bobby Molloy, like Blaney an ex-Fianna Fail renegade, could also be expected to harvest some of the Blaney votes. Likewise, given Blaney's 'republican' credentials and the ever-increasing *rapprochement* between a FF government and London, some diehard Blaney votes could be expected to fall to Sinn Fein in the person of Pat Doherty. Among minority party candidates were Ann Gallagher for Labour, at 27 the youngest candidate in the election, and Richard Douthwaite for the Green Party who was advocating among other things the abolition of income tax. This most traditional part of Ireland was expected to vote, however, on more traditional issues: delays in paying EU subsidies to farmers, the condition of rural roads and the allocation of structural funds to the region.

The addition of an extra seat to Leinster made party electoral calculations difficult to make in this eastern constituency. Twelve candidates were fighting here for the four seats. Previous elections showed this to be territory for Fianna Fail and Fine Gael but the Labour challenge was always strong and succeeded in taking a seat in 1979. The unpredictable nature of this constituency had caused the parties to introduce 'personalities' and 'big names'. Fine Gael drafted in a former IFA chairman Alan Gillis and women's rights champion Monica Barnes while Fianna Fail deployed junior agricultural minister Liam Hyland. Sinn Fein relied on its party's General Secretary Lucilita Bhreatnach who proved to be a lively debater in seminars and on the media. European issues and rural issues often overlap in this constituency. Sellafield provides electoral ammunition for the Greens and other parties. The issue of neutrality brings Sinn Fein and the Greens together but provides some discomfort for Labour and Fianna Fail where a traditionally pro-neutrality stance will in-evitably be undermined by the need to re-negotiate Ireland's policy on Euro-pean security in the Inter-Governmental Conference (IGC) of 1996 and, most probably, under an Irish presidency.

The campaign

As in all EP elections in Ireland the campaign issues that provided the ammu-nition between the political parties ranged from broadly idealistic proposals relating to European integration down to the more parochial concerns of specific constituencies within Ireland. All the major parties alluded to the need to bring the EU 'nearer to the citizen'. This concern was expressed most notably in the FG proposals to have the Commission elected by the EP by proportional representation, more modestly through the PD suggestion that only the President of the Commisison be so elected, down to the more muted FF preoccupation with the 'rights of smaller member states'. Linkages between a variety of EU policies and specifically Irish concerns were made by many of the candidates. For Paddy Lane, an outgoing MEP in the Munster constituency, the real debate was not about 'potholes and premia payments' but the role of Ireland in a new enlarged EU of 15 to 16 member states. 'How can we cope with our own unemployment problem if we also have to tackle rampant unemployment elsewhere?' and in the context of the EU's Nordic enlargement he said that the new Europe might try to adopt a liberal approach in areas of health and morality: 'We, as Irish MEPs, must highlight the importance of the central role of the family. We should never be afraid to protect the virtues of the family particularly in an arena that recently voted in favour of married homosexuals and married lesbians adopting children' (*Nenagh Guardian*, 21 May 1994).

The PD candidate, Des O'Malley, proposed that a scheme whereby Dublin families had been resettled in the West of Ireland could, if applied throughout the EU, be especially beneficial in countries like France where rural depopulation is an even greater problem than in Ireland. Such a scheme would not only relieve the housing problems of major cities but it would also contribute to the 'revitalization of rural Ireland with young families and the provision of better lives for city dwellers in the Irish countryside'. If elected, O'Malley would enlist the support of the European Liberal, Democratic and Reformist Parties (ELDR) group in the EP: 'What is needed now are the resources to reverse the tragedy of the decline in rural communities. The inherent strengths and supports which are part and parcel of rural life can help city folk to develop in a manner which a million social workers could never hope to achieve' (*Nenagh Guardian*, 21 May 1994).

In the run-up to the IGC in 1996, most parties took up some position on the question of European security – always a contentious issue in Ireland because of the country's traditionally neutral stance. Both the PDs and FG advocated upgrading Ireland's role as observer in the WEU to full membership while FF promised simply to 'monitor' the Western European Union (WEU) through Ireland's observer status. Significantly, perhaps, no major party regarded Irish neutrality as an immutable set of circumstances.

The environment played a major part in the campaign rhetoric especially on the eastern side of the country where broadly-based concern exists about the deteriorating quality of life in urban areas and a specific concern about nuclear waste being dumped in the Irish Sea off the British coast. The rising appeal of Green Party activists in local government in Leinster undoubtedly influenced the extent to which the major party manifestos tackled the problem of nuclear pollution – the convergent point between the parties being the need to use EU institutions and EU legislation as a lever to exert pressure on the British government. The fact that Ireland elected two Greens among its 15 MEPs underlines both the saliance of this issue and the inability of the major parties to co-opt the Green agenda on to their own policy platforms.

One of the most publicized campaign issues to surface was the desirability or otherwise of MEPs holding the dual mandate. This debate caused tensions not only between parties but also within parties. On one side of the debate were those who argued that no one could do both jobs properly at the same time. Senator Brian Crowley (FF) who won the highest vote in the election said 'politicians must lead by example if we are serious about our unemployment crisis'. If elected to the EP, he would resign from his seat in the Senate and 'give one job my total commitment'. Likewise, Pat Cox (Independent) in the same constituency of Munster, said he would resign from the Dail if re-elected to Strasbourg: 'This would take immediate effect from the onset of the European mandate'. The arguments used by those prepared to exercise the dual mandate were several. The most commonly expressed rationale was the necessity of holding a by-election following the resignation of a new MEP from the national parliament. For example, Jim Kemmy (Labour) said 'I will not resign my seat because the party could lose the by-election'. Another argument was that a politician had a duty to his constituents to complete his term as a national representative. Liam Hyland (FF) said of his constituents 'I owe it to them – even if it involves an additional physical burden. That's what they expect me to do.' The dual mandate could also be interpreted as a channel of communication between Ireland and the EU. Jim Higgins (FG) explained it in this way: 'I don't see any problem with MEPs holding onto their Dail seats. If anything, it would help them become better informed. It would enable them to bridge the information gap between the Dail and the European Parliament.' The controversy flared most publicly at a party meeting in the Munster constituency where two FF candidates, Brian Crowley and Gerry Collins, clashed after Crowley had said 'you could not properly serve both the European Parliament and the Dail' since the whip in the national parliament might require the presence of an MEP at the expense of his attendance at an important vote or debate in Strasbourg.

The Munster constituency was also the scene of another campaign issue that could be classified as entirely one of personalities – but none the less crucial for that, in the minds of voters. The decision of Pat Cox, a sitting MEP, to resign from the PDs and stand as an Independent in Munster against his former party leader, Des O'Malley, became a *cause célèbre* not only in Munster but throughout the country. No other single issue occupied as much media attention as this one. The eventual victory of Cox over O'Malley left a legacy of personal bitterness between the two former political colleagues and caused deep dissension in the ranks of the PDs between those who were sympathetic to Cox's personal ambitions (he had topped the poll in the EP election in 1989) and those who supported the veteran politican O'Malley – a former minister, founder and first party leader of the PDs.

All in all the EP election campaign in Ireland was muted, spasmodic, disjointed and often dominated by issues and events that had little to do with the future evolution of the EU and the role of the EP within it. Many voters regarded the election as simply an opportunity to make a mid-term judgement on the coalition government's performance. The cross-party consensus on EU membership made it difficult for voters to distinguish between party platforms. In the event, they voted for personalities instead. One newspaper headline captured the mood when it said 'Euro candidates struggle to bury their similarities' (*Sunday Business Post*, 15 May 1994).

The results

The turnout in the election was the lowest of the four EP elections held in Ireland since 1979. At 44 per cent, the turnout in Ireland was higher than only three other EU countries: Netherlands, Portugal and Britain, and markedly lower than the EU average of 56 per cent although the latter figure was inflated by complusory voting in Belgium, Luxembourg and Greece. The low poll in Ireland was attributed by commentators to an increasing awareness on the part of the voters that they have very little power or influence over the decision-making institutions of the EU. In this respect, Ireland's voters proved to be little different from many other EU electorates where the 'back wash' of scepticism left over from the ratification of the Maastricht Treaty had clearly eroded popular enthusiasm for the EP elections. The public awareness of the 'democratic deficit', even if its finer points were not always fully appreciated, had left its mark. In Ireland, also, the broadly permissive consensus in favour of EU membership and the lack of serious policy differences between the political parties produced an election campaign that was characterized mainly by personalities and the only policy issue to raise the political temperature, namely that of the dual mandate, can hardly be said to be a great ideological question. There is, however, a limit to how far one can push the argument that inter-party consensus produced electoral apathy. After all, in Britain, where EU membership still stirs strong political feelings, the turnout was less than in Ireland. It may be that, in Britain, the real divisions are within parties and not between them and, indeed, that the EU is not an issue that voters get very excited about. If so, this would explain why the Danish turnout (at 52.5 per cent) was substantially higher than in Britain or Ireland. In Denmark, EU issues rank high on the electoral agenda and divergences between the political parties are much more pronounced.

Within Ireland, turnout tended to be higher outside Dublin than within the metropolitan area and this was attributed to the abstentionism among urban working class voters and the greater salience of EU policies (eg on agriculture and regional policy) in the West.

Table 7.1 Euro-election results in Ireland

Party	Seats	Vote %
Fianna Fail	7	35.0
Fine Gael	4	24.3
Greens	2	3.7
Labour	1	11.0
Independents	1	6.9
Progressive Democrats	0	6.5
Others	0	8.4

Although governments traditionally do badly in EP elections, Fianna Fail actually increased both its number of EP seats from six to seven and its percentage of the vote from 32 per cent to 35 per cent. There was, however, a strong contrast between its performance in Dublin and its performance outside the capital. Outside Dublin, FF won six out of the available 11 seats while in Dublin only one of the four seats went to FF in the person of Niall Andrews, brother of the Minister for Defence. Niall Andrews had won the highest first preference vote in Dublin in the 1989 election and was now entering the EP for the third time as a FF MEP. His career has not been without controversy. He publicly supported the campaign to free the Birmingham Six and has been a member of both CND and the Anti-Apartheid movement in Ireland. Although an MEP continuously since 1984, he succeeded in attracting a certain amount of media attention in Ireland by exposing minority causes that the FF party did not officially or publicly subscribe to. Party in-fighting in Dublin had a deleterious effect on support for FF which dropped 8 per cent in the EP election in contrast to an increase elsewhere in the country. The perceived imposition of Olive Braiden had antagonized party supporters and this had been made worse by her call for the dismissal of her running-mate, John Stafford. Elsewhere in the country, the FF campaigns had been remarkably free of rancour; and the Taoiseach's high profile in the Northern Ireland ' peace process' coupled with more encouraging news on the economy, contributed to surprisingly strong support for a government party in mid-term. Nowhere was the FF success more obvious than in the Munster constituency. Here, Brian Crowley, aged 30, became Ireland's youngest ever MEP and the recipient of the highest number of first preference votes in the 1994 election. Crowley, a senator and son of a former FF TD, had been confined to a wheelchair since the age of 16. Crowley's success was due to a number of factors, all of them personal: his good looks, his disability, his energy, a TV performance on *Questions and Answers* but, above all, his newness to politics. His success was out of all proportion to the party he represented and underlines the strong impact made by personalities in Irish Euro-elections.

However, personality could also have a negative effect as FF discovered to its cost in the by-election (held on the same day as the EP election) in Mayo West.

The FF candidate here was Beverley Cooper-Flynn, the 28-year-old daughter of Ireland's EU Commissioner, Padraig Flynn. Despite being a safe seat for FF, the voters elected the FG candidate instead, partly, it seems, because they resented the 'dynastic' implications of the Flynn candidacy, and partly because Beverley Cooper-Flynn was not domiciled in the constituency (the 'parachuting' of candidates in this election provoked much adverse comment). Although Labour retained its one MEP (Bernie Malone) and increased its nationwide share of the vote by 1 per cent, the loss of the Dublin South Central constituency in a by-election held on the same day as the EP election, and the fall in the party's nation-wide support of 8 per cent since the preceding general election (1992) contributed to a mood of soul-searching in the party. The loss of Dublin South Central to a Democratic Left candidate, and a fall of nearly 20 per cent in the Labour vote there, was particularly hurtful, since it confirmed what many Labour backbenchers had been thinking for some time; namely that Labour's separate identity in the Coalition Government was at risk and that the traditional support for Labour in Dublin had defected towards parties that promoted a more authentic socialist agenda.

Among other factors contributing to Labour's poor performance were the 'passports-for-sale' affair, the tax amnesty (whereby tax evaders had been allowed to regularize their position at a reduced rate of tax) and the credibility of Mr Spring himself, who was perceived as having let the Taoiseach make the running on Northern Ireland and been too willing to accept FF dominance of the nation's economic agenda. There were, however, some brighter aspects to Labour's performance. It was pointed out that Labour had increased its share of local authority seats by 20 per cent (reflecting a hard core of support for the party) and had not performed badly in relation to previous elections with which comparisions should have appropriately have been made. After a period of political stagnation during which the Fine Gael leader, John Bruton, had narrowly survived an attempt to unseat him in February 1994, Fine Gael derived much-needed comfort from the results of the EP election. First, the Party retained its four seats in the EP and increased its nationwide share of the vote by 2 per cent. Second, its percentage of the vote in the EP election was almost exactly identical to its share in the 1992 general election (24 per cent). Third, in the two by-elections held simultaneously with the EP election, Fine Gael performed remarkably well: in Mayo West they took the seat from Fianna Fail; and in Dublin South Central they were the runners-up. The success of the party not only strengthened the position of John Bruton, the party leader, but also revived the morale of the entire party to the extent that it could now honestly look forward to the next general election.

The success of Fine Gael can be largely attributed to the experience of its candidates (exemplified by Banotti in Dublin, and Cushnahan in Munster) and the fact that there were no accusations of 'parachuting' candidates as happened with both FF and Labour, although in Leinster the sitting MEP (Paddy Cooney) withdrew when three candidates were selected for the constituency. Rivalaries between FG candidates succeeded in maximizing the vote in all four constituencies and the candidates were carefully selected to complement each other. For example, in Munster, Raftery's farming background and Cork base balanced Cushnahan's Limerick home and regional policy experience; and in Leinster, Alan Gillis, with farming support, balanced Monica Barnes whose strength lay in the urban vote and among women. The fact that FG came close to winning second seats in Dublin, Leinster and Munster, bore witness to the party's renewed fortunes and a carefully planned campaign.

The Progressive Democrats were another party wounded by the results of the EP election, but in this case the wounds were made worse by the personalities involved. Of all the Dail parties, the PDs suffered most in the EP elections. The Dublin candidate received only a few votes more than Sinn Fein, each with 3 per cent. In Leinster, the PD vote fell to 4.8 per cent (from 8.42 in 1989) and in Connacht-Ulster the PD candidate Bobby Molloy saw the party's vote fall by nearly 4 per cent from the 1989 level. In Munster, where the party had scored the highest first preference vote in the whole country in 1989, the party's founder saw his chance of an EP seat slip away on the twelfth count in favour of Pat Cox, a sitting MEP and only recently Deputy Leader of the PDs. The 'Pat Cox Saga' cost the PDs dear. Cox's decision to stand as an Independent in Munster on the day nominations closed raised probably the most contentious personality issue in the entire election. The electoral defeat of Mr O'Malley was all the more bitter for being his first in 26 years and coming only on the twelfth and final count after leading Mr Cox by over 3,000 in the first count. O'Malley's defeat has raised questions about Mary Harney's leadership of the party and indeed the future of the party itself in the wake of its worst electoral performance in its nine years of existence. Personal relations between O'Malley and his erstwhile party political colleague Pat Cox have inevitably become sour. When conceding the seat to Mr Cox, he observed with masterly understatement 'I will not be seeking his company in future'.

No party derived as much satisfaction from the results of the EP election as the Greens. From having no MEPs after the 1989 election, the party won two seats in the 1994 election with only 3.7 per cent of the vote nation-wide. However, their vote was highly concentrated in the east of the country. In Dublin, to everyone's surprise, including the Greens themselves, their candidate Patrica McKenna came top of the poll with 14.5 per cent of the vote. In Leinster, Nuala Ahern won the fourth seat on the seventh and final count. These EP election successes from the Greens ran counter to Green fortunes in several other EU countries, among them Italy, the Netherlands and France. In Ireland, the Green Party has also made inroads in local elections especially in Leinster where concern about Sellafield has given the party a vote-pulling issue. The success of the Greens also runs counter to the conventional wisdom either that concern about the environment is on the wane or, if it is not, the major political parties have subsumed the issue into their own policy agendas. All the major political parties devoted a section to 'green' issues in their EP election manifestos, but it was the Green Party that benefited most from environmental concerns among the electorate.

The aftermath

The lack of a distinctive European focus during the campaign was not unprecedented in Ireland and not unparalleled in other parts of the EU. It is possible to discern a mixture of purely domestic politics and purely European themes mingling with issues that were essentially domestic but dressed in European clothing. Throughout the campaign opposition parties, and especially Fine Gael, attempted to discredit the government by highlighting the so-called 'citizenship for money' scandal. This was essentially a reference to allegations, later confirmed, that Irish passports were sometimes issued without the usual formalities to those prepared to make major investments in Ireland. In the event, not much of this mud stuck, and FF actually emerged better from this EP election than they had from the last. The electoral system encourages intra-party rivalry and this was exacerbated, in some cases, by pitching candidates against each other whose geographical base or ideological persuasion were divergent rather than convergent or who represented contrasting or conflicting tendencies within the same political party. Several observers have made the point that Irish politics have not been Europeanized as a result of over 20 years of EC membership; instead we have witnessed the assimilation of European issues into the domestic political scene. Certainly, the aftermath of the 1994 EP election in Ireland was analysed in the media almost exclusively from the perspective of the main political parties. Although FF regards itself as lucky to have survived an election that is normally regarded as a mid-term test of government popularity, the same cannot be said of the coalition partner, Labour. The implications of the poor result for Labour are that the party has become too over-shadowed by FF and too ready to support FF policies. Many of the hopes placed in Labour, at the time of its 1992 general election success, have not been fulfilled; and Mr Spring's own credibility has taken a hard knock. As Foreign Minister, he will have a prominent role in reappraising Irish foreign policy in the context of difficult decisions that need to be taken at the IGC in 1996. Even if he handles this difficult assignment competently, there is no guarantee that this will persuade potential Labour voters to forgive or forget failures in domestic policy. By contrast, the position of John Bruton, as Leader of FG, was reinforced by the party's performance in the EP election. Against all the odds, the party looks like a credible alternative for floating voters in the next general election. The PDs were severely bruised by the European election and their future may lie in a merger with another party.

Looking further afield, what impact will these elections have on Irish membership of the EU? The answer must be very little. In an enlarged EP of 567 members, the Irish delegation of 15 can have only a limited influence. On the other hand, the EP functions in a way that favours individual MEPs and their participation in committees more than national representation *per se*. In the European People's Party (EPP), four FG MEPs join one Ulster Unionist and 18 British Conservatives in a transnational grouping that spans all the member states and is second only to the Socialist Group in size, the latter having one Irish member in the person of Bernie Malone. The ELDR claims Pat Cox despite his resignation from the PDs; and the two Irish Greens join 21 other Greens from six different countries. The seven FF MEPs join the former Gaullist colleagues in the EDA grouping. Five Irish MEPs were elected vice-chairs of EP committees at the first session of the newly-elected Parliament; Bernie Malone (Foreign Affairs and Security); Mary Banotti (Cultural, Youth, Education and the Media); Joe McCartin (Budgetary Control); Pat Gallagher (Fisheries); and Nuala Ahern (Petitions). The first session of the new parliament gave it an early opportunity to flex its muscles on the appointment of the new Commission President. Although there was only a narrow majority in favour of Santer's appointment, all the Irish MEPs except the two Greens, voted in favour.

The narrow margin of approval was, however, a sign of how much had changed, but also how little. The fact that the EU governments had virtually foisted a compromise candidate on the parliament with little consultation indicated how much the Union's post-Maastricht malaise still lingers; but the willingness of the new parliament to inflict the snub of reluctant approval was, perhaps, a portent of a more muscular democracy in the future.

The new Parliament will be anxious to assert its authority with new powers emanating from the Maastricht Treaty. The forthcoming IGC will provoke discussions on institutional reform in the wake of another enlargement of the EU. Although the EP has often been in the forefront of pressure for change, and will undoubtedly provide a forum for debate on the need for an EU constitution, Irish MEPs have not, in the past, been very prominent in such discussions. Irish public opinion is uncertain about how much power the EP currently possesses and is lukewarm about giving it more. It would not be surprising, therefore, if Irish MEPs took a fairly cautious line in those discussions. On the other hand, on matters of concern to Ireland, such as unemployment, fisheries, education, regional policy and agriculture, one can expect individual Irish MEPs, irrespective of their party political persuasion, to make a mark in committees and in plenary debates.

In Ireland, EP elections have become part of the domestic political process. Governments are judged; smaller parties are given more support than they would normally receive; and personalities loom larger than either parties or policies. If allowances are made for the idiosyncratic features of European elections, they provide a valuable insight into the workings of the political system.

Note

1.   The author wishes to thank Bernadette O'Sullivan, Centre for European Studies, University of Limerick, for research assistance.

8

Italy

Philip A Daniels

Background

The 1994 Italian elections to the EP took place against a backdrop of political and electoral turbulence. Since the early 1990s the political landscape in Italy has undergone a profound transformation which has seen the disintegration of a number of traditional political parties and the emergence of new political formations. The 1994 national elections, held 11 weeks before the Euro-elections, produced a victory for the right-wing alliance of parties and signalled an electoral breakthrough for Silvio Berlusconi's Forza Italia (FI).

The new coalition, led by Prime Minister Berlusconi and comprising FI, the National Alliance (AN) and the Northern League (LN), marked a shift to the right in Italian government. The inclusion in government of five ministers from the far right National Alliance (formerly the neo-Fascist Italian Social Movement) caused disquiet among a number of Italy's European partners and provoked direct criticism from the EP and Commission President Jacques Delors. In May 1994 the EP narrowly passed a resolution, sent to Italian President Oscar Scalfaro, calling on the new Italian government to be loyal to the fundamental values of the EU. The President and the government dismissed the EP's resolution and complained that it represented an unacceptable and unwarranted interference in Italian domestic affairs.[1] At the same time, the new government was expected to shift Italian European policy away from the traditional and largely consensual pro-Europe stance towards a more critical appraisal of the integration process and Italy's role in it.

The campaign: parties, candidates and issues

The notorious complexities of the Italian party system have been given a new twist following the political transformation of the early 1990s. A number of traditional political parties have disappeared or have adopted new names, while at the same time new national and regional political formations have appeared on the scene. This shake-up across the political spectrum was clearly evident in the 1994 EP elections in which 19 political formations presented lists (compared to 14 for the 1989 elections), many contesting Euro-elections for the first time.

The bewildering choice of parties on offer to the electorate was partly a result of the continued use of proportional representation (PR) which encouraged small parties to stand. In the national parliamentary elections held on 27 and 28 March 1994, PR had been replaced by a mixed electoral system in which 75 per cent of the seats were allocated on a first-past-the-post method and the remainder by PR. This shift towards a largely majoritarian electoral system had encouraged the formation of three competing electoral coalitions of the left, the centre and the right. With the return to PR for the elections to the EP the three electoral alignments dissolved into their constituent parts. The Pole of Freedom and Good Government, the right-wing alliance which had secured a parliamentary majority in the national elections and formed the new government, did not present joint lists for the Euro-elections. The Pannella-Reformers lists stood alone while the Christian Democratic Centre (CCD), a new party formed following the dissolution of the Christian Democrats, presented joint lists with Forza Italia. On the left, the principal parties which had formed the Progressive alliance in the national elections (the PDS, the Network, Communist Refoundation and the Greens) presented separate lists in the Euro-elections. The rump of the Socialist Party, which had also formed part of the Progressive Alliance in the national elections, presented joint lists with the Democratic Alliance. At the centre of the political spectrum, voters could choose among the PPI (the principal inheritor of the Christian Democratic tradition), the Segni Pact, the PRI, the PSDI and the Liberals. Of the 19 lists contesting the EP elections, 16 presented candidates in each of the five constituencies.

In total, 1,331 candidates stood for the 87 seats allocated to Italy in the EP. This overall figure includes a number of candidates standing for election in more than one constituency: for example, Prime Minister Silvio Berlusconi headed the Forza Italia list in each of the five constituencies (even though his ministerial office would preclude him from taking a seat in the EP in the event of his election).[2] In addition to Berlusconi, 11 other candidates presented themselves for election in each of the five constituencies: Umberto Bossi (Northern League), Enrico Ferri (PSDI), Gianfranco Fini (National Alliance), Anna Sartori Gremmo, Gianvico Pirazzini, Carlo Riva Vercellotti and Alberto Seghesio (all Lega Alpina Lumbarda), Marco Pannella (Pannella-Reformers), Carlo Ripa Di Meana (Green Federation), Mario Segni (Segni Pact) and Franco Stevenin (Union Valdotaine). Italy fielded the lowest percentage of female candidates, just over 14 per cent compared to the EU average of almost 27 per cent.

All the leaders of the principal parties stood as candidates although past experience indicated that few, if elected, would be likely to take a regular and active part in the EP's work. Many of the parties fielded the usual selection of prestige candidates: Forza Italia included Giampiero Boniperti (the former president of Juventus football club), Franco Malerba (an astronaut on the American shuttle), singer/actress Ombretta Colli and General Luigi Caligaris in their lists; Carlo Ripa di Meana, a former MEP and European Commissioner, stood for the Greens; for the PDS, Maurice Duverger, a French political scientist, was standing for re-election and actor Enrico Montesano was included in the party lists.

Only 35 of the 81 Italian MEPs elected in the 1989 Euro-elections stood again as candidates in 1994. This exceptionally high turnover was largely attributable to the turmoil in the Italian party system since spring 1992 and, in particular, to the rapid decline of the DC and PSI which had been deeply implicated in a series of corruption scandals. Of the 26 MEPs elected for the DC in 1989 only four were standing again for the party's successor, the PPI, while only two of the PSI's 11 MEPs elected in 1989 were candidates in the 1994 election. The most stable Italian party in the EP, in terms of continuity of MEPs, was the PDS with 15 of the 22 MEPs elected in 1989 on the list of its predecessor, the PCI, contesting the 1994 elections:[3] in addition, one MEP elected for the PCI in 1989 was standing in the 1994 elections for Communist Refoundation and another for the Solidarity list. A notable feature of the 1994 elections was the number of MEPs who had switched allegiance from one party list to another, a reflection of the dramatic changes in the Italian party system in the post-1989 period. For example, Eolo Parodi, elected for the DC in 1989, stood as a candidate for Forza Italia in 1994; Luciana Castellina, elected on the PCI lists in 1989, stood for Communist Refoundation in 1994; Marco Taradash, elected in 1989 on the list of the Anti-prohibitionist League (a movement to liberalize drug laws), was forced to leave the Green group in the EP (following his support for the right-wing alliance in the Italian national elections in March 1994) and stood in the 1994 Euro-elections for the Pannella-Reformers list.

The campaign for the 1994 Euro-elections was rather lack-lustre and failed to generate much interest among the electorate or in the press. A number of factors accounted for the low-key campaign: first, the long, intense campaign for the March 1994 national elections and two years of frenetic political change had left electors weary of politics; second, party finances had been heavily depleted in the national election campaign; third, the voters' lack of interest in the EP elections was symptomatic of a decline in the Italian public's enthusiasm for European integration; and fourth, the opposition parties appeared resigned to the inevitability of a victory for the right-wing governing coalition.

The parties did little to enliven the campaign. As in previous Euro-elections, national issues overshadowed European themes and the parties tended to focus on domestic policies and politics which merely rehearsed the themes of the March parliamentary elections. The parties' formal election literature addressed European issues but these rarely became a focus for profound interparty debate during the campaign. In their attempts to attract voters the parties focused inevitably on pressing domestic political issues rather than remote concerns about the EP. Only those European issues which had a direct bearing on domestic politics figured to any extent in the campaign. The PDS, for example, emphasized the parallels between European and domestic political priorities and portrayed the EP elections as a direct choice between the right, which favoured a deregulated, business-dominated, free-market Europe, and the left which supported a 'social' Europe based on rights and citizenship. In addition, the PDS argued that a victory for the parties of the right would distance Italy from its principal partners in the EU, a development which the party alleged was already occurring as a result of the inclusion of neo-fascist ministers in the Italian government. On the right, Prime Minister Berlusconi attempted to turn the vote into a referendum on his government; he appealed to voters to give a strong endorsement to the governing coalition as a way of enhancing Italy's bargaining position and standing in the EU. This message was clearly conveyed in Forza Italia's campaign slogan – 'make Italy count for more in Europe'.

Results

The recent electoral reforms in Italy, introducing majoritarian principles for both national and local elections, did not extend to Euro-elections which retained the system of PR. For EP elections Italy is divided into five large constituencies with the 87 seats (up from 81 in the last EP) allocated on the basis of population: the North-west (Lombardy, Piedmont, Liguria, Val d'Aosta) returns 23 MEPs, the North-east (Trentino–Alto Adige, Friuli–Venezia–Giulia, Emilia–Romagna) 16, the Centre (Marche, Umbria, Lazio, Toscana) 17, the South (Abruzzi, Molise, Puglia, Basilicata, Calabria, Campania) 21, and the Islands (Sicily and Sardinia), ten. The parties present lists of candidates in each constituency (up to a maximum of the number of seats available) and seats are allocated to the parties on the basis of PR. Voters may also indicate preferences for a candidate or candidates on the list for which they have voted. The number of preference votes available to the elector varies according to the number of MEPs elected in the constituency; in the North-west voters may express up to three preferences, in the North-east, Centre and South up to two preferences, and in the Islands constituency a single preference.

The 74.8 per cent turnout in the 1994 Euro-elections was the third highest in the EU (surpassed only by Belgium and Luxembourg) but was down significantly from the 81.5 per cent recorded in the 1989 EP elections. In addition, in 1994 over 2.5 million ballots (5.4 per cent) were spoiled or blank. The rise in rates of abstention is a general long-term trend recorded in both national and local elections. The sharp drop in turnout for the 1994 Euro-elections was symptomatic of the lack-lustre campaign, the parties' failure to mobilize support, voter fatigue following a series of local and national elections and the rise in anti-European sentiments among the Italian public.

Thirteen of the 19 party lists contesting the 1994 Euro-elections won seats in

Table 8.1 Euro-election results and 1994 general election results in Italy (Chamber of Deputies)

Parties	Euro-election 1994 % Votes	Seats	General election 1994 % Votes cast
Forza Italia	30.6	27	21.0
National Alliance	12.5	11	13.5
Northern League	6.6	6	8.4
Pannella-Reformers	2.1	2	3.5
PDS	19.1	16	20.4
Communist Refoundation	6.1	5	6.0
PSI/Democratic Alliance	1.8	2	3.4*
Green Federation	3.2	3	2.7
Republicans (PRI)	0.7	1	–
The Network	1.1	1	1.9
PSDI (Social Democrats)	0.7	1	0.5
Italian Popular Party	10.0	9	11.1
Segni Pact	3.3	3	4.6
SVP (South Tyrol People's Party)	0.6	1	0.6
Liberals (PLI)	0.2	–	–
Others	1.4	–	2.4
Total	100.0	87	100.0

Electorate: 47,489,843
Turnout: 35,505,023 (74.8%)
Valid votes: 69.3%
Invalid votes: 5.5%

* Stood separately in 1994 general election.

the EP. The most significant features of the result were: the millions of voters who switched party allegiance in the few weeks between the national and European elections; the dramatic rise in the vote for Forza Italia which emerged as Italy's largest single party less than six months after its formation; the decline of the left; the poor performance of the PPI, the principal successor to the DC; the decline in the vote for the Northern League; and the virtual electoral demise of historic parties such as the PSI, PSDI and PRI.

The most notable result of the EP elections was the spectacular performance of FI which gained a clear victory while all the other main parties lost votes. It increased its share of the vote from 21 per cent in the March national elections to 30.6 per cent in the Euro-elections, an addition of more than 2 million votes.[4] The party emerged 11.5 per cent ahead of its nearest challenger, the PDS. Forza Italia's success was spread evenly, indicated by the movement's leading position in 15 of the 20 regions and in 72 out of 94 provinces (compared to the 37 in which it led in the March national elections). In the North-west Forza Italia won 34.5 per cent of the vote, in the North-east 27.8 per cent, in the Centre 25.6 per cent, in the South 30.4 per cent and in the Islands 36.1 per cent. The party took first place in seven out of the ten largest cities (Turin, Milan, Venice, Trieste, Genoa, Naples and Palermo) and Berlusconi secured the highest number of preference votes (around three million). Before Forza Italia's success in the EP elections, only the former Christian Democrats and the Communist Party had attained more than 30 per cent of the vote in any post-war Italian election.

A number of factors account for Forza Italia's dramatic success. The party clearly benefited from a 'bandwagon effect' following its strong showing in the March national elections and Berlusconi's installation as Prime Minister at the head of a right-wing coalition. On the eve of the EP elections, Berlusconi appealed to voters to give an endorsement to his new government in order to allow it to govern and to strengthen its influence in the EU. More than any other political force, Berlusconi's movement had captured the mood of an electorate seeking change to the pattern of Italian politics and a break with the leading parties of the old regime. Forza Italia relied on a network of more than 14,000 sports and social clubs (affiliated to the party) to mobilize support and made extensive use of the television networks owned by Berlusconi's Fininvest company. Its budget for the campaign far exceeded that of its rivals: some estimates indicated that Forza Italia had spent 15 times more than the PDS and possibly more than all the other parties put together. Berlusconi's movement became the rallying point for much of the centre and right electorate, attracting former Christian Democrat, Socialist, Social Democrat, Liberal and Republican voters. His amorphous electoral appeal, embracing traditional values and a new style of politics, simultaneously attracted a broad though somewhat contradictory constituency. Forza Italia did particularly well in Southern Italy where large numbers of erstwhile DC and PSI voters, wedded to clientelistic modes of politics, have shifted allegiance to the new parties of government. Berlusconi's movement also advanced in northern Italy where the promise of tax cuts, deregulation and reform of the state has struck a chord with the electorate. These two bases of support co-exist uneasily and will be difficult to hold together in the face of painful economic choices. Exit polls indicated that Forza Italia had taken large numbers of votes from their allies in the national government: 21 per cent of the Northern League's voters in the March national elections switched support to Forza Italia, while 14 per cent of the AN's support in March voted FI in the EP elections. In addition, evidence from exit polls suggested that FI also took votes from the Segni Pact, the PSI, the Pannella List, the PPI and parties of the left.

The EP results were a setback for the Northern League which saw its vote fall from 8.4 per cent in the national elections to 6.6 per cent in the EP elections, a loss of more than a million votes. In the North-west, the League's electoral heartland, the party's vote declined from 19 per cent of the vote in the March national elections to 14.8 per cent in June. In Lombardy, the LN was the second largest party with 17.7 per cent of the vote but trailed well behind FI which won 35.2 per cent. A similar result occurred in the Veneto region where FI won 31.5 per cent of the vote compared to the LN's 15.6 per cent. In Milan, where the LN had won over 40 per cent of the vote in the 1993 administrative elections, the party slipped to third place behind FI and the

PDS. In general, the League lost heavily to FI which, in its critique of the old political class and wasteful public expenditure, to some extent appeals to the same electorate. In addition, as a national party FI has a potential and an appeal that the regionally-based League is unable to match. The Northern League's entry into the new coalition following the March 1994 elections posed a number of tactical difficulties for a political movement with an essentially anti-system appeal and the internal disagreements over the LN's role in government undermined its performance in the Euro-elections. Bossi, the party leader, fearful that the LN in government would lose its identity as a protest movement, frequently disrupted the coalition in its early days. He attacked both principal coalition partners alleging, for example, that Berlusconi's FI was nothing more than a recycling of the old, discredited political elite. Bossi's disruptive tactics backfired, however, and a large number of LN voters, seeking governmental stability, switched support to Berlusconi. The electoral setback for the League reduced its bargaining power in the coalition and made the party keen to avoid a political crisis which would provoke early elections.

The National Alliance, part of the right-wing government coalition, also suffered an electoral setback with a decline from 13.5 per cent of the vote in the March national elections to 12.5 per cent in the Euro-elections. The losses, more than a million votes, were largely concentrated in the South (down 2.6 per cent compared to the March national elections) where significant numbers of AN voters hitched on to the Forza Italia bandwagon. Nevertheless, the AN attracted, on average, around a quarter of the vote in the South and Islands and remained the leading party in Rome. Gianfranco Fini, the party leader, attracted almost 2 million preference votes nation-wide and the highest number in the South.

The EP elections represented a further setback for the parties of the centre. The PPI, strongly pro-European and direct descendant from the DC, saw its vote decline from 11.1 per cent in March 1994 to 10 per cent in the Euro-elections. The PPI emerged as the leading party in only two provinces, Avellino and Potenza, and its total vote was only about a third of that won by its predecessor, the DC, in the 1989 EP elections. The result was greeted with some relief by the party which had feared an electoral annihilation in the face of competition from FI. In the aftermath of the EP elections, the PPI was divided internally over whether the party should seek a *rapprochement* with the governing right-wing coalition or position itself in the centre of the political spectrum and leave open the possibility of a future alliance with parties of the left. The Segni Pact lost more than a quarter of the vote it had polled in the March national election, declining from 4.6 per cent to 3.3 per cent. The parties of the centre lost heavily in southern Italy and in the North-east, formerly electoral bastions for the DC. In the North-east, an area with a traditionally strong Catholic sub-culture, the combined vote of the PPI and the Segni Pact was only 14 per cent, a fall of 2.6 per cent on their combined vote in the March elections.

The parties of the left, heavily defeated and demoralized in the March national elections, could draw little comfort from the results of the Euro-elections. The combined vote for the parties which had formed the Progressive alliance in the March national elections fell from 33.7 per cent to 32 per cent, a fall of approximately 2.6 million votes, and estimates suggested that one in seven left-wing voters in the national elections switched to the right in the EP elections. The PDS, the successor to the PCI and the leading party of the Italian left, polled 19.1 per cent compared to its 20.4 per cent in the March national elections. The PDS vote declined across the country with the partial exception of 'the Red Belt' of Central Italy where the party could draw upon the deeply implanted left-wing sub-culture. The PDS did badly in a number of cities where left alliance candidates had won in the 1993 municipal elections: in Rome, for example, the PDS was relegated to third place in terms of votes. The party led in only 19 provinces in the EP elections compared to 35 in the national elections. The largely negative campaign of the PDS, with its call for a vote to block the 'arrogance' of the government, did not attract support to the party. In addition, despite the far-reaching reforms undertaken by the party in recent years, the PDS and its leader, Achille Occhetto, were associated with the old, largely discredited party regime. In the aftermath of this latest electoral setback for the party, Occhetto, the architect of the transformation from the PCI to the PDS, resigned as leader and was replaced by Massimo d'Alema.

The other parties in the Progressive alliance of the left had a mixed set of results. Communist Refoundation, the hardline faction of the PCI which had opposed the formation of the PDS, increased its vote marginally from 6 per cent in the national elections to 6.1 per cent in the Euro-elections. The PSI-Democratic Alliance coalition was unable to halt the rapid electoral decline of the Italian Socialists, polling only 1.8 per cent of the vote in the EP elections compared to a combined vote of 3.4 per cent in the March national elections. Post-election estimates indicated that as much as 44 per cent of the Socialist vote in the March national elections deserted the party in favour of Forza Italia. This disappointing result, the latest in a series of electoral setbacks following the Socialist Party's deep implication in corruption scandals, precipitated the resignation of Ottaviano Del Turco as leader of the PSI and Willer Bordon as the leader of the Democratic Alliance. The Greens were the only opposition party to record a significant success with an increase in their share of the vote from 2.7 per cent in the March national elections to 3.2 per cent in the EP elections, while La Rete, led by the anti-Mafia mayor of Palermo Leoluca Orlando, saw its vote fall from 1.9 per cent to 1.1 per cent.

Of the three remaining lists to gain representation in the EP, the Pannella List (the Pannellas-Reformers) saw its vote fall from 3.5 per cent in the national elections to 2.1 per cent. The Republicans (PRI) and the Social Democrats (PSDI) each won a single seat in the EP but the lifeline provided by the system of proportional representation used in the EP elections could not disguise the parties' virtual extinction as electoral forces in the wake of their involvement in corruption scandals. The Liberals, a historic party and frequent participant in post-war governments, have also been discredited by allegations of corruption; the party polled fewer than 55,000 votes and failed to secure a seat in the EP.

A comparison of the results of the 1989 and 1994 EP elections illustrates the rapid transformation of the Italian party system. In 1989 the DC got 32.9 per cent of the vote and 27 seats in the EP while in 1994 the PPI and the Segni Pact, the new centre parties, polled a combined vote of only 13.3 per cent and took 12 seats in the EP. The collapse of the Socialist Party was equally striking: in 1989, the PSI won 14.8 per cent of the vote and 12 seats in the EP but in 1994, standing with the Democratic Alliance, its vote had fallen to only 1.8 per cent and it secured only two seats. While there was little overall change on the left in terms of votes and seats there was a redistribution of support among the parties: in 1989 the PCI won 27.6 per cent of the vote and 22 seats, while in 1994 the party's principal successor, the PDS, won 19.1 per cent and 16 seats and Communist Refoundation 6.1 per cent and five seats. Finally, the recent advance of the far right is fully reflected in the comparison of the 1989 and 1994 EP elections: in 1989 the MSI won 5.5 per cent of the vote and four seats in the EP while in 1994 the National Alliance, successor to the MSI, won 12.5 per cent and 11 seats.

The transformation of the Italian party system inevitably produced an exceptionally large turnover in Italy's representation in the EP and had a significant impact on the make-up of some of the Parliament's political groups. Of the 87 MEPs elected in Italy in June 1994 only 21 had sat in the previous Parliament. This high turnover, including many Forza Italia MEPs new to politics, produced a significantly more inexperienced and fragmented Italian representation in the EP. Competition among Italian parties and unease in the EP about political developments in Italy complicated the formation of political groups in the Parliament. Forza Italia, the largest single Italian party with 27 MEPs, had initially sought membership of the European People's Party (EPP) but the political group, sensitive to the delicate issue of FI's collaboration with the far-right National Alliance in the Italian government, gave little encouragement. Press reports suggested that Chancellor Kohl blocked FI's adhesion to the EPP fearing it would cause domestic political embarrassment in the run-up to the German elections in October 1994. The German SPD also warned that FI's membership of the EPP would damage relations between the two leading party groups in the EP. In addition, the PPI, a member of the EPP, gave a lukewarm response to the suggestion that Forza Italia should join them in the same political group in the EP. As a result Forza Italia formed its own group, Forza Europa, which was ready to develop informal parliamentary links with the EPP. The ill-feeling in the EP towards FI, largely as a consequence of its alliance in national government with the far right, was clearly demonstrated when the party failed to secure the chairmanship of any of the EP's committees: indeed, the Belgian Socialist MEP Claude Desama was reelected chairman of the EP's Committee on Energy, Research and Technology, a position which should have gone to FI's candidate, Sandro Fontana, in accordance with the technical distribution agreement.

The other Italian parties represented in the EP joined a variety of political groups. The far right National Alliance, keen to project an image of a post-fascist party, rejected a parliamentary alliance with the French National Front and opted instead to locate itself among the non-attached. The party could not disguise the fact, however, that its representation in the EP included a number of hardline, neo-fascists, at least two of whom had been investigated for serious acts of political violence. The six Northern League MEPs entered the Group of the European Liberal, Democratic and Reformist Party along with Giorgio La Malfa, the leader and sole MEP of the Republicans. The League MEPs had formerly adhered to the EP's Rainbow Group but were forced to quit as a result of the party's participation alongside the National Alliance in the Italian national government. The three MEPs elected for the Segni Pact became the second Italian party, along with the nine PPI MEPs, to join the EPP. The PDS, the former PCI, after a long process of transition is now a fully-fledged member of the group of the Party of European Socialists while Communist Refoundation, the hardline breakaway from the PCI, is part of the Group of the Confederal European United Left. Leoluca Orlando, the Network's single MEP, joined the three Italian Greens in the EP's Green group while Marco Pannella's Radicals joined the European Radical Alliance. Enrico Ferri, leader of the PSDI, was excluded from the Group of the Party of European Socialists following his support for the National Alliance in elections in Sicily.

The three principal parties of the Italian government coalition (Forza Italia, the National Alliance and the Northern League) are in different EP party groups. This is not untypical but for once none of the Italian governing parties is in one of the EP's big party groups and only the LN of the coalition parties is in a traditional EP party group. This is likely to mean that Italian governing parties will have a more marginal role in the EP for the foreseeable future. In addition, the widespread parliamentary hostility towards Forza Italia and the National Alliance may add strains to an already tenuous domestic political alliance.

Conclusion

The 1994 Italian elections to the EP were a low-key affair focused primarily on domestic political issues and themes. In an introspective campaign, the parties paid lip-service to European issues but only debated those themes, such as market deregulation and a social Europe, which had a resonance on domestic political divisions. The importance of the vote was judged mainly in terms of its impact on national rather than European politics: for example, the intense competition for votes among the coalition partners reflected each party's desire to improve its relative standing in the government. The results confirmed the rightward drift of the Italian electorate: the governing coalition secured a combined vote of nearly 52 per cent with FI clearly the leading party with 30.6 per cent of the vote. Berlusconi received the electoral endorsement which he had sought and, with his position strengthened, he was able to threaten new parliamentary elections if the LN continued to disrupt the governing coalition.

The rise of the right has produced a novel situation in Italian politics in which the principal parties of opposition, the PDS and the PPI, are generally more pro-European than the governing coalition. While the LN favours a Europe of the regions, both FI and AN are critical of key aspects of European integration. The foreign minister, Antonio Martino (FI), epitomizes the government's new approach: a member of the Thatcher-inspired Bruges Group and a free-market economist, he favours the single market but attacks European regulations (for example, the social chapter) and the centralized bureaucracy in Brussels. The hints of change in the Italian government's approach to Europe prompted speculation that Britain and Italy would develop a closer alliance within the EU: this notion appeared fanciful, however, when Britain failed to get Italy's support in blocking the nomination of Jean-Luc Dehaene as the new president of the European Commission.

The new intake of Italian MEPs is on the whole less pro-European than its predecessors largely as a result of the demise of the Christian Democrats and the PSI coupled with the electoral breakthrough of Forza Italia and the National Alliance. The AN, for example, is nationalist in outlook, favouring a confederal Europe of strong national-states and opposed to the Maastricht Treaty. Over the years Italian MEPs have given strong and consistent support to the strengthening of the EP's institutional role and this is unlikely to diminish since it is based, in large part, on a continued desire to check Franco-German domination of the EU's decision-making processes.

Nevertheless, there is evidence to indicate the emergence of a more critical and sceptical approach to European integration among both the Italian public and the country's political class.[5] The first signs of this more lukewarm approach were evident in the debate about the convergence criteria for EMU contained in the Maastricht Treaty. In particular, the rules regarding the GNP/debt ratio, which will require fundamental and wide-ranging reforms to public expenditure and taxation in Italy, have provoked criticisms from across the political spectrum.[6] The lira's enforced exit from the Exchange Rate Mechanism in September 1992 undermined confidence in Italy's ability to meet the conditions required for participation in the single currency and raised fears that Italy would be relegated to a slow lane in the integration process. These fears appeared well-founded in September 1994 when a policy document issued by the German CDU rehearsed the possibility of a two-speed Europe in which France, Germany and the Benelux countries would move ahead in the integration process leaving only Italy, of the original founder members, consigned to the slower lane. The document was presented by Wolfgang Schäuble, leader of the CDU parliamentary group, but it was assumed to have had the endorsement of Chancellor Kohl. Antonio Martino, the Italian foreign minister, rejected the plan but it was seen widely in Italy as a realistic commentary on the lack of credibility in the government's economic policy.

The need to adjust the Italian political and economic system to the demands of European economic and monetary integration has intensified pressure for the reform of the country's politics and institutions. To some extent these external constraints have been welcomed by political and business élites who have been able to justify painful domestic economic policies as essential to Italy's future in Europe. Nevertheless, cuts in public expenditure, designed to reduce the public sector borrowing requirement and to tackle the pressing problem of Italy's accumulated stock of debt, have continued to provoke wide-spread public resistance and political infighting among the coalition parties. The painful choices required to keep Italy in the 'fast lane' of European integration may undermine public support for Europe and encourage political parties to seek electoral advantage by adopting a more critical stance towards Europe. The challenges of integration leave little room for Italy's traditional 'verbal' Europeanism in which the strong pro-European party consensus was rarely matched by a consistent implementation of European policies. Italy's relative lack of political influence in the EU is likely to be compounded by recent domestic political developments: first, the ties between the Italian and German Christian Democratic parties, so important in keeping Italy at the heart of the integration process, have been effectively lost; and second, the political composition of the Italian government is likely, at least in the short term, to deter other member state governments from developing close links with it.

Notes

The author would like to thank the British Academy for its generous financial assistance in support of the research on which this chapter is based.

1. Other events indicated the unease in Europe over neo-Fascist participation in the new Italian government. The issue was raised in a number of national parliaments and President Mitterrand of France and Jean-Pierre Cot, a French Socialist MEP, expressed concern. Jacques Santkin, Belgium's environment minister, delayed his arrival at a council of environment ministers as a protest at the presence of the Italian representative Altero Matteoli, a member of the neo-fascist National Alliance. In a similar protest, the Belgian deputy prime minister, Di Rupo, in charge of telecommunications, refused to shake hands with Giuseppe Tatarella, of the National Alliance, at a council meeting in Brussels.

2. Berlusconi's candidature provoked widespread criticism and accusations that he was cheating voters. Carlo Ripa de Meana, former Italian commissioner and a candidate for the Italian Greens, attempted to get the EP to declare Berlusconi's candidature inadmissible.

3. In addition, Pierre Carniti, who had been elected for the PSI in the 1989 EP elections, was a successful candidate for the PDS in 1994.

4. The dramatic changes in the Italian party system in recent years make it more mean-
    ingful to compare the 1994 EP elections with the 1994 national elections rather than
    with the 1989 EP elections.
5. Although public enthusiasm for Europe may have waned somewhat in recent years,
    opinion polls continue to show large Italian majorities in favour of the integration
    process: for example, a poll reported in June 1994 showed 72 per cent of Italians (the
    highest figure of any member state) favouring a more integrated Europe. See the *Finan-
    cial Times*, 1 June 1994.
6. For a discussion of the impact of the Maastricht Treaty on Italy see Philip Daniels,
    (1993) 'Italy and the Maastricht Treaty' in S Hellman and G Pasquino (eds), *Italian
    Politics: A Review* (Vol 8), pp 178–91, Pinter, London.

9

Portugal

Jose M Magone

Twenty years ago the Portuguese Revolution of Carnations initiated a process of democratization, which achieved its highest levels of political, economic and social stability for the country after its accession to the European Community/ European Union (EU) in 1986 (Lopes, 1994).

This positive conjuncture came to an end during 1993, when several small-scale industries and the agricultural and the fisheries sectors were struck by crisis. Rising unemployment resulted and continues to this day largely as a result of the implementation of the Single European Market, although blame is normally apportioned to the government for the economic situation. It is argued that it failed to prepare the most vulnerable economic groups (farmers, fishermen, textile and shoe industries in the north, and unskilled workers) for the new challenges that would confront Portugal in the Single Market. In some regions in Portugal, such as the southern province of Alentejo or the industrial town of Setúbal, around 20 per cent of the population is unemployed. The situation is so desperate in Alentejo that the population on the border with Spain decided symbolically to declare themselves Spanish citizens, because they felt left behind by the Portuguese government (*Expresso*, 23 April 1994: 94).

Social disarray in the rural areas, growing unemployment in the cities and crisis in the health, social and educational systems has been used by the opposition to pressurize the government to change policies. The governing liberal Social-Democratic Party (Partido Social Democrata-PSD) under Anibal Cavaco Silva was confronted over the past two years by several social protests (the largest one being the student unions against the introduction of university fees in public universities).

Against this background of social and economic crisis, the Euro-election campaign unfurled. Portuguese president Mario Soares played a prominent role and used his office to focus the government's attention on socio-economic realities. In the pre-campaign period President Soares intervened on several occasions to single out some urgent problems of Portuguese society. His 'open presidency' in mid-April was devoted to the problems of environmental damage in Portugal. He undertook a *tour de force* across the country with the

Minister for the Environment Teresa Gouveia to highlight major environmental problems and to argue for the introduction of policies compatible with
the logic of the idea of sustainable development in economic thinking and practice. On 25 April, he presided over the commemorations of the 20th anniversary of the Portuguese Revolution, in which his role in leading Portugal
towards democracy was honoured. More controversial was his participation in
a congress on *Portugal: Que Futuro?* (Portugal: What Future?) which aimed at
presenting an alternative both to the policies of the leading social-democratic
government and the opposition policies of the main challenger the Socialist
Party (Partido Socialista-PS). But his attempt to persuade the leadership of
the PS under António Guterres to combat more aggressively the policies of
the PSD government damaged his own popularity with the public.

Generally, Portugal needed to respond to the challenges of European integration. The main problem remains building up an efficient, complex and
flexible institutional-political setting to respond over the long term to the
major social and economic problems of Portuguese society.

The actors in the campaign

The elections to the European Parliament were dominated by the largest
parties represented in the Portuguese and European Parliaments. Ten small
parties also contested the elections. Some of them, such as the regionalist
Partido do Atlântico or the electoral platform Política XXI, were new formations with clear ideas about the European Union.

The liberal PSD had been in power since 1985. Prime Minister Aníbal
Cavaco Silva won an absolute majority in the legislative elections of 1987 and
1991. In the local elections of 1989 and 1993 and in the elections to the European Parliament of 1989, the PSD was successfully challenged by the PS. Currently, the PSD faces difficulties in overcoming the social and economic crisis
of the country. The party is very pragmatic and flexible in its approach. It
attempts to be a national party concerned with the modernization and development of the country. Nevertheless, this position has changed substantially since
1987. The turning point was the presidency of the Council of Ministers in the
first half of 1992, the first time Portugal had assumed this role. Upon accession
to the EC in 1986, it had not felt well enough prepared to assume the presidency. By 1992, the Portuguese government under Cavaco Silva was ready to
assume the mantle of a very self-confident and assertive presidency. The climax
was President Cavaco Silva's participation in the Rio Conference on Environment in May 1992.

This belatedly-found Europeanism of the PSD became more moderate in
the 1994 elections to the EP. The main slogan was 'Europe yes, Portugal
forever' which reflected support for the Maastricht Treaty as long as it did
not compromise national sovereignty, Portugal's cultural specificities or its
national identity. Apart from this qualification, the PSD broadly supported

integration and EU policies (particularly the structural funds) through the prism of the modernization and development of the country.

The leader of the PSD list Eurico de Melo was one of the oldest members of the party and a member of the Portuguese Parliament. In comparison with the mainstream of the party his position towards European integration was rather minimalist and favourable to the idea of a *Europe des Patries*. He stressed the importance of the 1996 Inter-Governmental Conference (IGC) in defining the future outlook of the European Union. The other main candidates had different views on integration. Some supported wholeheartedly the process of European integration. This group included former Democratic Social Centre (Centro Democrático Social-CDS) MEP Lucas Pires and Carlos Pimenta. These divergencies and discrepancies within the party were interpreted by observers and the opposition as indicative of a major difficulty in the Social-Democratic Party in defining itself clearly in terms of the European venture (*Expresso*, 16 April 1994: 5).

The Socialists have been clear advocates of European integration. The party fought their first elections after the Revolution in 1976 on the slogan *A Europa está connosco* (Europe is with us). It was former Prime Minister Mário Soares who submitted the application for EC membership in 1978. The European project has been since then a constant element of the Socialist discourse. But internal party dissent during the 1980s and 1990s divided the party in the electoral contest against the rival PSD. During the pre-campaign period, PS leader António Guterres had to counteract interference by President Mário Soares who, through the controversial congress in early May, tried to force the leadership of the party into a more frontal and radical position towards the PSD government.

The PS campaign was synchronized with the campaign of the other Socialist parties in the 12 member states comprising the Party of European Socialists. Even so, the Euro-elections were primarily seen as a test of the party's popularity before the forthcoming legislative elections scheduled for October 1995. The leader of the PS list António Vitorino was a judge in the Constitutional Court and was seen as a strong supporter of European integration. Other names on the list such as João Soares, the son of the President, the trade unionist leader José Torres Couto, the former Communist José Barros Moura and the member of the Portuguese Parliament António Campos were considered wholehearted supporters of European integration. José Barros Moura's work in the European Parliament was well-known. He worked extensively on European social policy and was able to build up a reputation before he was expelled from the Communist Party and had to renounce his seat. The choice of the candidates for the new list was overshadowed by the self-exclusion of João Cravinho, MEP from the PS list. He felt personally offended by the rather diffuse position of leader António Guterres in relation to the PSD. João Cravinho was well known among the emigrant circles of the European Parliament and in Lisbon as a fierce critic of the policies of PSD-leader Aníbal Cavaco Silva, particularly regarding the use and abuse of the structural funds (*Expresso*, 23 April 1994: 4).

The Communist Party (Partido Comunista Português-PCP) traditionally opposed European integration. The party considered itself to be a national party defending Portugal's sovereignty. This position can be traced to the origins of the party as the main opposition party to the dictatorship before 1974. The preservation of the memory of the Portuguese Revolution of Carnations and the party's social achievements (eg the occupation of the *latifundia* in the province of Alentejo by the land labourers) became the Communist Party's reference point in the 1980s. The whole discourse focused on this topic. Such rigidity and dogmatism led steadily, but inevitably, to the decline of the PCP. Most analysts attribute this to the erosion of the party's social support as it failed to attract new young members. Moreover, in relation to the events of Eastern Europe and the former Soviet Union, the PCP was unable to deal with its past. (Gaspar and Rato, 1992). The new Secretary-General of the PCP, Carlos Carvalhas, continued to refer to the European Union as the 'Europe of the bankers and bureaucrats'. Although he supported Social Europe, Carvalhas opposed what he saw as the erosion of national sovereignty (*Avante*, 3 March 1994: 18). The PCP contested the elections in a coalition alliance with the Green Party. The Democratic Unitary Coalition (Coligação Democrática Unitária-CDU) was led by Luis Sá. He was personally against Maastricht but for a Social Europe and embodied the Coalition's reticence to embrace a federal Europe (*Expresso*, 30 April 1994: 4; *Portugal e a CEE*, Jan–June 1994: 3).

The Social-Democratic Party-People's Party (Centro Democrático Social-Partido Popular-CDS-PP) became the most dominant party in the pre-campaign and campaign period. The leader of the party, Manuel Monteiro, changed the outlook of the party when he came to power in 1992. His line paralleled closely that of the *L'Europe des Patries*. His party was expelled from the European People's Party in 1993 because it followed an anti-Maastricht nationalist line. Until his nomination as leader of the party, the CDS followed closely the model of Christian democracy. All three former MEPs of the CDS left the party and became independent members of the European People's Party. Lucas Pires became a direct opponent to Manuel Monteiro. As head of the list, Monteiro was able to present his nationalist programme around the slogan 'Viva Portugal'. The election manifesto opened with the phrase: 'The European elections are a clear choice between sovereignty and federalism'. Thereafter the programme explicitly mirrored the Gaullist design of a confederal Europe. The manifesto called for a referendum in 1996 and also for strengthening the role of national parliaments at European level. It advocated a return to unanimous voting in the Council and a concomitant weakening of majority voting (*Viva Portugal*, 1994). Apart from these anti-Maastricht and anti-federalist positions, Manuel Monteiro drew attention to increasing Spanish influence in the Portuguese economy and suggested that this could endanger Portugal's national identity and sovereignty.

Among the ten tiny parties contesting the European elections, the maoist Movement for the Reconstruction of the Party of the Proletariat (Movimento para a Reconstrução do Partido Proletariado-MRPP/PCTP), the Democratic People's Union (União Democrática Popular-UDP) and the Movement for the Unity of the Workers (Movimento para a Unidade dos Trabalhadores-MUT) had their origins in the ideological Communist splits of the 1960s and 1970s. All three parties followed the line of the Communist Party and rejected Maastricht. The Trotskyist Socialist Revolutionary Party (Partido Socialista Revolucionário-PSR) headed by Maria Helena Silva focused its campaign on social Europe, racism and xenophobia around Europe. The Monarchic People's Party (Partido Popular Monárquico-PPM) stressed the idea that Portugal should promote the Lusitanian Community by strengthening ties with the Portuguese-speaking African countries, Brazil and even Japan. It saw subsidiarity as a safeguard to national sovereignty. As to political union, it argued that Portugal needed to attain a certain level of economic development before it could participate in such a project. The Democratic Renewal Party (Partido Renovador Democrático-PRD), founded in 1985, presented a critical manifesto in relation to the European Union, but on the whole supported European integration.

The other four parties were newcomers to the Euro-elections. The surprise was the electoral formation Politics XXI (Política XXI) led by 20-year-old Ivan Nunes. It consisted of a group of independent candidates, ecologists and non-aligned militants from the left. They ran on a ticket denouncing the logic of the professionalization of politics. They were very pro-European and advocated further democratization of the Union by introducing a Charter of Rights of the European Citizen and the strengthening of the powers of the European Parliament. They proposed a second chamber of the nations for the European Parliament. Nevertheless, Politics XXI were very concerned about what was considered 'Fortress Europe' and called for a Europe open to the rest of the world (*Expresso*, 16 April 1994: 6). The ecologist Movement of the Earth Party (Movimento do Partido da Terra-MPT), founded in autumn 1993, first appeared in the earlier local elections. In the Euro-elections the party was fairly supportive of the EU Commission's Fifth Environmental Programme which was based upon the principle of sustainable development. A referendum in 1996 was also a central issue of its electoral manifesto. Last, but not least, the new Party of the Atlantic (Partido do Atlântico-PDA) led by the high school teacher António Aragão de Freitas originated on the Portuguese island of Madeira. The party followed a regionalist and federalist programme and called for the introduction of a second chamber of the regions in the European Parliament. The PDA opposed any revision of Maastricht.

The campaign: 'the federalism of the President'

The pre-campaign period was dominated by the actions of the President. As early as 12 April he presented his views on Europe in the French newspaper *Le Figaro* where he called for a federal Europe, the adoption of a European

Constitution, the introduction of the office of European president and the building up of transnational party and trade-union structures. These views were criticized by all major parties as too radical (*Expresso*, 16 April 1994: 3). Most of the parties put forward European issues in the Euro-election campaign. In particular, the future design of the European Union was passionately discussed with reference to Portugal. The main parties – PSD and PS – remained highly ambivalent on the issue of European Union. Consequently, both the CDS-PP of Manuel Monteiro and the Communists were able to campaign on an anti-Maastricht and anti-loss of national sovereignty platform. A survey conducted during the pre-campaign period showed the popular appeal of such a position: the CDS-PP leader was considered to be the most popular head of list of the four main candidates (*Expresso*, 30 April 1994).

The governing PSD had difficulties getting its campaign off the ground. It took relatively long to get its election machine into action. The secretary-general of the PSD was heavily criticized inside the party because of the PSD's disorganized campaign. But during the last three weeks of the campaign, Prime-Minister Cavaco Silva rallied to the side of the PSD in supporting its candidates seeking election to the European Parliament. Nevertheless, the head of the list Eurico de Melo was seen as the least well-prepared candidate of all main candidates. His knowledge of the European Union was seen as very weak. The PSD had major difficulties in fitting into and accommodating the European campaign of the group of which they were members in the European Parliament. They refused to accept the slogan of the Liberal Democratic Reformist-Group *Mon Pays: l'Europe*. Apart from this, it was speculated that the PSD wanted to leave the LDR and join the numerically stronger and more powerful European People's Party. Evidence for this assumption was adduced from the visit to Portugal of the leader of the Spanish People's Party, José Maria Aznar in support of the PSD (*Expresso*, 23 April 1994: 24; *Expresso*, 30 April 1994: 1).

The Socialists were seen during the whole pre-campaign and campaign as the favourites. A poll two weeks before the elections gave the PS 39.5 per cent of the vote in comparison with the PSD's 28.2 per cent, the CDS-PP's 7.8 per cent and the Communists's CDU 7.2 per cent. Nevertheless, their campaign was not strictly European. They used the occasion to criticize the government and especially its economic record since 1992. The head of the list António Vitorino and the secretary-general António Guterres travelled the land presenting the message that the only vote that hurt the PSD was a vote for the Socialist Party (*Expresso*, 28 May 1994: 4). This message was well received in the areas where the PSD was dominant, such as in the peripheral provinces of Trás-Os-Montes. The Communists tried to mobilize their declining social support among the farm labourers of Alentejo and the working class of Setúbal and Lisbon.

The 1994 Euro-election campaign was dominated by television. Since 1993 Portugal has had four channels. Apart from two state channels (RTP and TV2), a channel of the media tycoon Pinto Balsemão (SIC) and a channel close to the Catholic Church (TVI) were founded. These four channels organized several debates between the four main candidates. The general impression was that the parties took the opportunity to clarify their positions in relation to each other. Manuel Monteiro and António Vitorino were considered the best prepared for the European Parliament. Manuel Monteiro used his anti-Maastricht position to criticize the two big parties for being indistinguishable from each other on Europe. The main Communist candidate was unable to take advantage of these television discussions.

On the whole, the campaign was rather moderate and seen as less important than the legislative, presidential and local campaigns. Europe and the European Parliament are still a second consideration for the national political élite. Some days before the elections, the government feared that this could be also the feeling of the majority of the population. It was estimated that turnout would be low with an abstention rate around 60 per cent (*Expresso*, 10 June 1994: 1 and 24). This was confirmed on the day of the elections. The long holiday weekend was the main reason for the poor turnout, but the economic situation had severely curtailed early optimism as to the benfits to be gained from European integration.

The results

Portugal uses proportional representation (PR) for elections with a national list. Voting is voluntary. Abstention was high on the day of the Euro-elections. In a survey carried out for the weekly newspaper *Expresso*, the main reasons given for staying away from the polls referred to lack of interest in politics, health problems, discontent with the corresponding party or dislike of the candidates (*Expresso*, 18 June 1994: 1). What the Socialists feared most was a low turnout. In a sense, they were defeated by the opinion polls. Even television projections on election day predicted that the PS would stay between four and eight points ahead of the the Social Democratic Party. It is likely that many potential PS supporters remained at home because the polls suggested the party was in an unassailable position. The high level of abstentionism mostly affected the Socialist party. All predictions assumed that the abstention rate would be similar to that in 1989 (48.9 per cent). The marginal victory over the PSD was disappointing for the Socialist leadership which saw these elections as a dry-run for the legislative elections of 1995. Nevertheless, compared to 1989, the PS increased its share of the vote by almost 6 per cent and won two extra seats.

The PSD was content with the results having expected a far worse result. It did not lose in relative terms. On the contrary, it gained over 2 per cent more in the share of the vote and did not lose any seats. The Socialists were very worried that Anibal Cavaco Silva might not secure his absolute majority result of 1991. Manuel Monteiro's CDS-PP became the third largest party. Electoral geographical analysis shows that while the CDS-PP, which had until then been

Table 9.1 Euro-election results in Portugal

Parties	EP-elections 1989 %	EP-elections 1989 Seats	EP-elections 1994 %	EP-elections 1994 Seats
PS	28.5	8	34.8	10
PSD	32.7	9	34.4	9
CDS-PP	14.1	3	12.5	3
CDU	14.4	4	11.2	3
Other	10.1	–	7.1	–
Total		24		25

12 June 1994: abstention: 64.4 per cent; turnout: 36.6 per cent
9 June 1989: abstention: 51.1 per cent; turnout: 48.9 per cent

Source: Ministry of Inner Administration quoted from: European Report supplement no 1958–15 June 1994; *Expresso Revista*, 18 June 1994, p 52; Eleição Para o Parlamento Europeu, 1989. Escrutínio Provisório-Resultados (Lisboa: Ministério da Administração Interna 1989).

a predominantly rural party, was able to win votes too in urban centres, its share of the vote fell compared to 1989. The CDS-PS lost 2 percentage points, but was able to hold on to its three seats. The Communists lost one of their seats to the Green Party. Their strongholds in the south of Portugal are gradually disappearing. All other small parties remained below one per cent of the vote and failed to win seats in the EP.

The majority of Portuguese MEPs are new to the EP. Only one-third has been an MEP before. The lack of continuity is high compared to 1989 when 48.84 per cent of MEPs were returned. Also the number of female MEPs fell from three to two. No CDS-PP member had ever been in the EP before (Magone, 1993: 12). This can be explained by the ideological shift of the party from Christian–democracy wholeheartedly supporting the project of the European Union to the anti-Maastricht stance and nationalism of Manuel Monteiro. All the former MEPs left the party, but continued to be members of the European People's Party. Thirty-two-year-old Manuel Monteiro served as MEP until end of 1994 and has now returned to the national arena to prepare for the legislative elections. The other elected MEPs are Professor Rául Rosado Fernandes and the former President of the Council of Aveiro José Girão Pereira. The three MEPs will become part of the group of the European Democratic Alliance.

In the Socialist Party, trade union leader José Torres Coutowas was re-elected to the EP. Several other well-known politicians are in the Socialist group, including João Soares, Carlos Lage and António Campos. The former communist MEP José Barros Moura was elected as an independent on the Socialist list. The Portuguese Socialists will join the European Socialist Party. In the Social Democratic Party the most prominent member is the former Minister of Agriculture Arlindo Cunha. The former MEP of the CDS Francisco Lucas Pires remains with his status as an independent in relation to the Social Democratic Party. The PSD is thinking of leaving the Liberal

Table 9.2   Continuity of Portguese MEPs

	PS	PSD	CDS	CDU	%
Elected before 1994	3	4	–	1	8	32
Elected for the first time in 1994| 7	5	3	2	17	68
	10	9	3	3	25	100

Democratic Reformist Group and of joining the European People's Party. In the Communist Party both Carlos Carvalhas, the present secretary-general, and José Barros Moura had to be replaced by the party. The head of the list, Luís Sá, and Sergio Ribeiro became the new Communist members. They will become members of the Communist Group, jointly with the French and Greek communists.

Conclusions

The Portuguese Euro-election campaign was muted and sober. Most of the discussion addressed European issues, particularly the future design of the European Union. The two big parties seemed to classify the EP elections as a secondary consideration compared to legislative, presidential and local elections. The EP still seems to be portrayed as a 'luxurious place of exile' for Portuguese MEPs (Gillespie, 1989: 109). It seems that the initial idealism that motivated the MEPs of 1986, 1987 and 1989 is being replaced by MEPs who are less convinced about the latest developments in European integration. After eight years of membership, the Euro-optimism of 1986 has faded and been replaced by more down-to-earth discourse.

Some Portuguese MEPs are dedicated Europeans. It is expected that José Barros Moura will contribute to advancing European social policy because of the expertise he has developed since 1986 in the EP. Carlos Pimenta (PSD) can also continue his good work on environmental policy. All the other candidates are unknowns. Time will reveal their potential. All four parties are interested in augmenting the role of the European Parliament in securing the greater democratic accountability of the other institutions to elected representatives.

References

Actividade dos deputados do PCP no Parlamento Europeu. In *Portugal e a CEE*, January–June 1994.
Centro Democrático Social-Partido Popular (1994), *Viva Portugal. Manifesto Eleitoral.*
Coligação Democrática Unitária (1994) *Encontro Nacional sobre as Eleições Para o Parlamento Europeu*, Lisboa.
European Elections: Patchwork European Parliament Emerges from June 9-12 Poll (1994). In *European Report*, Supplement No. 1958 – June 15.

Gaspar, C and Rato, V (1992) *Rumo à Memória. Crónicas da Vida Comunista*, Lisboa, Quetzal.

Gillespie, R (1989) Spain and Portugal. In Lodge, J (ed), *The 1989 Election of the European Parliament*, London, Macmillan, pp 107–25.

Lopes, J S (1994) *Portugal and EC Membership Evaluated*, London, Pinter.

Magone, J M (1993) *The Iberian Members of the European Parliament and European Integration. Their Background, Their Attitudes and the Prospects for Transforming Elite Cultures*, Bristol, Centre for Mediterranean Studies, Occasional Paper No 7.

Manifesto Eleitoral do Partido Ecologista 'Os Verdes' Para as Eleições ao Parlamento Europeu (1994), Lisbon.

Ministério da Administração Interna (1989) *Eleição Para o Parlamento Europeu 1989. Escrutínio Provisório-Resultados*, Stape, Lisbon.

Partido Social Democrata (1994), *Linhas Programáticas*, Lisbon.

The Times (1989) *Guide to the European Parliament*, Times Books, London.

10

Spain

John Gibbons

Background

Spanish membership of the EU has been strongly marked by increased integration in the European economy. Such growing integration is reflected especially in patterns of trade in goods and services (eg the EU accounted for 71 per cent of Spanish exports in 1991) as well as in foreign investment where substantial increases have also occurred.[1] EU policies have replaced many of the previous domestic protectionist systems resulting in significant shifts especially in agricultural, regional, competition and monetary policies. Spain has also been a net recipient of EU funds. In the period since the 1989 European elections major EU initiatives including the advent of the Single European Act (SEA) and Treaty on European Union have augmented the transfer of economic and political control from Madrid – as from other European capitals – to Brussels. Against such a backdrop, the 1994 European elections might have been expected to provide an occasion of widespread public debate and evaluation of Spain's membership of the EU. Indeed, no clearer prompt for such a debate could be forthcoming than the major change in fortune of the Spanish economy from those early years of membership between 1986 and 1991 when it enjoyed faster growth than the average of its European parties to more recently between 1991 and 1993 when it fared worse than the European average. With figures for 1993 showing 23.4 per cent unemployment (the highest among OECD countries) and a fall in GDP of 1 per cent indicating the worst recession for three decades, there was clearly much that was controversial about Spain's direction, both politically and economically, in the EU. Slight indications of improvements for exports and unemployment in March 1994 could not alter public perception of a deeply troubled economy before the onset of the Euro-election campaign in the last days of May 1994.

However, the state of the economy was one of just a number of woes which competed for the attention of parties and public opinion in the run up to the elections of 12 June. Most in evidence was the widely perceived weakness – since the general election of 1993 – of the government of the Socialist Party

(PSOE) led by Felipe González, dependant as it was for its very survival on the votes of the Catalan nationalist party Convergència i Unio (CiU). The continued support of CiU was contingent upon Catalonia gaining a string of concessions for that region — both political and financial — which regularly raised the ire of many in Spain's 16 other 'autonomous communities' or regional political structures. Andalucia, one of those other autonomous communities and heartland of the Spanish Socialist Party's electoral support, held elections on the same day as the Euro-elections to decide the make-up of its regional parliament and regional government (Junta), fuelling even more than usual the widespread public perception of it being the object of special favour (with examples cited including public investment associated with Expo '92 in Sevilla and the Madrid–Sevilla rapid express train). Small wonder then that in the eyes of many in the rest of Spain, the destiny of the country in Europe and elsewhere was to all intents and purposes held in the hands of the political power-brokers of Barcelona and Sevilla.

Moreover, seeking to build on the electoral advances that they made in the 1993 general elections, the opposition parties, notably the conservative Partido Popular (PP) and the left-wing coalition of Isquierda Unida (IU) were provided with more substantial sticks than the vagaries of the economy with which to beat the government. Helpful in this respect was the outbreak of corruption scandals right at the heart of government which came to the forefront in the weeks and months before the Euro-elections. Most prominent was the case of Luis Roldán, the first civilian head of the Civil Guard nominated to that post by a Socialist government, who disappeared to a secret venue in Africa under a cloud of suspicion of embezzling state funds resulting in the resignation of two of González' ministers. Second, were the allegations against Mario Rubio, the ex-governor of the Central Bank of Spain who faced charges of having channelled into secret bank accounts investment gains from 'insider dealing' in stocks and shares. Thus while some political élite-level debate saw discussion of essentially European issues, such as the single currency question or the danger that Spain would find itself marginalized with significantly weaker voting rights in an EU expanded northwards to include the new Nordic members, the voting public were in fact much more enlivened by political matters closer to home. Part of the reason for this lay in weaknesses inherent in Spain's political system.

The actors

Political parties in Spain proved unable to sustain a high level of debate on European issues once the European election campaign got under way. The promise of enhanced power for the newly elected EP as well as an extra four seats (giving Spain a total of 64 seats) failed to animate much public interest in the institution and quickly drew the parties back to the more familiar debating territory of national issues. Part of the difficulty lay in the complex electoral system which Spain has used for European elections although it is only fair to add that this has also offered some interesting voting possibilities. The existence of a single country-wide constituency whose members are elected through proportional representation (PR) by a party-list system has meant that candidates are often too remote from and unknown to an electorate familiar with a provincial constituency system in general elections. Additionally, many small regional parties have found it necessary to join forces in an electoral bloc so that they might stand a chance of gaining sufficient votes to win seats against the nationally-organized parties.[2] One such bloc – Coalicion Nacionalista – consisted of parties from the following regions: the Basque Country (Partido Nacionalista Vasco), the Canary Islands (Coalicion Canaria), Valencia (Unio Valenciana); Aragon (Partido Aragones); Galicia (Coalicion Galega) and the Balearic Islands (Unio Mallorquina). While some of the campaigns in the Spanish national media have taken place in the name of such broad blocs, the campaign at the level of those regions with parties in the blocs has been conducted by the relevant regional party. Additionally, ballot papers in relevant autonomous communities when referring to such blocs have carried the names of the local party or parties after the name of the bloc to which they belong, eg the bloc of the European People's Coalition (Por la Europa de los Pueblos) was referred to on the ballot papers in Catalonia, Valencia and Aragon – in Catalan – as Per L'Europea de les Nacions (Esquerra Republicana de Catalunya – Accio Catalana).

Although complex, the system adopted for the Euro-elections did offer the opportunity of greater voting opportunities for some electors such as migrants within Spain. For example the many natives of Galicia or their families living in Catalonia could if they so wished vote for Xosé Manuel Beiras' left-wing nationalist party BNG (Bloque Nacionalista Galego) which over recent years has built up considerable support in regional and general elections in Galicia, thus boosting the votes of that party from beyond its regional core support. Even so, the task for a regional party such as BNG to win one of the 64 Euro-seats in a country-wide constituency was a very difficult one.

Another obstacle to the arousal of public interest in the campaign was the fact that generally only those candidates at the top of the various party lists tended to be major public figures in Spain. The head of the PP list, Abel Matutes, had reached a degree of prominence as an EC Commissioner for Energy and Transport and as a successful businessman in Ibiza but was not as well known politically as Fernando Morán, at the top of the PSOE list, the former foreign minister and an intellectual from the left of his party. Like Morán, the head of the lists for IU and the CiU – Alonso Puerta and Carles Gasòliba respectively – were both former members of the EP seeking re-election. Regional figures tended also to have some prominence such as Max Cahner, the first Catalan candidate on the list of the European People's Coalition who was a former culture minister in the Generalitat, ie the regional government of Catalonia. However, the Euro-candidates tended to be over-shadowed by party leaders during the campaign who in turn were to varying degrees absorbed by various national/regional concerns for the duration of the Euro-elections. These included for instance the major divisions which existed in the PSOE between the left-wing *guerristas* led by Alfonso Guerra the former Vice-President of Spain who resigned from that position in 1991 amid a tangled web of corruption allegations surrounding his brother but remained on as the Socialist Party vice-secretary general to challenge Felipe González and the more moderate band of *renovadores* (renewers) within the party. González managed to achieve a truce between the two party factions at least for the duration of the European and Andalucian election campaigns. However, he could not ignore the fact that under-performance in those elections would carry the threat to his administration of a renewed post-election challenge at a time when he was disadvantaged by the corruption scandals, the jaded image of his party which was losing him urban and youth votes especially to the PP, high levels of unemployment and serious tensions with the unions who were so disenchanted with government plans to make employment contracts more flexible that they held a national strike in January 1994. Much of this scenario was apparent in the general elections of 1993 which the PSOE survived but not without a surge of support for the PP and IU.

Led by José Mariá Aznar, the PP had to help the public overcome the many taboos associated with voting for the post-francoist right in Spain. Its stated electoral aim was to defeat the PSOE by gaining the first majority for the right since before González came to power in 1982. However, Aznar was widely recognized to lack the personal charisma which in the past so helped González to many electoral victories, and thus a failure of PP, the so-called 'Populars', to win a majority of votes in the Euro-elections of 1994 carried with it the threat of a possible challenge to his leadership.

IU aimed to break the two-party mould by revealing the weaknesses of the Socialist credentials and apart from attracting many union members and disenchanted PSOE supporters it hoped to continue to gain from its clean political image in contrast to those parties tainted with corruption scandals and allegations, especially the PSOE and to some extent the PP. The CiU had one overriding concern in the European elections which was to gain public approval in Catalonia for its actions since the general election of 1993, especially the policy of supporting the minority government of Felipe González. If it failed to at least maintain its electoral position, then the Catalan coalition party would have to fundamentally re-think its tactics. The CiU also saw greater advantage for Catalonia in the outcome of an even more electorally-weakened PSOE, from which could be extracted yet more financial and political autonomy: but not so weak that González might feel obliged to call a general election.

The decline of the Centro Democratico y Social (CDS) (evident in its 1.8 per cent vote in the 1993 general election) was rapid after the departure of its leader Adolfo Suarez, former prime minister and one of the key figures in Spain's transition to democracy. The main question to be answered in these elections with respect to the CDS was to where would the majority of its 7.2 per cent of the national vote and five seats won in the 1989 Euro-election go? The same question surrounded the idiosyncratic José Mariá Ruiz-Mateos whose personal vendetta against González and his government had won his group two seats in 1989 but who was unlikely to achieve the same in 1994. The Andalusian Regional Party, the Greens and Herri Batasuna also faced a challenge to maintain their seats in the EP while many other small groupings contesting the elections and ranging from Carlists and Falangists to the Natural Law Party were without much chance of gaining a seat.

In the midst of more immediate preoccupations party canvassers found it difficult to concentrate on matters as apparently remote as European issues, but that is not to suggest that they were not in possession of distinct policy approaches on European questions.

Electoral manifesto issues

According to whether the party programmes or election campaign speeches are examined, the issues important to the parties participating in the Euro-elections seem to vary considerably. The former tended to provide an analysis of the European matters of most concern to the party in question while the latter usually revealed a fixation with national matters. A brief survey of published party programmes is instructive as to the party positions on issues in Europe.

The PSOE, whose MEPs have made up a significant proportion of the Socialist bloc in the EP, has always emphasized its strong European credentials. In this election it did so in its 24-page programme with the unadorned title *The European Manifesto, 1994* which pointed to the fact that it was the Socialists (with the head of the party-list Fernando Morán, then Foreign Minister) who conducted Spain's entry into the EC in 1986. The programme was made up of an extensive series of intentions wishfully entitled 'The Europe that we want, which put a particular focus on the forthcoming prestigious occasion of Spain's presidency of the EU in the second half of 1995 leading up to the Inter-governmental Conference year of 1996 where it hoped that Spain would maintain and reinforce the prestige and power it believed had been achieved through the party's work in Brussels. It was optimistically suggested that a strong group of Spanish Socialist MEPs sent to work with the Socialist group in a more powerful EP would facilitate this situation. More specific matters were also raised by the PSOE in its programme, for example the promise to promote the case of the autonomous communities for a greater degree of participation in decision-making in relation to EU matters: an issue intended to win the PSOE some more votes in the regions where the regional parties were making a strong case for the greater application of the principle of subidiarity.

The PP which has been part of the European People's Party (EPP) in the EP gave its 65-page programme a more emphatic title than its main opponents, namely *Strength in Europe*.

Although it included a rather long drawn-out account of the workings of various institutions and policies of the EU, it was also peppered with well-argued criticisms of the Socialists' action in the EU as well as in Spain and offered proposals for change. It made concrete recommendations on the steps required for the convergence of the Spanish economy with the leading group of EU economies. Specific suggestions to enhance competitiveness in the Spanish economy were laced through the programme. Tax reforms were mooted to encourage savings and investments and to eliminate the disincentives of fiscal disparities between Spain and other member states. More criticism was heaped on the government of the Socialist Party for its handling of public expenditure deemed by the PP to be out of control. Thus the programme moved back and forth from Madrid to Brussels offering a critique and commentary on each level. Blame was also laid at the door of the government for its failure to renegotiate a good deal for – among others – Spanish farmers and fishermen. So for agriculture the 'Populars' proposed a re-negotiation of the milk quota system: ideas destined especially for the ears of Spain's dairy farmers in the north. Under a section entitled 'Europe of the Citizens' the programme of PP focused on family values, identifying the need to protect the family and in this vein offered proposals for a common EU code on violent and pornographic movies.

The electoral programme of IU which has been an independent group in the EP was entitled *Europe Move!* It offered the electorate the longest and most detailed of the manifestos covering in some cases policy issues beyond the remit of the EU let alone the Spanish government, eg the wider role of NATO. Considerable attention was also paid to the question of the democratic-deficit and proposals were made to change the Treaty on European Union to allow citizens to initiate EU legislation by means of a referendum. Other matters raised by the left-wing coalition included the case for increasing the community budget to enhance its spending, especially on EU social policies. It also demanded a modification of the goals of economic convergence to give priority to the battle against unemployment in the EU.

The CiU which is itself really a coalition of two Catalan parties Convergència Democrática de Catalunya (CDC) and Unión Democrática de Catalunya (UDC) has belonged to two different EP groups reflecting its different ideological tendencies, the former affiliating to the Liberals and the latter to the EP. The somewhat odd nature of their arrangement becomes more apparent when it is remembered that since the general election of 1993 the CiU has been propping up the Socialist government in Spain. However, notwithstanding such multiple allegiances the CiU did have a common programme *Both Strong in Europe!* clearly focused on European issues with a particular eye to the role of Catalonia in Europe. Central to the programme was a demand for the participation of the Generalitat in the decisions of the EU Council of Ministers. It also called for a strengthening of the powers of the Committee of the Regions and an improvement in the links between Catalonia and European institutions generally. The Catalan language was also promoted with calls for its recognition as an official language of the EU.

The CiU programme emphasized the importance of developing the principle of subsidiarity and thereby ensuring that powers and competencies conceded to the Generalitat by central government in the autonomous process would be maintained at the regional level and not removed to Brussels. Other significant reform proposals mooted included the creation of a single President of the EU and a more powerful EP.

The PNV programme *It's Time to Join Forces*, like that of CiU, was also distinctly European in its outlook but its nationalism was more vehement than its Catalan counterpart. It emphasized the importance of self-government for the Basque country and demanded participation for Basque representatives not only in the EU Council of Ministers but also in other processes such as the 1996 Inter-governmental Conference. Like the CiU it recommended a more powerful EP with members elected in Spain from regional constituencies rather than the current single country-wide constituency. It also called for the acceptance of the Basque language as an official language of the EU. Before the 1994 election, the PNV MEPs formed part of the European People's Party in the EP.

Foro-CDS, the rather tattered remains of the Social Democratic Centre party, fought to defend its five seats in the EP's Liberal bloc on a programme of policies entitled *Changing the policy process to construct a Europe of Citizens*. Its content was idealistic and wide-ranging, covering issues beyond the realm of the EU including proposals to have a directly-elected Spanish presidency, the reform of the system of financing political parties and more encouragement to equal opportunities in public office. On Europe, it advocated a stronger European Parliament with powers equal to those of the Council of Ministers, greater public access to the proceedings of Council meetings and all its decisions by majority voting.

In conclusion, the larger parties tended to be vaguer in their proposals than the smaller ones who usually had quite specific agendas although the PP offered more detailed analysis than the PSOE. All parties emphasized at least to some extent the need to deepen European integration and to strengthen the EP with the PP being less committed on this aspect. All except the PNV expressed worry about the consequences for existing member states of expanding the EU northwards and eastwards. Only IU offered a fundamental critique of the EMU objectives in the context of the European recession while the CiU suggested greater flexibility in the timetable for the adoption of a single currency. Whether the issues raised in the party manifestos could be said to have revealed Euro-idealism, -realism, -sceptism or just simply naïvete, the fact of the matter was that these issues were largely subsumed beneath the more pressing matters occupying the mind of the party activists once the campaign got under way.

The campaign issues

What were the pressing domestic matters that faced the electorate on 12 June? One question raised constantly during the campaign leading up to this date was what if anything the Euro-elections signified for the future stability of an already unsteady government. Aznar and the 'populars' argued that the Euro-elections were effectively a national plebiscite and that the socialists might have to call a general election if – as was widely predicted in the media – it polled badly. At the very least it would have to submit to a vote of confidence, according to Aznar. González declared this to be nonsense and suggested that the opposition parties respect what he called 'the rules of the game' saying that he knew of no other member state where the outcome of the Euro-elections had provoked a general election and whatever the outcome he was not proposing to call one.

While the PSOE was keen at its meetings and rallies to talk up its chances of retaining seats and votes in the elections it was aware that the outlook for the party was poor. Apart from playing down the significance of the election, it adopted a number of tactics to deal with the prospect of humiliation at the hands of the Popular Party which set a target of a half a million more votes than the Socialist Party, quite remarkable when one considers that the PSOE gained almost 1 million votes more than the PP only 12 months previously. At times, it flatly denied the accuracy of statistics and opinion polls and in contrast suggested that the position of the PSOE was improving as the election campaign progressed and undecided and undeclared voters finally, albeit grudgingly, opted for the government party. On other occasions, it admitted the weakness of its position but argued that this was merely a consequence of the effects of the tardiness of the (slight) economic recovery to make an impact on the lives of the public, a matter that would change with the imminent success of the policies of the government. A few days before the election the argument was floated by sources within the PSOE that a drop of more than 4 per cent in its vote could actually provoke a dangerous crisis in government and for Spain, while a drop of more than 8 per cent would be disastrous and would almost certainly mean a general election in October. Thus, by alternately denying and admitting to the significance of the Euro-elections for national political reasons, PSOE attempted to cajole and frighten voters into casting their ballots in favour of the governing party on election day.

CiU meanwhile, anxious not to undermine the *status quo* which had reaped considerable rewards for Catalonia, was careful not to join the PP bandwagon and have too much read into what opinion polls suggested would be a slump in the PSOE vote. Jordi Pujol, the CiU leader, argued that the elections were simply European and not a test of who should run Spain. He dismissed the idea that the government would have to modify its actions as a consequence of the outcome of the Euro-elections or the Regionals in Andalucia. What was less audible from the Pujol camp was the certainty that CiU would itself have to rethink its support for the González government if Catalans gave his party the thumbs down in the Euro-elections. To avoid such an outcome, at a rally in

Barcelona, Pujol was at pains to remind his Catalan audience that the CiU had no personal, ideological or historical interest in supporting the Socialists and that their only interest was to do what was best for Catalonia. Early in the campaign the PP tried to put a different slant on CiU's relationship with the PSOE, but its efforts temporarily backfired. Mercedes de la Merced, a Madrid councillor and third on the PP list, floated the idea in a newspaper interview that the country would disintegrate like Yugoslavia as the government gave in to the pressure of the regional nationalists to stay in power and that it could be held to ransom in future by whatever 'loco' became President of the Generalitat after Pujol. In the same speech de la Merced attempted a rewriting of the history of the Franco era by favourably comparing the ideas of Franco's National Movement to Christian democratic ideas. Outrage from the Catalans at any suggestion that they would elect a madman as President was matched only by the rather gleeful attack on the PP by parties of the left and especially by Alfonso Guerra, the political hitman of the PSOE, who declared that as they suspected all along PP represented the friendly face of Spain's fascist tradition – the defender of 'franquismo' – a suspicion when conjured up by the PSOE in previous elections had served it well by escalating fear of the right. The CiU accused the PP and PSOE of creating a moral and intellectual vacuum, within which fascism could actually emerge, by whipping up emotions about corruption and allegations of fascism instead of concentrating on real European issues.

While PP had to apologise for the de la Merced incident on the grounds of her youth and political naivete, it did not dent the confidence of that party which believed for most of the campaign that 'its hour had come' and that the imminent victory would mark a consolidation of Spain's democracy (although for the Socialists this had already occurred in 1982 with the party's first electoral victory and transfer of the reins of power by UCD to PSOE as the main opposition). The PSOE was pilloried at every opportunity for the corruption scandals in its midst, especially the Roldán and Rubio cases and the subsequent ministerial resignations which had recently engulfed the government. The media, which had been responsible for publicizing the cases, provided a lively analysis of these events scanning the international horizons and producing such headlines as: 'Sex for the Anglo-saxons and money for the Latins: scandal hit governments across the Western world'. PP worked hard at making the charge stick that there was a serious problem of corruption, that the situation had deteriorated since the 1993 general election and that González should be held politically responsible for creating an environment allowing such practices to occur. Their argument was made even more forceful by the resignation of the highly respected legal figure Balthazar Garzon, who had been elected to parliament as a leading figure in the PSOE list in the 1993 election with the task of cleaning up corrupt practices in government only to resign shortly before the European elections in frustration at the slow progress of his reform initiatives. González and his supporters stuck to the argument that the party had been infiltrated by self-seekers and that they had a duty to themselves and the country as a whole to eradicate this 'enemy within', thus conveying the notion of a concerned, responsible and statesman-like leader embarking on something of a moral crusade. The PSOE were also not slow in responding with their own personal attacks on PP whenever it seemed appropriate. Thus an attempt was made to stick an allegation on Abel Matutes of involvement in a shady land deal. Charges of attempted vote-buying by the PP were also floated but never with the success of those various allegations levelled against the PSOE. The PP's real credibility problem lay in the image of Aznar who was portrayed by the media as lacking the charisma and oratorial skills possessed by González, and who was caricatured by the PSOE as a rather dull figure with few original ideas on how to run the country or its economy let alone its relations with the rest of Europe. At a rally in Valladolid (Aznar's home territory), González chose to stick the knife in his opponent by rather viciously questioning his suitability for the post of President of Spain. But the public visibility of such vitriol emananting from the normally statesmen-like González, indicated his own neuroticism about the outcome of the election.

Also affecting the direction the debate took during the campaign were the TV debates. The subject of such debates was also to merit some adverse comments by parties. The CiU and IU accused the PSOE and PP of damaging Spain's democratic pluralism by allowing a sort of TV battle of 'gladiators', ie between the heads of the two main party lists — Morán and Matutes — which left out the other political groups. The PP and PSOE for the most part also refused to participate in TV debates alongside HB in the Basque country and Galicia because of its support for ETA violence.

While not shunning contact with HB to that extent, PNV suggested that bomb attacks like the one that killed General Juan José Hernandez in the middle of the Euro-election campaign showed how ETA cynically invited the electorate to cast its vote for HB. IU's campaigns in both the European and Andalucian elections were focused on the aim of breaking the two-party mould of the PP and the PSOE by raising its declared profile to 15 per cent of the vote, ie 2–3 per cent more than the 1993 general election. It predicted, correctly as it turned out that IU, would hold the balance of power and that there was every likelihood that its candidate for the presidency of the Junta of Andalucia, Luis Carlos Rejon, would defeat the Socialist Party incumbent Manuel Chaves. As a consequence it argued that the results of the Andalucian elections were actually more important than those to the EP. PSOE recognized that IU would eat into its support across the country and especially on the left of the party where discontent with the market-orientation of the PSOE government was growing. To try to check the progress of IU which was verified by opinion polls during the campaign, González attempted to discredit the left-wing of the party notably at a rally in Malaga (Andalucia) where he compared its model of socialism to that of Ceauşescu's Romania and contrasting it with that of PSOE which offered a modern social democratic realism after the model of other West European Social Democratic parties. At a rally in Ouiedo (Asturias) Alfonso Guerra tried to convince waverers that voting for

IU would split the socialist vote thus damaging the left as a whole and help the PP. The IU leader Julio Anguita made much of trade union tensions with the government, evident particularly in the disenchantment that had built up in the previous six months over high unemployment and the government's labour law reforms which were aimed at creating a more flexible workforce.

In the midst of such national campaign issues Europe and the EU faded somewhat into the background. Nevertheless, at some local election meetings especially in rural areas awareness of EU policies and the relevance of the elections to the EP grew during the campaign through particular discussions on aspects of policy: the Common Agricultural Policy 'set aside' policy for cereal growers; fishing quotas in coastal areas; transfrontier programmes near to Portugal; and EU steel production policy and the loss-making ENSIDA and HUMOSA steel industries in Asturias. Generally, though, the level of public knowledge and interest in the activities of the EP was very low according to various media surveys and attendance at political meetings (except in Andalucia) reflected that fact. Efforts, especially by Socialist Party candidates to caution against indifference and abstention from voting by a section of the electorate reflected their own special fear that it was the Socialists who would most feel the effects of apathy among the electorate on 12 June. Aznar and PP meanwhile warned supporters against relaxing their efforts (despite their confidence) fearing a repeat of the 1993 general election when the Socialists gained crucial ground in the last few days and scraped through to victory. But both major parties did engage in at least some Euro-posturing to embellish their otherwise rather inward-looking campaigns. Felipe González and Helmut Kohl in a Hispano–German summit kept each other company while other European leaders were busy celebrating the 50th anniversary of the Normandy invasion. The summit served to remind the Spanish public (or at least those who were not already confused by the sight of González posturing with his friend Christian Democrat leader Helmut Kohl, while the PSOE's allies in Germany the Social Democrats were busy trying to defeat him in the elections) that González was also one of the favourite, if not willing candidates, for the EU presidency to succeed Jacques Delors. González publicly and repeatedly refuted the idea during the campaign on the grounds that there was much work to be done at home. In reality, by even declaring himself to be a candidate for the EU job, he would have weakened his position at home and would have been portrayed as a captain deserting a sinking ship.

PP showed that they too had a familiarity with the highest echelons of the European political stage, inviting Giscard d'Estaing to attend and speak at rallies in Barcelona and other venues. However, the PSOE candidate Morán gave short shrift to the PP visitor saying that d'Estaing had blocked Spanish negotiations for entry to the EC in 1981.

The results

With a turnout of 59.58 per cent, electoral interest in the 1994 European elections in Spain lay between that of 1989 at 54.16 per cent and 1987 in which it was 68.9 per cent. However, there were significant regional variations. For instance, the province of Jaén in Andalucia (assisted by strong interest in the regional elections) had a turnout of 75.7 per cent, the highest on mainland Spain while La Coruña in Galicia had the lowest with 50.0 per cent. These elections marked the first time the PP won more votes than PSOE (with a 1.8 million majority) far exceeding its own campaign aim of 0.5 million more votes. In fact, the PP gained more than the combined votes of the PSOE and the Catalan supporters of PSOEs minority government. Secure in his position as leader of the PP as a consequence of the majority, Aznar publicly challenged the legitimacy of the González government. The PSOE meanwhile dropped to a level of support it last attained in 1977–9 when CDS was in power but it insisted that this was just a 'protest vote' and meant that while many of its voters had supported IU or stayed at home its core support was still solid and the others would return once the political scandals had been dealt with and the effects of the improved economy became more widespread.

CiU increased its vote, winning at the expense of the PSOE, (which it overtook in Catalonia for the first time) as well as the CDS whose vote, as predicted, collapsed and lost five EP seats. Rejecting the PP calls for a vote of confidence in the government, 'business as usual' was the message to the González government from Pujol and CiU whose extra seat actually owed as much to the increase in the number of seats for Spain as to its powers in attracting votes.

IU more than doubled its vote with considerable help from disenchanted union members and former PSOE supporters, thus strengthening Anguita's claim to the mantle of the left of the political spectrum. The result reinforced the position of the left wing *guerristas* in the PSOE against González *renovadores* to the extent that they called for a cabinet reshuffle with promotions from among their ranks. The PSOE also lost many seats in Andalucia. This defeat, actually, was more humiliating for González than the losses suffered in the Euro-elections.

In the Basque country, HB lost its European seat while the PNV in the Coalicion Nacionalista gained one, giving it two altogether and suggesting that ETA violence during the campaign had adversely affected HB. As predicted, the Ruiz-Mateos phenomenon had somewhat fizzled out losing the two 'protest' seats, while the Greens and the Andalusian Regional Party lost their seats through the vicissitudes of small-party internal divisions and the fundamental weakness of regional parties in the face of competition from the major party groups.

Conclusion

Notwithstanding a drop in the number of seats they won for the Socialist Group in the EP, when the dust had settled on the elections the PSOE found themselves to be the third largest component of that group, up a place since

Table 10.1   Euro-election results in Spain

	1994			1989		
	Votes	**%**	**Seats**	**%**	**Seats**	**Group in EP**
Popular Party	7,426,189	40.21	28	21.7	15	EPP
PSOE (Socialists)	5,665,537	30.67	22	40.2	27	PES
United Left	2,486,550	13.46	9	6.2	4	Ind
Catalan Party	861,897	4.67	3	4.3	2	LDR/EPP
Nationalist Coalition (Regional Parties)	517,882	2.80	2	1.9	1	EPP
European People's Coalition (Regional Party)	237,521	1.29	–	1.9	1	RBW
Social Democratic Centre Party	182,512	0.99	–	7.2	5	LDR
Basque Party	179,361	0.97	–	1.7	1	Ind
Andalucia Regional Party	139,994	0.76	–	1.9	1	RBW
Galicia National Party	132,051	0.76	–	–	–	–
Greens	107,731	0.68	–	–	–	–
Ruiz Mateos (Financier)	82,069	0.44	–	3.9	3	EDA
Other Regional Party				1.9	1	Green
Others	230,910	2.41	–	–	–	–
Total	18,256,204	100	64	100	60	

Seats: 64 (60 in 1989)
Turnout: 1994: 59.58
         1989: 54.6
         1987: 68.9
Electorate: 31,145,446
Votes cast: 18,554,316
Valid votes: 18,256,204
Invalid votes: 298,112

Source: European Parliament (1994) European Elections, 1994; Results and Elected Members, 15 June.

1989 due mainly to the sharp demotion of the Italian Socialists. Gains in other member states, notably Britain and Germany meant that despite those losses, the Socialists remained the largest group in the EP after all results were declared. A significant reduction of status and influence for the PSOE in Europe was not therefore a likely outcome. (Indeed, it flexed its muscles at the first opportunity by voting against its socialist colleagues in support of the nomination of Jacques Santer as President of the European Commission, thus coming to the aid of Helmut Kohl who was the chief architect of his candidacy.)

In contrast to the PSOE, the position of the PP in terms of seats was considerably enhanced in the European People's Party. The Spanish party was now the second largest segment of that group after the German Christian Democrats, up two places from 1989 due in fact to the sharp losses inflicted on that group by the electorates of Italy and Britain. However, the Spanish gains on the right were somewhat overshadowed by the fact that the EPP still remained in second place overall; the right of the political spectrum in the EP generally continued to be divided and thus weakened by the number of different party groups. So, the advances made by the PP were not likely to result in it being rewarded with significantly more influence in the EP.

CiU and the PNV slightly enhanced their positions numerically in the EP, but perhaps more important for the regions they have been representing was the Spanish Constitutional Court ruling announced during the campaign which strengthened the position of the autonomous communities in their direct dealings with the EU.

'Protest' voting which partly found expression in Spain through the Ruis Mateos group in the 1989 elections found more conventional channels in 1994, although it flourished elsewhere in Europe. Left-wing protest against the widely perceived corruption and ineffectiveness at the heart of the PSOE government found expression in IU, whose chief task was to try to challenge the two-party hegemony in Spain. In the EP, the effectiveness of IU hinged on its ability and willingness to secure post-election alliances. To begin with, it succeeded in securing one of the 14 EP vice-presidencies as did two other Spanish parties (the PP and PSOE).

In conclusion, the elections did not mark a watershed in terms of Spain's presence or influence in the European Parliament. They did however mark a watershed for the PP and the moderate right which for the first time won more votes country-wide than the PSOE, so breaking the 'taboo' which had blocked their path since the days of Franco. It is for this more than anything else that the European elections of 1994 will be most remembered in Spain.

References

A more detailed account of the electoral system for the European elections in Spain is to be found in Almarcha Barbado, A (1993) *Spain and EC Membership Evaluated*, London, Pinter.

Salmon, K *The Modern Spanish Economy*, ACIS, Vol 5, No 1, pp 52–3.

11

The United Kingdom

Neill Nugent

Background

Europe and British politics

'Europe' has been an important and divisive issue in British politics since the EC was constituted in the 1950s. In a manner which has not been paralleled in any other member state, the 'European dimension' has been a source of immense controversy both between the major parties and also within them.

The period between the 1989 and 1994 EP elections saw the European issue loom larger than perhaps ever before. Three aspects of the issue, themselves in practice closely related, principally accounted for this.

First, the Treaty on European Union (TEU) — the Maastricht Treaty — generated considerable political debate and friction. In pursuing a generally minimalist, integrationist stance during the negotiations in the Inter-governmental Conference (IGC) and at Maastricht itself, in securing opt-outs from the Social Chapter and from the commitment to a single currency, and in helping to ensure that the concept of subsidiarity was entrenched in the Treaty, the Prime Minister John Major sought to hold his sceptical party together. In this he was generally successful, for although many Conservative MPs expressed their concern over aspects of the Treaty, in crunch votes during the ratification process the hard-core of Conservative 'dissidents' were reduced to a handful. This hard-core was enough, however, to make UK ratification of the Treaty difficult, for the main opposition parties, though generally supportive of the Treaty, were critical of aspects of it — the Labour Party was particularly opposed to the Social Chapter opt-out, and took advantage of opportunities to register its dissatisfaction on the matter. The government made life no easier for itself by delaying ratification until after the outcome of the second Danish referendum was known — which meant that the final Parliamentary vote was not taken until July 1993: 20 months after the Treaty had been agreed and 18 months after it had been signed.

Second, the 'social dimension' of Community policies and policy intentions was a constant source of friction between the Conservative and Labour parties following Mrs Thatcher's rejection of the Social Chapter at the December 1989 Strasbourg Summit. The Conservatives consistently opposed any extension of social policy at Community level, arguing both that decisions in this policy area should be taken at national level and that Community policy proposals were misguided in that they would undermine economic competitiveness. Labour, rather like the Commission and the governments of most other member states, saw Community social policy as a necessary complement to the more competition-based policies of the Single European Market programme.

Third, the Community's evolving plans for Economic and Monetary Union (EMU) were much to the fore, not least as a source of division within the Conservative Party. Britain entered the Exchange Rate Mechanism (ERM) of the European Monetary System (EMS) in October 1990 – Mrs Thatcher, it later emerged, having been faced with threats of resignation from her Foreign Secretary and Chancellor if she continued to block entry. It was, however, less than a wholehearted entry, and it certainly did not remove EMU from the political agenda; Mrs Thatcher's openly expressed opposition to EMU played an important part in her downfall in November 1990. John Major ensured at Maastricht that no firm commitment was given by the UK to entering the third stage of EMU (which involves the creation of the single currency) when it is projected to begin in the second half of the 1990s; and – to the barely disguised delight of many Conservative MPs – sterling was forced to leave the ERM during the currency crisis of the autumn of 1992.

Each of these three issues – the nature and significance of the Maastricht Treaty, the social dimension, and EMU – were still being much debated up to, and were so during, the 1994 EP elections.

Electoral fortunes

The principal features of the 1989 EP elections were as follows: satisfactory though not outstanding results for Labour – its 38.9 per cent of the United Kingdom (UK) vote and 40.1 per cent of the Great Britain (GB) vote enabled it to defeat the Conservatives in a national election for the first time since October 1974 (the GB vote excludes Northern Ireland); poor results for the Conservatives – their 33.0 per cent of the UK vote and 34.7 per cent of the GB vote was their lowest percentage in any national election in the post-war period; extremely bad results for the Social and Liberal Democratic Party (the then name of what is now called the Liberal Democratic Party) – its 6.2 per cent UK vote and 6.4 per cent of the GB vote signalled a confirmation of the decline that it (in the guise of the Social and Democratic Alliance) had experienced in the 1984 EP and 1987 general elections and seemingly suggested that its hopes for a breakthrough into the electoral mainstream were as far away as ever; and spectacular results for the Green Party – its 14.5 per cent of the UK vote and 14.9 of the GB vote brought it from virtually nowhere (0.6 per cent of the GB vote in the 1984 EP elections). The single member constituency first past the post electoral system, which was used for all seats other than the three allocated to Northern Ireland, produced its customary distortion of ratios between votes cast and seats gained: Labour won 45 of GB's 78 seats, to make it the largest national party group in the EP; the Conservatives won 32; the Scottish National Party (SNP) won one; and the Social and Liberal Democrats and the Greens won none.

For most of the period between the 1989 and 1994 Euro-elections, British electoral politics were set in a pattern whereby opinion polls and local elections (there were no EP by-elections) showed the following: Labour was in the lead, with usually 40–45 per cent of the vote, though occasionally as high as 50 per cent was touched; the Conservatives were struggling, with less than 40 per cent, and in 1993–4 with less than 30 per cent; the Liberal Democrats were usually within 5 per cent either way of 20 per cent; and no other national parties – including the Greens, who rather withered away after the 1989 EP elections – made any significant impact. Within these global figures, an important pattern began to emerge in parliamentary by-elections, with the electorate coming to see the Liberal Democrats, rather than Labour, as the main challengers to the Conservatives in most of the south outside London.

Poor opinion poll and by-election results were crucial to the decision of the Conservative Party to replace Margaret Thatcher by John Major in 1990. Evidence suggests that the decision was correct, for not only did the Conservatives manage to win the 1992 general election, albeit with a reduced majority, but research indicates that an important reason for that win was a lack of attribution to John Major's government of blame for the problems of the British economy: Mrs Thatcher's replacement by Mr Major was perceived by many voters as not just a change of Prime Minister but as a change of government.

As the 1994 Euro-elections approached, talk of repeating 'the trick of 1990' – that is, of replacing the leader – was again being heard in Conservative circles. The main reason for the talk was the same as before: very poor opinion poll ratings, with Labour comfortably ahead in the 42–46 per cent range, and with the Conservatives vying with the Liberal Democrats for second place in the 25–30 per cent range. When local elections in May 1994 confirmed the opinion poll findings, the EP elections looked as though they could become not just the customary mid-term and second-order test of the government, but a real threat to the position of the Prime Minister.

Electoral arrangements

The government made it clear from an early stage that it was not prepared to depart from the electoral arrangements which had been used in 1989: that is to say, all mainland constituencies would be contested on the single member constituency first past the post system, and the three seats in Northern Ireland would, to ensure the Nationalist minority gained a seat, be contested on the basis of one constituency and the single transferable vote.

Difficulties arose with the electoral arrangements when it was decided at the December 1992 Edinburgh European Council meeting that, as part of the general enlargement of the EP which was deemed to be necessary following German unification, the UK would be allocated six extra seats, bringing its total number of seats up to 87. There were three particular difficulties, each of which was related to the short time that was available to make the necessary arrangements.

The first difficulty was the basis on which the seats should be allocated. An easily manageable solution, which many advocated, was to distribute them according to some proportional formula. Not surprisingly, given the Government's traditional opposition to proportional representation (PR), this was rejected in favour of the creation of new European constituencies — five in England and one in Wales.

The second difficulty arose from the decision to create extra seats: how could this be done quickly and effectively? The solution that was chosen was to give the task of creating and redrawing boundaries to specifically created bodies: the European Parliamentary Constituency Committees for England and for Wales. The Committees announced their preliminary recommendations in November 1993 and, following time for the lodging and consideration of appeals, their final decisions in January 1994. Considerable changes were made between the two stages, with the Labour Party, which co-ordinated its appeal submissions to the Committees on a regional basis, seeming to have most success in persuading the Committees to its viewpoint. The Committees' final recommendations resulted in boundary changes in every Welsh constituency and in all but 17 of the English constituencies.

The third difficulty was one that had to be faced by the political parties: where new seats were created there was little time to select candidates, and where boundaries were redrawn the parties had to decide what to do about already selected candidates. In general, the latter problem was dealt with by fitting already selected candidates into those new Euro-constituencies where most of their previous constituencies lay.

The candidates

There were a total of 534 candidates for the 87 UK seats, including 17 in Northern Ireland. The three main parties — Conservative, Labour and Liberal Democrats — contested all of the 84 mainland constituencies. Other parties putting forward a large number of candidates were: the Natural Law Party (followers of the teaching of the Maharishi Mahesh Yogi) — 87 candidates; the Green Party — 84 candidates; the UK Independence Party — 25 candidates; the Liberal Party (Liberals believing they embodied true and traditional British Liberalism) — 20 candidates; the SNP — eight candidates (that is, all the seats in Scotland); and Plaid Cymru — five candidates (that is, all the seats in Wales).

The procedure used by the three main parties for selecting their candidates was similar in some respects and different in others. One similarity was that where contests for the candidacy occurred, shortlists were drawn up by Euro-constituency executives of various kinds from lists of candidates approved by the central party organizations. Another similarity was that the final choices from shortlists were made by ballots of ordinary party members living in the component Westminster constituencies. An important difference was that Labour's procedures offered more opportunity than did those of the Conservatives for sitting MEPs to be challenged and de-selected: in the event, though a few were openly challenged, none was de-selected.

As to the characteristics of the candidates of the major parties, three merit particular mention. First, a very high proportion of sitting MEPs sought to be returned: 25 of the 32 Conservative MPs and 40 of the 45 Labour MEPs. Second, there was the customary absence of well-known or prominent political figures: the most recognizable were two newcomers to European elections – Edwina Currie, the high profile Conservative MP stood in Bedfordshire and Milton Keynes, and Glenys Kinnock, the wife of the former Labour leader, stood in South Wales East. Third, there was no increase in the number of women candidates in winnable seats – a fact which was partly explained by Labour, which required at least one woman to be on each short-list where there was a contest for the candidature, re-selecting most of its sitting MEPs without contests.

The issues and the campaign

Election campaigns in Britain are normally officially conducted for between three and four weeks, but the 1994 EP campaign was truncated when, the week before the campaign was due to begin, the Labour Party leader, John Smith, suddenly died of a heart attack. Each of the major parties announced that, as a mark of respect, they would suspend all campaigning until after Smith's funeral, which meant that the official campaign only lasted for two and a half weeks.

Smith's death had a softening effect on the campaign in that the personal criticisms of party leaders, which are such a part of elections in Britain, were not so prevalent. Labour did not deny itself attacks on what it sought to present as John Major's lack of leadership, but the matter was not pressed as hard as otherwise it probably would have been. As for Labour itself, it had only an acting leader – Margaret Beckett – and the leadership issue was largely sidelined, with the potential leading candidates all agreeing not to announce their candidacy or to openly campaign until after election day.

In addition to John Smith's death and its aftermath (despite the near silence of Party figures themselves on the matter, there was inevitably much media speculation on who would be the next leader of the Labour Party), two other episodes also served to distract attention from the election campaign. First, the death at the end of the first week of the campaign, in a helicopter crash on the Mull of Kintyre, of 29 people, including 25 senior figures in the security services in Northern Ireland, received great media attention and was the subject of extensive comment. Second, in most of the week immediately prior to polling day, media attention was much taken up with the D-Day 50th anniversary commemoration ceremonies: the BBC and the tabloid press in particular gave this massive coverage.

As for the campaign, the main themes were much the same as those which had prevailed in the May local elections: Labour focused on its familiar theme that Britain was ruled by an incompetent, worn-out party, which was led by an indecisive leader who presided over a deeply divided Cabinet and Parliamentary Party; the Liberal Democrats made much the same criticisms of the Conservatives as Labour, but sought to present themselves, not Labour, as the main opposition to the Conservatives in the south, and especially the south-west; and the Conservatives based their defence principally on the grounds that the economy was showing clear signs of recovery, and that in any event all would be much worse under Labour (on whom the Conservatives, not wishing to boost Liberal Democrat credibility, except as Labour fellow travellers, targeted most of their attack).

'European' issues were deliberately kept in relatively low profile by each of the main parties. For the Conservatives, too much focus on Britain's relations with Europe was likely to draw attention to internal party divisions on the matter: divisions which reached up to the Cabinet itself. For Labour, more political capital was likely to be gained by focusing on the Conservative's record in government, than in emphasizing an issue which might, because of Labour's generally pro-integrationist stance, be less than attractive to many voters. For the Liberal Democrats, too much concentration on European issues might arouse voters' suspicions of the long-standing Liberal Democrat advocacy of a European federal system.

Insofar as the parties did set out their positions on Europe during the campaign, they were very much along the lines that had not only evolved gradually over the years but which in many ways had been sharpened during and since the Maastricht debates. The tone of the Conservative campaign was encapsulated in the Prime Minister's Foreword to the Conservative Manifesto, *A Strong Britain in a Strong Europe*: 'We are clear that our national interest lies in Europe. . . . But that does not mean always accepting what our partners want. We will fight for the kind of Europe we want: not a European superstate, but a Europe of nation states, working together. . . . The Labour and Liberal Parties both threaten British people with more centralism, more Euro-spending, more Euro-taxes, more restrictions. They would merge Britain in a Socialist superstate'. Labour's stance was less suspicious than that of the Conservatives, as the title of its manifesto – *Making Europe Work For You* – implied. While emphasizing that Labour would not, as the Conservatives claimed, surrender what remained of the national veto, it was stressed that there was a greater need to take advantage of the opportunities Europe

offered, but to do so not just via market-related policies but also via a much
broader policy framework. In the words of the manifesto 'That is why we
totally reject the Conservatives' attempts to make Britain the low skill, low
wage sweatshop of the European Union. . . . We want an integrated and cooperative Europe, grounded in strong communities with democratic rights
and freedoms for all its citizens. We want a productive and prosperous
Europe, where people have the right to fulfilling employment, full social
rights, a clean and safe environment and security for themselves and their
families.' As for the Liberal Democrats, candidates were briefed by the Party
leadership not to alarm voters by loose talk of the desirability of a United
States of Europe. Much of what the Liberal Democrats had to say was not so
different from Labour, apart perhaps from more emphasis being given to the
need for political reform in the EU so as to make it more effective, more democratic, and more decentralized. Emphasis was placed on the need for Britain to
play a full part in Europe and stress was given to the necessity of undoing the
damage which it was alleged the Conservatives' half-hearted attitude had
inflicted on Britain's interests in Europe. As the Party leader, Paddy
Ashdown, claimed in the Foreword to the Liberal Democratic manifesto,
Unlocking Britain's Potential: Making Europe Work For Us, 'The Conservative approach to Europe has given Britain a bad deal. The UK has failed
to secure its rightful place in Europe. It has failed to make the most of British
membership and take a lead in building the new European Union'.

Beyond the three main parties, other parties pursued a variety of issues and
themes. The national parties of Scotland and Wales proclaimed the political,
economic, social and cultural advantages of independence within the context
of a Europe of sovereign nation states. Votes for the nationalist parties would,
it was claimed, help to bring that independence about. In the words of the SNP
manifesto, which was entitled *Power For Change*, 'A massive SNP vote, and
the election of a strong team of SNP Euro-MPs on 9 June, will not only
strike panic into the Tory Government in London. It will show Europe that
Scotland is serious about becoming a full and equal member of the European
family – and will serve notice of Scotland's intention to take our rightful
place at the heart of Europe.' In Northern Ireland, the Unionist, Nationalist
and other parties advanced their traditionalist positions, without too much
reference to the European dimension of the elections.

The results

The percentage of the electorate turning out to vote on polling day was little
different from five years previously: an average for the UK as a whole of 36.4
per cent in 1994 as opposed to 36.2 per cent in 1989. The highest turnouts were
in Northern Ireland (48.7 per cent), Wales (42.8 per cent), and the south-west
(42.5 per cent), and the lowest turnouts were in the north-west (30.2 per cent),
Yorkshire/Humberside (31.2 per cent), and London (32.7 per cent). Somewhat

Table 11.1   Euro-election results in the UK

	1994			1989		
	Votes	%	Seats	%	Seats	Group in EP
Labour	6,753,860	42.67	16	38.9	45	PES
Conservative	4,248,531	26.85	18	33.0	32	EPP
Liberal Democrats	2,552,730	16.13	2	6.2	–	–
Green Party	494,561	3.12	–	14.5	–	–
Scottish National Party	487,239	3.08	2	2.6	1	RBW
Plaid Cymru	162,478	1.03	–	0.7	–	–
Democratic Unionist Party	163,246	1.03	1	1.0	1	Ind
Social Democratic and Labour Party	161,992	1.02	1	0.9	1	PES
Ulster Unionist Party	133,459	0.84	1	0.8	1	EPP
Others	669,321	4.23	–	1.4	–	–
Total	15,827,417	100	87	100	81	

Seats: 87 (81 in 1989)
Turnout: 36.4% (36.2% in 1989)
Electorate: 43,443,944
Votes cast: 15,827,417

Source: *Results and Elected Members*, European Parliament Directorate-General for Information and Public Relations (adapted).

surprisingly, and for the first time since EP direct elections were initially used in 1979, the UK did not have the lowest turnout of the member states: in both the Netherlands and Portugal the turnout was 35.6 per cent.

As for party political fortunes, the election results were fairly good for Labour, were poor for the Conservatives, and were disappointing for the Liberal Democrats. Beyond the three main parties, other parties, apart from regional specific parties, generally polled badly.

Labour, with 42.67 per cent of the UK vote and 44.24 per cent of the GB vote, gained its highest share of the vote in a national election since the 1966 general election. As compared with the 1992 general election, it achieved an 11 per cent or more swing from the Conservatives in every part of the country apart from Scotland (7.4 per cent), Wales (9.9 per cent), and the south-west (9 per cent). Crucially, in terms of its future electoral prospects, it won seats in East Anglia, the Home Counties, and the south-east: areas that had seemed increasingly to be beyond its reach. Its increased share of the vote as compared with 1989 (up from 38.9 per cent for the UK and 40.1 per cent for GB) enabled it to increase its representation in the EP from 45 to 62. This made it even more than previously by far the largest national party group both in the EP as a whole and in the Group of the Party of European Socialists (PES).

The Conservatives received their lowest share of the vote in a national election since universal suffrage was established: 26.85 per cent of the UK vote and

Table 11.2 Euro-election results in Scotland

	% vote		Seats	
	1994	1989	1994	1989
Conservative	14.5	20.9	–	–
Labour	42.5	41.9	6	7
Liberal Democrats	7.2	4.3	–	–
Scottish National Party	32.6	25.6	2	1
Greens	1.6	7.2	–	–
Others	1.6	0.1	–	–

Seats: 8 (8 in 1989)
Turnout: 37.9% (40.1% in 1989)

Table 11.3 Euro-election results in Wales

	% vote		Seats	
	1994	1989	1994	1989
Conservative	14.6	23.4	–	–
Labour	55.9	48.9	5	4
Liberal Democrats	8.7	3.2	–	–
Plaid Cymru	17.1	12.9	–	–
Greens	2.0	11.2	–	–
Others	1.7	0.4	–	–

Seats: 5 (4 in 1989)
Turnout: 42.8% (40.6% in 1989)

Table 11.4 Euro-election results in Northern Ireland[1]

Candidate	% vote		Seats	
	1994	1989	1994	1989
Paisley, Rev I (Democratic Unionist Party)	29.16	29.9	1	1
Hume, J (Social Democratic and Labour Party)	28.93	25.5	1	1
Nicholson, J F (Ulster Unionist Party)	23.84	22.2	1	1
(Sinn Fein[2])	9.86	9.2	–	–
Clark-Glass, M[3] (Alliance)	4.14	5.2	–	–
Others	4.07	8.0	–	–

Seats: 3 (3 in 1989)
Turnout: 48.67% (48.9% in 1989)

Notes:
1. In Northern Ireland, MEPs are elected by proportional representation from one constituency covering the whole Province. Percentages in this table refer to first preference votes.
2. Unlike other parties which, apart from the Natural Law Party, put forward just one candidate, Sinn Fein put forward three candidates in 1994. The 9.86 percentage given in the table represents the combined Sinn Fein vote. In 1989 Sinn Fein put forward only one candidate: Danny Morrison.
3. The 1989 Alliance candidate was John Alderdice.

27.83 per cent of the GB vote. As compared with the 1992 general election, the Party's vote fell in every part of the country by at least 11 per cent, with the biggest losses being in the south-east (18 per cent), and London, East Anglia, and the East and West Midlands (where in all cases it fell by 16 per cent). The 18 seats which were won marked a decline from 32 in 1989 (and indeed from 45 in 1984). Of the 18 winning candidates, several had very narrow majorities and only two had majorities of over 5 per cent. Amongst the defeated candidates was Sir Christopher Prout, leader of the Conservative MEPs.

For the Liberal Democrats the results were mixed. On the one hand they gained their first ever directly-elected MEPs, with two successes in the south-west. (There should have been three successes in the south-west, but one candidate lost by 700 votes in a seat where another candidate, standing as a Literal Democrat, polled 10,203 votes. This result led to a legal challenge.) On the other hand, the Liberal Democrats' overall share of the vote, which was 16.13 per cent of the UK vote and 16.77 per cent of the GB vote, did not live up to hopes or expectations. To be sure it was much better than the disastrous 6.2 per cent of the UK vote and 6.4 per cent of the GB vote which the Social and Liberal Democratic Party had gained in the difficult circumstances of 1989 (when the Party was seeking to establish itself in the wake of the demise of the former Alliance between the Liberals and the Social Democrats), but it was down by 1 per cent compared with the 1992 general election and by 10 per cent compared with the local elections which had been held just one month before the EP elections. A pronounced feature of the Liberal Democrat vote was its regional concentration, with the range varying from 7 per cent in Scotland, 9 per cent in Wales and 11 per cent in the north-east, to 25 per cent in the south-east and 33 per cent in the south-west. This regionalism does nothing for the Party's claims to be a genuine national party, but it does enable it to win seats: in the 1984 EP elections a more even spread of the vote resulted in the Liberals gaining no seats, despite winning 19 per cent of the total vote.

The nationalist parties of Scotland and Wales had mixed fortunes. The Scottish National Party, with an overall share of the vote in Scotland of 32.6 per cent, gained its highest ever vote in a national election, beating the 30.4 per cent it achieved in the October 1974 general election when it won 11 seats at Westminster. This one third of the vote considerably enhanced the SNP's claim to be the leading challenger to Labour north of the border and also enabled it to win an extra seat in the EP (Scotland north-east being added to the stronghold of Highlands and Islands). In Wales, Plaid Cymru again failed to win a seat. Its overall 17.1 per cent of the total vote masked the customary division between the north and the north-west (where it won 33.8 per cent of the vote in the constituency of Wales North and 25.4 per cent in Wales Mid and West) and the south and the south-west (where its highest vote in the three constituencies was 10 per cent).

In Northern Ireland the results were much as in 1989, with the three sitting MEPs being re-elected, and with the voting percentages being little changed apart from a small increase in the vote for the Social Democratic and Labour Party candidate, John Hume.

Of other parties, the Green Party was the most successful, with 3.12 per cent of the UK vote. This was up from the 1.3 per cent it had gained in the 1992 general election, but considerably down from the spectacular 14.5 per cent it had won in the 1989 EP elections. Only 3 of its 84 candidates managed to poll the 5 per cent that was necessary to save the £1,000 deposit that all EP candidates were required to pay. The main reasons for the Party's decline between the two elections were the improved fortunes of the Liberal Democrats (the Greens had picked up much of the Liberal Democrats 'protest vote' in 1989), the withdrawal from high profile politics of the Party's 1989 leaders, and perhaps an increased 'green awareness' by the main parties. The UK Independence Party won an overall share of 1 per cent of the vote, but an average of 3.3 per cent in the 25 constituencies it contested, and 5 per cent or more in four constituencies. The Natural Law Party gained an overall 0.6 per cent of the vote, and did not come near to saving its deposit in any constituency.

Conclusion: the impact and consequences of the elections

The 1994 Euro-elections in the UK had both domestic and European implications. In the short term, the major domestic implication was to relieve the pressure within the Conservative Party for either a switch in policy direction or for there to be a change in the leadership. The opinion polls before the election had been so bleak — with many projecting the number of Conservative MEPs being in single figures — and Conservative Central Office had so dampened down expectations, that 18 successful candidates could be projected as being not too bad.

In the longer term the principal domestic implications were in terms of the fortunes and prospects of the main political parties. The Conservatives clearly had a long way to climb if they were to re-establish themselves before the next general election: but there was time in hand given that the EP elections might well prove to have been nearer the last general election than the next one. Labour enhanced its position as a potential party of government, not least by the progress it made in much of the south. For the Liberal Democrats the elections were disappointing, notwithstanding the gaining of their first seats in the EP: they did not make the major breakthrough they hoped for, and indeed they looked more than ever to be a third force with limited regional concentrations. In Scotland, the SNP demonstrated that they posed a real threat to Labour in seats which Labour must win if it is ever again to win a general election.

As for the European implications, the UK results acted as something of a counterbalance to the predominant trend in most of the other member states. The increased Labour representation helped to offset the losses which several of the constituent parts of the PES suffered elsewhere — notably in Italy,

France and Spain. In recognition of its numerical strength within the PES Group in the EP, Pauline Green, the former leader of the Labour Group, was chosen to be PES leader in the new Parliament. Paralleling these implications for the PES Group in the EP, the near halving of Conservative representation partially offset Centre Right gains in other member states, notably in Germany, Spain and Italy.

12

Prospects for a European Party System after the 1994 European Elections

Christophe Lécureuil

It is interesting to evaluate the current state of development, role and potential future influence of transnational party federations within the 'European political system' after the fourth elections to the EP, which took place in a new political environment occasioned by the entry into force of the Treaty on European Union. Transnational organizations acquired official recognition through the introduction of Article 139(a) of the Treaty, which states: 'political parties at European level are important as a factor for integration within the Union. They contribute to forming a European awareness and to expressing the political will of the citizens of the Union.' Transnational parties were granted further legitimacy through the establishment of a European citizenship (Article 8 of the Treaty), put into practice through the Council Directive of 6 December 1993 on the right to vote and conditions of eligibility at European elections. The Council Directive aims to give some uniformity to the diverse national electoral systems employed in the member states for Euro-elections by granting European citizens the legal right to vote and be candidates in their country of residence. This encouraged transnational parties to deepen their cooperation and expand their membership. According to F Froment Meurice (EPP, French), the Directive constituted 'the first translation of Europe towards its citizens, which resulted from the creation of a European citizenship contained in Article 8.B of the Treaty on European Union, and showed the 200 million voters that Europe was no longer an abstraction'.[1]

Clearly, these innovations brought by the Maastricht Treaty modified the European political environment. They created a dynamic framework in which transnational party federations developed renewed impetus and ambition. Willy De Clercq, President of the European Liberal, Democratic and Reformist Party (ELDR) emphasized that he wanted to create a 'European Party, as the "backbone" of the political groups in the European Parliament and involving citizens in the integration process'.[2] Similarly, the Party of

European Socialists (PES) positioned its communication strategy around the promotion of a citizens' Europe.

Does the reality match the rhetoric? Some hoped that transnational organizations would develop into the kind of organizations with the kind of functions and roles ascribed to traditional national political parties. It was hoped, for example, that they might perform the grand forum, interest articulation, political recruitment functions associated with member states' parties and that they would be able to provide leadership and representation at European level. The 1994 Euro-election results and the institutional framework of the European Union provide pause for thought. Such views are over-optimistic. So to what extent can transnational party federations, both inside and outside the European Parliament, initiate and contribute to the development of a European party system?

Historically, the three most influential political families of the Western European political spectrum quickly developed into the first pan-European parties in the early 1950s in tandem with the first steps in European integration. These political families were: the Christian Democrats, the Liberals and the Socialists.[3] The establishment of structured transnational groups at the supranational level occurred in June 1953, within the framework of the ECSC's Common Assembly which evolved into the European Parliament. Gradually, new transnational organizations and supranational party groups emerged inside the European Parliament and evolved with the successive enlargements of the European Community.[4] However, early splits and defections among these groups demonstrated that belonging to the same political family – whether on the left or right – did not automatically mean that the component parties shared the same vision of European integration or that they adhered to a single ideological definition of what they stood for. Indeed, as early as 1965, the French Gaullists of the RPR deserted the Liberal Group to found the European Democratic Union, joined in 1973 by Fianna Fáil.[5] Later on, the entry of British Conservatives to the European Parliament underscored divisions over ideological affinity when they did not create a joint Conservative group with French and Irish conservatives, but instead founded another group, the European Conservatives. National political problems as well as the antipathy of other centre and centre-right parties to aligning themselves with British Conservatives also played a role in dividing them from what some saw as their 'natural' ideological allies – the Christian Democrats.

On the other side of the political spectrum, the Communists – trying to come to terms with two conflicting views over European integration – faced enormous difficulties in developing transnational cooperation but eventually managed to form a group in October 1973. On the one hand, encouraged by Italian Communists, the Euro-Communists supported the establishment of a 'European Communism', while more orthodox, pro-Moscow (and hence anti-EC and anti-Nato) French Communists opposed a liberal and federal Europe. These clashes persisted until the late 1980s and resulted in the creation of two separate groups after the 1989 European elections, the United European Left and Left Unity.

These preliminary remarks demonstrate that, at European level, the defini-tion of common political platforms among national parties proved difficult for many reasons including historical differences and specific national contexts. Currently, and although transnational groups have gained in homogeneity, the EP's party groups bring together national political parties with sometimes remote ideological affinities. For instance, the members of the PES group in the EP range from the former Communists of the Italian PDS to the German SPD. The European People's Party (EEP) group has the same characteristic, with member parties from the center-right like the French CDS and the German conservatives of the CSU.

Types, structure and membership of transnational parties

Two types of transnational political organizations can be distinguished at Euro-pean level, which operate within two specific environments and thus have different functions. These divide between the EP's party groups and the trans-national federations. The former are often referred to as supranational parties, the latter as transnational party federations. The EP's groups, which link MEPs from the same political family or tradition on a transnational basis, may be regarded as the most influential transnational political groups, since their members are directly elected, and because they have the potential to influ-ence and shape policy decisions given the growing legislative powers granted to the EP.

Between 1979 and 1989, in the EP the number of groups oscillated between seven and ten, coming down to eight (linking around 100 national parties) again in 1992 when various national MEPs switched party group. Given the increase in the number of MEPs, from 518 to 567 and the entry of new member states to the EU by 1 January 1995, the EP's Rules of Procedure were modified in respect of rules governing the size of a group wishing to gain the official status of a party group. The new rule provides that a political group can be founded on the basis of at least 26 MEPs originating from one member state, 21 if from two member states, 16 if from three, and finally, 13 if the MEPs come from four or more countries.[6]

The functions of these supranational party groups logically revolves around their role and duties within the EP and their parliamentary and executive responsibilities. They are central to the functioning of the EP, since they are involved in the nomination of the President and Vice-Presidents, the Com-mittee Chairmen and other important positions like quaestors and rappor-teurs. In fact, the political groups have similar roles to the traditional work of parties in national parliamentary assemblies. The political groups' position is further enhanced by the fact that the EP's budget provides important funds to finance their activities: in 1990, this sum represented 15 per cent of the EP's total budget.[7] The funds are allocated to each group according to a formula with a fixed minimum amount per political group and a variable sum depending on the number of MEPs and languages used. These funds are intended to cover secretarial activities, but also actions in the field of political information about the role and work of the EP and its political groups.

The second type of pan-European political party is constituted by transnational federations or parties, which gather political parties of the same families and serve as a link between the EP groups and the member parties which are not represented in the EP, or those from non-EU states of similar political persuasion. Party membership includes organizations from European countries which do not belong to the EU but which generally benefit from an association agreement or are likely to join the Union in the future. Again, the three main transnational organizations feature the Christian Democrats, gathered around two structures, the Union of European Christian Democrats (EUCD) and the EPP; the Socialists within the Party of European Socialists (PES), and the Liberals, under the European Liberal, Democratic and Reformist Party (ELDR).

In February 1994, the Christian Democrat sphere encompassed 50 European parties with differing affiliative status and membership. The EUCD/EPP comprised 13 member parties from the EU. Four more Scandinavian parties held the status of 'permanent observers' to the EPP (created in 1976).[8] The EUCD (founded in 1965) itself is composed of 15 member parties and 15 observers, largely representing organizations from Central and Eastern Europe. The principal objective of the EUCD is to develop and enhance its working relations with Central and Eastern European political parties in order to support the current democratic process and the transition to a market economy. At its Dublin Congress on 14–16 November 1990, the EPP also declared the same priority in a resolution stating that 'dialogue and systematically broadening contacts with parties in Central and Eastern Europe is a top priority'. The ELDR is currently composed of 17 full members, three affiliated members from Finland and Sweden[9] and six observer parties from Central and Eastern European countries.[10] Finally, the PES now has 20 member parties, including organizations from the Scandinavian countries which are to join the Union,[11] four associate members from Iceland, Switzerland and Malta[12] and five observers from Israel, Malta, Turkey and San Marino.[13]

In terms of internal organization, the transnational parties have similar structures and organs, which broadly-speaking correspond to a secretariat, an executive and a legislative body in which all the member parties are represented. The EUCD functions around the General Secretariat, the Political Bureau and the Council.[14] The ELDR Party Statutes contain institutional provisions which set up a secretariat (the Bureau), an executive body (the Council) and a legislative assembly (the Congress). Similarly, the PES structure includes a Secretariat, dedicated to administrative questions, a Bureau, which stands for the executive, and a Congress, which meets every two years to adopt the PES general political orientations. In addition, the Socialist Party Leaders hold semi-annual Conferences in order to synthesize general orientations and define common positions on current issues. As an example, on 9 December 1993, the

PES Leaders adopted a Declaration entitled 'The European employment initiative' designed to become the central theme of their European elections campaign.

Despite the fact that transnational parties have now established working structures and internal rules of procedure, generally they all suffer from the same problems as most international organizations. First of all, and due to the very nature of the EU, transnational parties confront a dual political structure which dramatically complicates cooperation as well as their positioning and function. On one hand, as successive Euro-election campaigns have shown, national party politics regularly take over European politics, eventually blocking transnational initiatives to fight on common platforms, let alone implement them at a national level. On the other hand, the transnational 'position' is already occupied by the EP's political groups. Given the fact that MEPs are directly elected by the European electorate, non-parliamentary transnational parties are almost automatically excluded from this privileged relationship with the electorate and national parties. Yet, they do have a role in trying to assist in mobilizing voters to turn out. Secondly, these party federations are financially dependent on contributions from their individual members and from the EP's Groups. This makes it difficult to adopt an independent status and high profile. Furthermore, unlike national political parties, they lack a network to fund and back up their activities. Lack of financial independence clearly limits the possibilities of political action.

Finally, transnational party federations face similar difficulties to those of international organizations when it comes to the question of effective decision-making. Until recently, the decision-making process was characterized by the adoption of decisions on the basis of consensus, implying that the outcome usually corresponded to the lowest common denominator, especially since the number of member parties kept on increasing. In order to raise their profile, transnational federations improved their decision-making systems by introducing majority voting. This facilitated the adoption of common platforms for the 1994 Euro-elections. However, as the 1994 Euro-elections demonstrated, questions of coherence and consistency still arose when member parties became embroiled in and captured by national debates and agenda.

Role and impact of party federations

The activities of non-exclusively parliamentary transnational parties are traditionally confined to two main sectors: to extend their membership outside the Union's scope as mentioned earlier, and to support Euro-elections by drafting common manifestos and coordinating the parties' campaigns in the respective member states. Logically, this activity was favoured by the introduction of direct and universal suffrage in 1979. Gradually it became associated with the official start of the campaign. However, these election manifestos are but part of the official campaign literature. Individual parties produce most of this type of campaign material. For the 1994 campaign, four transnational political groups drafted common programmes and coordinated European campaigns: the Christian Democrats, the Socialists, the Liberals and the Greens.

A comparative study of the main transnational parties' manifestos reveals a few similarities concerning the proposed programmes. First, the manifestos tended to underline general objectives and policies rather than clearly put forward concrete measures to realize them. This follows from the fact that the implementation of manifestos can only be achieved by MEPs and then indirectly if the Commission advances appropriate legislative proposals. Moreover, the content of manifestos necessarily reflects compromises made between the parties during the drafting process. For example, the PES manifesto did not constitute a real electoral programme, but instead 'a framework in which our future policies will be fleshed out', as Willy Claes, President of the Party of European Socialists stated in the introduction to the PES manifesto. He added that it was to be considered as 'an instrument that may be used during the Euro-election campaign by all the member parties, but not as a final point for the campaign'. In fact, the manifesto clearly left it to the member parties whether or not to use its guidelines on employment in the course of national campaigns. French Socialist Michel Rocard acknowledged that the means listed for combating unemployment were not accepted by all the member parties. Indeed, unlike the French Socialists neither the British Labour Party, nor the Greek Socialists (PASOK), intended to make part-time work the campaign priority.[15] The way unemployment was treated in the manifestos generally illustrates this point. The EPP manifesto set the priority to 'combat unemployment through an economic policy based on the principles of the social market economy'. The ELDR manifesto was as vague when demanding that 'unemployment must be a major goal of the Union's social and economic policies', while for the PES, the aim was 'to concentrate all efforts on a massive reduction in unemployment [. . .] through a co-ordinated European strategy'. Clearly, the aim was not to fix the priority, but to achieve agreement on the means to reduce unemployment. A major obstacle to drafting concrete policies by transnational parties lay in the various approaches available to tackle the issue, themselves dependent on a specific national context. In addition, the EP's lack of a right of legislative initiative only reinforces this tendency to promote general objectives. The operational counterpart is almost necessarily absent.

However, while it is easy to criticize the 1994 manifestos as bland, overly generalized, and lacking in operational finesse, the quality has improved compared to past campaigns. This is because the parties have drafted other papers that were relevant operationally which might be considered to be actual electoral programmes. The EPP 'Action Programme 1994–1999', entitled *Europe 2000: unity in diversity* illustrates this move towards concrete policy proposals. The other party federations also published this type of material. The ELDR issued a booklet called *Building a citizens' Europe*. In it, the Liberals put forward specific proposals. The PES adopted a programme entitled *Put Europe to Work*, defining ways of decreasing unemployment in the Union.[16] In future, it is likely that transnational parties will continue to develop these policy-oriented programmes instead of simple manifestos which now seem to correspond more to statements of general principles and objectives than to traditional and effective campaign material.

Another comment regarding the European elections manifestos concerns their ideological aspect. Progressively, it seems that transnational parties tend to reproduce the ideological cleavages which divide these political families in terms of themes and priorities. This is an advantage in that partisan political activity and competition generate new ideas and may foster the electorate's interest. It may prove beneficial to the EP as its powers increase and as it becomes crucial for political parties to commit themselves on concrete European policies. Again, the issue of unemployment illustrates this point. Whereas the Christian Democrats highlighted the need for free competition and enterprise to combat unemployment, the Liberals stressed the desirability of lower company taxation and the Socialists underlined, among other points, the benefits of part-time employment. Compromise will have to be sought but in the meantime, a debate must be initiated to explore possibilities for appropriate action at the EU-level.

However, ideological diversity and plurality does not preclude the parties from identifying and prioritizing issues in the same or a similar way. For the 1994 Euro-election, the PES, EPP and ELDR agreed that priority had to be given to employment, competitiveness and institutional change. But this was not surprising given that first, all EU states were and are affected by the economic crisis; and second, the loss of public confidence in and alienation from national political parties in general and European integration in particular, represented a global and not a peculiarly national trend. Consequently, in order to try and redress disenchantment, the electoral programmes took positions on questions like subsidiarity and the democratic accountability of the Union. Another common feature of the 1994 campaign was the way in which traditional parties Europeanized and accentuated environmental protection in recognition of the impact that this issue had made over the last few years and in the expectation that commitments to improving environmental protection would attract additional support.[17]

As the EP gradually emerges from the role of an 'opposition' institution in the legislative procedure to the role of co-equal legislative partner with the Council, it will have to make clear its priorities in respect of legislation on matters dealing with society choices. Mindful of this, transnational party federations have slightly changed the emphasis of their programmes from an almost exclusive support for an accretion of the EP's powers, (which remains an important goal), to medium- and long-term policy priorities. What were they? They are sketched out briefly below.

The Christian Democrats' five priorities during the 1994 campaign included: the fight against unemployment; the improvement of the economy; actions for the environment; internal security; and peace. Apart from these general policy objectives, the EPP also stressed the need for an improved institutional system and the need to draft a European Constitution, bearing in mind the fundamental principles of subsidiarity, effectiveness and democracy which they insisted should constitute the basis for a Federal Europe respecting national and regional identities. The Liberal manifesto, *Building a citizens' Europe*, included proposals on the completion of economic and monetary integration through economic convergence and tight national budgetary control, the introduction of a social and employment policy and an appeal for an economy based on a sustainable environment. The Liberals highlighted the need for more democracy in the Union, especially through the establishment of a full co-decision procedure between the EP and the Council. The European Socialists' manifesto prioritized job creation, the strengthening of social and economic cohesion, equality between men and women, peace and security, as well as the fight against racism and organized crime. Again, a major feature in the manifesto was the commitment to modifying EU decision-making structures. Stressing that the June election constituted an historic opportunity for the EP to exercise democratic control over the Commission, the PES called for a right of initiative to be granted to the EP, the introduction of a generalized co-decision procedure and qualified majority voting in the Council.

Between bi-polarization and fragmentation

A preliminary remark regarding the 1994 elections results concerns the number of political groups in the EP which increased from eight to nine (see Table 12.1). Two political groups disappeared: the Group of the Technical Right led by J-M Le Pen did not secure enough members to re-form its group and these MEPs are now listed with the Non-Attached, along with three representatives from Belgium's Vlaams Blok and National Front. The 11 Italian members of the National Alliance (former MSI) have not yet initiated any link with the French National Front to form a joint group. As far as the Rainbow Group is concerned, it joined the newly created Group of the European Radical Alliance. At the same time, three new groups emerged: Forza Europa, Prime Minister Berlusconi's party (27 seats), led by Giancarlo Ligabue, the European Radical Alliance, chaired by Frenchman J F Hory and mostly composed of French Radicals with 13 seats out of 19, and the Europe of Nations Group of P De Villiers, who, along with four Danish anti-marketeers and two Dutch members, gained 19 seats in the new assembly. Fragmentation within the French and Italian political lines had a major impact on the EP's overall structure, although the general balance of power between the main political groups was not dramatically affected: the PES Group remains the largest group with 198 members, instead of 180, followed by the EPP Group which now boasts 157 MEPs, as opposed to 162 in January 1994. The ELDR Group

Table 12.1   Evolution of the EP party groups from July 1989 to July 1994

Groups/date	July 1989	April 1992	January 1993	January 1994	July 1994
Party of European Socialists (PES)	180	179	198	198	198
European Peoples' Party (EPP)	121	161	161	162	157
Liberal, Democratic and Reformist Group (ELDR)	49	45	45	44	43
European Democrats	34	–[1]	–	–	–
Green Group	30	27	27	28	23
United European Left (UEL)	28	29	–[2]	–	28
European Democratic Alliance (RDE)	20	21	21	20	26
Rainbow Group	13	16	16	16	–[3]
Technical group of the European Rights	17	14	14	13	–
Left Unity	14	13	13	13	–
Forza Europa	–	–	–	–	27
European Radical Alliance	–	–	–	–	19
Europe of Nations	–	–	–	–	19
Non-Attached	12	13	21	24	27
Total	518	518	518	518	567

1. In April 1992, the European Democrats joined the EPP Group.
2. In January 1993, 20 members of the United European Left joined the PES Group, the others were listed as Non-Attached.
3. The Rainbow Group Members joined the European Radical Alliance.

still remains the third largest with 43 seats, and was joined by the six Italian members of the Lega Nord.

However, the restructuring of the traditional political lines in two member states, France and Italy, as well as the preponderance of the British Labour Party, modified the internal balance of power within each political group. This may lead to important orientation changes (see Table 12.2). The French Right, although it campaigned on a common list for the elections, did not join the EPP Group as agreed before the elections. Fourteen RPR member reformed the European Democratic Alliance with the help of the seven Fianna Fail MEPs, as well as two Greek and Portuguese MEPs. The 27 members of Silvo Berlusconi's majority, by founding the Forza Europa Group, and the poor showing of the British Conservatives (19 members) denied the EPP additional weight. This situation left the EPP dominated largely by the German and Spanish delegations, with respectively 47 and 30 seats out of 157. Similar balance of power changes occurred in the PES as the French Left was returned divided and weakened when the French Socialists lost seven seats. The PES Group Presidency went to Pauline Green, leader of a 63-member strong British Labour contingent which will inevitably dominate the PES even though the next largest national contingent comprised 40 German Social Democrats.

The 1994 Euro-elections confirmed the emergence of a contradictory trend in European politics. On the one hand, the clear bi-polarization of European political life has been accentuated: the two main groups have an absolute majority in the EP. This phenomenon really began during the third legislature when national delegations like the Italian Democratic Party of the left and the British Conservatives aligned themselves with or joined the main groups, namely the PES and EPP. Indeed, small contingents or groups have quite rightly considered that their influence could be maximized within large groups, particularly through the opportunity of securing positions in them for their MEPs as Committee Chairmen and Vice-Chairmen. In the new European Parliament, out of the 20 Committees, the PES Group holds nine Committee Chairmanships, the EPP Group seven, while the European Democratic Alliance, the ELDR, the European United Left and the Greens have one each.[18]

On the other hand, a gradual fragmentation of political representation can be observed at European level, partly due to national political turmoil and proportional representation, but also to a growing anti-European feeling in the electorate. As mentioned, another set of groups has emerged, characterized by their national or single party pattern. These groups are: Forza Europa, the European Democrats, the European Radical Alliance and Europe of Nations. If these political groups do not represent a large number of MEPs as a whole, they do reflect this growing process of fragmentation. As a result, the new EP may be caught by the more/less Europe debate which is currently very much alive in the member states and whose relevance will rise again in view of the 1996 Inter-governmental Conference and its brief to shape the EU's future institutional framework. If some observers believe that this potential destabilizing factor can be qualified by the fact that the two main groups, the PES and EPP, possess an overwhelming majority with a total of 355 votes, whereas an absolute majority can be achieved with 284 votes, the recent narrow margin in favour of new Commission President Jacques Santer clearly demonstrated that fragmentation is also a component of the large and apparently homogeneous political groups. The endorsement of Santer showed that within the same political family or group, divisions could emerge: the 22 votes difference can be attributed to the rather strange coalition which included Christian Democrats, Spanish and Greek Socialists, as well as extreme-right members. Such a combination further demonstrates that transnational party cohesion, even within the EP's structure, is still elusive and chaotic.

Towards a European Party system?

The bi-polarization versus fragmentation process which emerged from the 1994 Euro-elections raises questions concerning the future development and role of transnational parties in the Union. One of the weaknesses faced by transnational parties today in Europe derives from the fact that many of their members see their primary responsibility and accountability in terms of their own member state or national party. It was striking in the 1994 Euro-elections to see that four political groups were founded, or maintained, along national lines for the Gaullist Group. The primary attachment to the national setting, while logical given that MEPs represent a national constituency, still inhibits the emergence of a genuine European party system. Moreover, the 'European ideal' put forward by transnational groups is not always shared by MEPs within the constituent national parties or by the smaller parties in the European Parliament. Sir Norman Fowler, Chairman of the British Conservative Party, which drafted a 'British' manifesto for the 1994 Euro-elections, noted that the 'Tories had not made the commitment to respect the (EPP) manifesto, but would carry out their electoral campaign on the basis of a British Conservative manifesto'.[19] The British Conservatives were particularly opposed to the references and commitment made to the federal structure of the Union, economic and monetary union, and finally, to the social chapter.

In addition, research on what motivates voters to turn-out at Euro-elections regularly suggests that decisions are highly dependent on national issues.[20] Most observers acknowledge that electoral campaigns favour national questions; this is reflected in the media, by levels of public interest and in the political parties' agendas. Euro-elections are widely regarded as national tests of party or personal popularity. This was certainly the case in 1994 in France, with the Presidential election just a year ahead, in Germany, a few months before the general election, and finally in the UK and Spain, where the Prime Ministers' leadership was being challenged. Having said that, it remains obvious that national factors will never be completely eliminated from European ballots.

Another obstacle likely to block the development of transnational parties is their dependence on and accountability to national parties. First, it is important to note that national delegations of MEPs still hold regular meetings, particularly during plenary sessions, to define a national voting position. Consequently, it not uncommon for national delegations to flaunt the group position on certain sensitive issues. Besides, delegations are often 'pressurized' by their national counterparts when questions affecting national interests arise. The fact that MEPs have an independent mandate takes second place on some occasions to national party considerations. This allegiance is further enhanced by the Euro-elections nomination process: candidate nominations are carried out on a national basis by the central organization, which stresses accountability, even if it has often been observed that MEPs tend to gradually develop a European and independent spirit.

Finally, another obstacle to the development of a transnational European party system lies with the fact that the transnational parties do not fulfil the usual roles ascribed to political parties in national settings. They are not the link between the electorate and the government. Obviously, one reason why they are not is that the EU cannot be regarded as a traditional political system with a distinct separation of powers and a majority/opposition parliamentary structure. In these conditions, transnational parties respond to different needs and requirements than do their national counterparts. Moreover, in the absence of a structured institutional framework providing some space for political parties, transnational organizations do not rely on an established network of activists, and consequently lack a social basis to foster their image and activities at the local level. In addition, they are not involved in the day-to-day political life of their constituents, nor is their work structured around an institutional framework and agenda which is widely recognized by the electorate. This situation reinforces the tendency among national party leaders to afford Euro-elections a low status and a matching low level of financial support. Indeed, national political parties have generally been reluctant to commit resources to their European campaigns, due to the such factors as low turn-out, the limited media interest or the absence of key issues. Funding in the member states varies considerably.

In this specific European political environment where transnational parties cannot rely on a direct and privileged link between the electorate and the government, which would provide them with some legitimacy, or on an activist network guaranteeing visibility in the population, transnational parties have to find a 'middle way', where their views and actions can have a positive impact at national party and European levels, both on citizens, political parties and decision-makers. One way of positively using their structure and participating in European integration is clearly to support the integration process by informing and educating the electorate in order to increase awareness. Observers agree on the fact that the low turnouts for Euro-elections partly derive from a weak understanding of the Union system and political life. In this respect, party federations have the appropriate structure and scope to diffuse non-ideological information about the Union. Improved knowledge among the electorate about EU issues might boost turn-out. But these information dissemination, communication and education tasks have to be carried out on a continuous basis instead of every five years, just before the Euro-elections. This idea is reinforced by the fact that national parties have a different agenda and set of priorities, while the EP's groups will increasingly be concerned with their role within the legislative process of the Union. As a consequence, transnational organizations could intervene in the public debate and contribute to the creation of a sense of belonging and of a European political identity through a politically and socio-economically relevant translation into practice of Article 8 of the Treaty on European Union on citizenship. This task would be especially important in respect of future members of the Union and other European countries and would help to develop mutual understanding.

Second, given the different approaches not only to social, economic and political issues, but also to the direction the construction of the EU takes, transnational parties constitute an appropriate platform for the discussion and for the adoption of common positions on key European questions. The ELDR Statutes state that 'the purpose of the Federation will be to seek common position on all important problems affecting the European Community'.[21] Similarly, the PES objectives are to 'establish closer cooperation between members, the primary aim in order to play a decisive role in European integration'. Thus,

Table 12.2   Size of main national delegations within the PES and EPP groups

	Germany	France	Britain	Italy	Spain
PES (198)	40	15	63	18	22
EPP (157)	47	13	19	12	30

the harmonization of national viewpoints and interests represents another fundamental challenge that transnational parties can tackle. This challenge should not be underestimated as political parties must now develop strategies and policies at European level to match the growing importance of the European Union in terms of legislative activity.

Being still relatively free from internal party politics, transnational parties should also use their structures to set up long-term policy planning and think about major questions facing society. They could fulfil in the role of Euro-think-tanks for the national parties as well because the latter focus primarily and inevitably on national concerns. To this end, transnational parties have started to organize meetings prior to European Councils as a means of identifying and defining common approaches to European issues, and also as a way of trying to influence the Councils' debates and decisions. The EPP held a Congress in Brussels on 9 December 1993, during which the Christian Democratic leaders voiced their support for the White Paper on *Growth, Competitiveness and Employment* to be submitted by the European Commission to the European Council on 10 and 11 December 1993. EPP President Wilfried Martens noted that 'the leaders of the EPP expected the European Council to adopt concrete measures to end the economic crisis and begin the democratic and federal deepening of the European institutional system'.[22] Similarly, the European Socialists Party Summit on 9 December 1993 discussed and approved President Delors' White Paper. In this respect, it is worth mentioning that the PES Group of the EP set up a special committee to sketch out new possibilities to create jobs in Europe. The final report was presented to the Essen European Council in December 1994. It is clear from these initiatives that transnational parties can have a direct input into the policy debate and agenda. How influential they are in determining its shape and content depends on many factors including the receptiveness of national leaders and the experience of MEPs, some of whom are or have been party leaders, or hold ministerial or even prime minister's positions in their respective countries.

Conclusion

The European party system is clearly at an embryonic stage. Inevitably, national, ideological and institutional elements have inhibited the development of transnational parties. Given the specific European institutional framework, the role of these federations cannot be strictly analogous to those of traditional,

national political parties. They operate under a different 'constitutional' structure lacking both a central government and a single electorate. In this respect,
the absence of a uniform electoral procedure for Euro-elections, despite Article
138 of the Maastricht Treaty and the De Gucht Report on this question,
further complicates the position of these organizations.

However, change is inevitable for several reasons. First, with more legislative
power and control over the Commission, the EP's political groups will necessarily be more involved in EU policy-making. This will encourage greater
cohesion, discipline, thought and strategic thinking. The status of MEPs and
transnational parties in the member states may rise if MEPs can prove themselves adept at influencing and amending the substance of significant legislative proposals. Second, despite the recent emergence of national-oriented
political groups, major political parties have found it necessary to join European federations in order to preserve their influence. Still, transnational party
federations are dependent on the mixed institutional structure of the EU, being
both intergovernmental and supranational, which reflects on their own structures and activities. This situation also means that their members will certainly be drawn into the current debate on the powers and future of the
Union, which may lead to internal crises and perhaps divisions. In this
context, the future of these organizations will depend partly on the decisions
which will be made at the 1996 Inter-governmental Conference and on the
degree of adaptation of European citizens to the integration process.

Notes

1. European Parliament (1994), *Info-Memo, Special Elections*, DG of Information, Press
   and Public Relations, No 2, 10 February 1994, p 5.
2. ELDR Vade-Mecum 1993.
3. As an example, the International Socialist Movement set up in 1950 a 'Special Committee', gathering the Socialist parties from the future founding member states of the
   ECSC.
4. For further details on the early developments of transnational parties, see Jacobs, F,
   Corbett, R and Shackleton, M (1992) *The European Parliament*, Longman, London.
5. The group then became the European Progressive Democrats.
6. Article 29 of the *Rule of Procedure*, European Parliament, October 1993.
7. Jacobs, F, Corbett, R and Shackleton, M (1992), op.cit.
8. Det Konservative Folkeparti from Denmark, Kansallinen Kokoomus from Finland,
   the Conservative Party of Norway (Hoyre) and Sweden's Moderator Samling.
9. The Center Party of Finland, the Swedish People's Party of Finland and the Liberal
   Party of Sweden.
10. The Federation of Young Democrats and the Alliance of Free Democrats from
    Hungary, the Liberal-Democratic Party from Slovenia, the Hungarian Civic Party of
    Slovakia, the Radical Democratic Party of Switzerland and the Liberal Reform Party
    of the Former Yugoslav Republic of Macedonia.
11. The Finnish Social Democratic Party, Det Norske Arbeiderparti from Norway, the
    Socialist Party of Austria and the Swedish Social-Democratic Workers' Party.

12. The Social Democratic Party of Iceland, the Swiss Socialist Party and the Social Party of Cyprus (EDEK).
13. The Labour Party and the United Workers' Party from Israel, the Malta Labour Party, the Social-Democratic People's Party of Turkey and the Socialist Party of San Marino.
14. After several years of debate, the Political Bureau adopted the new EUCD statutes in 1991. *Report of the Secretary-General of the EPP/EUCD*, Brussels, 14 January 1993.
15. *European Report*, No 1901–11 November 1993.
16. *The EPP 'Action Programme 1994–1999'* was adopted at their Tenth Congress which was held in Brussels on 8–10 December 1993. The Socialist and Liberal initiatives were respectively adopted on 9 and 10 December 1993.
17. See the PES Group newsletter, *Agenda*, No 45, June 1994.
18. This question has regularly brought about criticisms on the 'D'Hondt' procedure, which is used to nominate Committee Chairmen. This mechanism, based on proportionality, means that the majority of positions go to the largest groups.
19. *Agence Europe*, 25 February 1994, p 5.
20. See the pre-European elections *Eurobarometers*, European Commission.
21. Chapter I, Article 1.
22. *Agence Europe*, 11 December 1993, p 5.

13

The Future of the European Parliament

Juliet Lodge

On 21 July 1994 the European Parliament nearly succeeded in denying approval to the member governments' nominee as Commission President, Jacques Santer. At a stroke, within little over a decade, MEPs had turned something that began as a change in internal procedure into a political tool. Paradoxically, it had been M Santer's countryman, Gaston Thorn who, as Commission President, had agreed tacitly to permit the MEPs to stage a kind of vote of investiture following his appointment. This had subsequently become entrenched and incorporated as a treaty amendment into the TEU.

It was perhaps inevitable that newly elected MEPs should try out their right to be consulted on the Commission President. It was indeed proper that they should challenge the nomination of Jacques Santer on procedural grounds. After all, the member governments had made a great deal of noise about promoting transparency and an open EU from the time of the Birmingham summit in 1992. But they had done precious little to realize it. If anything the contrary had occurred. The fiasco over the earlier nomination of M Dehaene at the Corfu summit merely served to undermine the credibility of such claims. The lame excuse that he was too much of a federalist for the UK to tolerate was also shown to be a sham. He differed little in terms of programme from M Santer.

However, the Party of European Socialists was right to take on the issue head on: MEPs had not been consulted over the Commission President. There were consequences for such an omission. These did not merely relate to the subsequent nomination of his fellow Commissioners. Rather, they related directly to: the legislative programme the Commission intended to pursue; the relationship between the Commission and the EP; and more poignantly still to the relationship between the two arms of the EU's bi-cameral legislature – the Council of Ministers and the European Parliament.

The close vote on the Commission President signalled MEPs' intentions to use the opportunities afforded them under the TEU to influence policy priorities and, equally importantly, to embarrass the governments into opening up closed procedures. The close vote was a signal to them that such a situation would not be tolerated in 1999 nor would secrecy surrounding subsequent legislation be lightly accepted: the governments' rhetoric on openness was being unveiled for what it was. MEPs were determined that their views on issues coming up before the 1996 IGC should not be ignored.

M Santer gave an early warning in August 1994 that he expected MEPs to have a greater influence over the appointment of the other Commissioners when he signalled his approval for their 'interrogation' of Commissioners-elect; and that a greater politicization of EP–Commission relations was on the agenda. In the event, the 'interrogations' were lack-lustre and disappointing. MEPs did not cross-examine the Commission nominees effectively. They failed to ask penetrating questions and some, by absenting themselves from the relevant committee's cross-examination, even failed to take the occasion seriously. It was also apparent that some Commission nominees were ill-prepared and unwilling to engage in a constructive dialogue. This was a far from promising start.

The EP responded by publishing a black-list of five Commission nominees: the Irish, Danish, Swedish, Finnish and one French nominees. While it was unlikely that the EP would actually refuse to sanction their appointments, MEPs were determined to flex their muscles and to secure a reallocation of contentious portfolios. Padraig Flynn had already allegedly compromised his portfolio (which included women's and equality issues) by his allegedly sexist remarks on Irish President Mary Robinson, and his support for the anti-abortion lobby in Ireland. By contrast, during the Delors Presidency, he had taken steps to advance aspects of judicial and home affairs. That portfolio had been allocated to Anita Gradin (Sweden) and it was felt that a swap might be appropriate. Edith Cresson (France) while impressive on part of her portfolio covering R&D had, allegedly, 'forgotten' her responsibilities in respect of education, training and youth. The Danish and other French nominees – Ritt Bjerregaard and Yves-Thibault de Silguy – respectively had also not satisfied MEPs. The overall effect of the débâcle was certainly to sensitize both the Commission and Council Presidents to the need to respect the EP's authority.

Santer had relished the appointment to the Commission of high-ranking politicians like Neil Kinnock, for example. He felt that this would add stature and influence to the Commission. Most member states had over the years appointed former prime ministers and government ministers to the Commission. However, it did not follow that such appointees' experience would necessarily enhance the Commission's performance: collegiality could be easily undermined by a lack of cohesion and rivalry. A counter-balance was needed in the shape of Commissioners not only in command of their portfolios but well-informed about MEPs' preferences and concerns. Good communication with the EP's main party groups was seen as essential by some Commissioners who understood the potential for developing a mutually supportive and politically effective alliance between the Commission and the EP.

A Commission comprising national heavy-weight figures and headed by a relatively weak Commission President is more likely to find individual Commissioners attracting media attention and political fire. They could compete with the President in some respects and certainly might be expected to develop a more overtly ideological relationship with the major parties within the EP. This would have important consequences for the EP–Commission relationship in particular and for inter-institutional relations in general. It could also lead to a clearer prioritization of policy issues if competition within the Commission became apparent in the public domaine. Certainly, member governments would find it more difficult to conceal their preferences. Interest in subsequent Euro-elections might also be enhanced. Against this, intra-Commission conflict could have negative repercussions on the development of the EU and on the promotion of coherence and efficient, effective policy-making and the transformation of the EU's institutional structure at a crucial point in its development. A fine balance would need to be struck between constructive conflict and conflict resolution and politically expedient opportunism practised by governments keen on maintaining the *status quo* or rolling back integration.

The developing relationship between the Commission and the EP in the run-up to the IGC will be particularly sensitive and important: sensitive in terms of testing each other's resolve to work constructively in the promotion of democratic, open and coherent political interaction to a common end; important in unveiling the opportunities for the development of a system of government for the EU commensurate to the tasks facing it. Both need to work together to maximize the impact of their inputs on the IGC's agenda and to show themselves as capable, authoritative, credible and trustworthy political actors to the public in whose eyes they have been roundly villified over the years, none more so than during the Maastricht ratification processes, in many states to the detriment of the development of a common will.

Inter-Governmental Conference (IGC)

For the first time in the history of IGCs, the European Parliament had secured two seats for itself at the IGC negotiating table. This placed it in a unique position to inject its views and priorities into the deliberations. It also afforded it the chance to ensure that inter-institutional and constitutional issues should not be swept aside on the specious grounds that further enlargement would impel yet further revisions to the institutions' composition, functions, powers and inter-relationship.

The EP's future depends upon its abilities to act politically – through the concerted action of its party groups – and to maximize its role through the exploitation of technical provisions. Indeed, the somewhat artificial distinction between political (and hence often sensitive) issues and technical matters

Table 13.1 Composition of European political groups by member state

Political group	B	DK	F	G	Gr	Ire	I	Lx	NL	P	Sp	UK	Total
Party of European Socialists	6	3	15	40	10	1	18	2	8	10	22	63	198
European People's Party	7	3	13	47	9	4	12	2	10	1	30	19	157
Liberal, Democrat and Reformist	6	5	1	–	–	1	1	1	10	8	2	2	37
European Unitarian Left	–	–	7	–	4	–	5	–	–	3	9	–	28
Forza Europa	–	–	–	–	–	–	27	–	–	–	–	–	27
European Greens	2	1	–	12	–	2	4	1	1	–	–	–	23
European Radical Alliance	1	–	13	–	–	–	2	–	2	–	1	2	19
Europe of Nations	–	4	13	–	–	–	–	–	–	–	–	–	19
European Democratic Alliance	–	–	14	–	–	–	–	–	–	–	–	–	14
Non-attached	3	–	11	–	–	–	18	–	–	–	–	1	33

(such as budgetary questions) is becoming increasingly murky. Policies have budgetary implications. The European Parliament's role in budgetary matters was, in the past, a vehicle for securing and then augmenting its rudimentary legislative influence and authority. This distinction no longer makes sense: the idea that the EP should be excluded from influencing policy decisions in general as a matter of course rather than on the say-so of the member governments must be abandoned in favour of recognizing its role as one arm of a functioning bicameral legislature. The balance of authority between the two arms may need changing and will be the subject of argument but no plausible case can be made any longer for delaying the entrenchment of a bicameral system. Only then can the requirements of efficiency, effectiveness, responsiveness, democratic legitimacy and openness (set forth in the 1980s by Spinelli and then by the Dooge committee and post-Single Act reports – such as those of Martin and Herman) be met.

Clearly, the EP needs to use the IGC in order to show that it is worthy of a place at the negotiating table and has realistic contributions to make to the process of consolidating the EU. It also needs to demonstrate a clear grasp of the complexities of the technical problems besetting the legislative processes under the Maastricht treaty reforms and show how these might be addressed in order to advance transparency and efficiency. In short, it must play a key role in reasserting the principle of a unitary system (the principle of *unicité*) in order to augment the EU's capacity to act into the next century. Its tasks therefore divide into two broad but interdependent categories: one relates to the agenda setting and political priorities, the other to the technical facets of the legislative processes. The inter-connectedness can only be properly recognized when the artificial separation between financial, budgetary and legislative matters has been erased and the pillar structure replaced by a single text. At the heart of this is the need to insist that all legislative matters should be subject to judicial review. This is perhaps the only effective way of ensuring openness.

Setting the political agenda

Aside from institutional and constitutional issues regarding power-sharing and the respective roles of the legislative bodies and consultative organs like the ESC and Committee of the Regions, the European Parliament must address and prioritize a series of policy matters. It must do so without losing sight of the overall need to enhance democratic accountability, legitimacy and open government at all levels of the EU's activities.

Without openness, the notion of citizens will remain an aspirational rather than operational goal. Too many critics are still able to claim that people in the EU are its subjects rather than its citizens. This is not merely a sophist point but relates to the view that uninformed individuals will always be subjects whereas those educated about government and society are empowered to participate as citizens in the socio-economic and political life of society. For the EU, which never aspired to educate individuals directly about its activities, their rights and obligations, the crux of the problem of public perceptions of the EU relates to public concern and suspicion as to both the legitimacy of the EU institutions to regulate their lives and the rightness of measures advocated and introduced through the EU. The presentation of the EU as meddlesome rather than as protective or facilitative creates a negative impression of the EU which has yet to be effectively counteracted. This is something that MEPs, as mediators between 'the government and governed', have to address both through their legislative activities and directly through the kind of issues they put on their own agenda and through the medium of their parties. While MEPs can be petitioned and receive and answer voters' and citizens' complaints about all manner of issues (many of which they have no power whatsoever to redress, not least because they fall outside the EU's competence), they also need to be seen to be effective in responding both to citizens' complaints and views and to those of lobbyists and pressure groups. Their own national experience may inevitably colour their response.

The possibility of citizens complaining against limited EU administrative acts is provided for in the new post of the Ombudsman (Millar, 1994; Casini *et al*, 1994). The EP's initial selection resulted in a deadlock between two candidates shortly before enlargement. The process was then re-opened in the expectation that countries – like Sweden – well-experienced in such matters would provide further candidates. However, somewhat exaggerated expectations of the relative openness of Scandinavian societies and systems of government compared to some of the older member states may yet be disabused.

From a political perspective, the EP's priorities must correspond in some measure to those of the public. If combating environmental decay and unemployment are high on the public's agenda, then MEPs must make an issue of them. To argue that the EP cannot be as effective as it may like in these areas because of its limited powers is a fair point. But it is also a lame one. MEPs have to force such issues on to the governments' and Commission's agenda and into the public arena. This means that they must take seriously not only their legislative responsibilities but their obligation to be the grand forum of the people and give voice to their concern.

This will inevitably mean that MEPs will have to risk embarrassing the governments at times: confrontation is a necessary part of the democratic political process. It is not to be equated, as it has been for too long and so often in the EC, with irresponsibility on the part of MEPs, thereby negating their legitimate quest to influence policy outcomes: something that could only be achieved in the past through the modest institutional reforms epitomized by the cooperation and latterly the co-decision procedures. Nor is it realistic any more to claim, as governments have done in the past, that MEPs' resistance or objection to their views and priorities renders them unfit to assume legislative power. This battle has been won. The TEU confirms that.

MEPs have a legitimate right to exercise genuine legislative functions and authority. Indeed, not until they did so through the cooperation and co-decision procedures did the efficiency and speed of the legislative process appreciably improve. However, it is not always clear to the people that MEPs do have such an influence and that their views, and notably their objections and amendments to either Commission or Council proposals, have altered policy outcomes in a particular direction. The ideological orientation of any input by the EP is also often lost in the public eye. This is partly because compromise and therefore cross-party voting typifies the process when MEPs succeed in amending draft legislation. It is also partly because the process itself is tedious, ill-reported, and is often concerned with technical matters. In the normal course of events, the fate of a government, or of a Commissioner, does not hang on the outcome of what MEPs do: their activities therefore seem to lack substance and even the presentation of successful amendments to policy initiatives seems to lack the cut and thrust presumed to exist in domestic politics.

Presentation

Presentational problems need to be addressed not merely to justify MEPs' existence and activities to the other institutions and the public but because much of MEPs' work does have an impact on the legislation finally adopted and implemented in the member states. MEPs' amendments are often in the public interest, something which is all too rarely apparent. Legislative outcomes are too often presented by the media as the product of the Eurocracy which is portrayed as impervious to rational argument, somewhat conspiratorial and lacking in transparency. However, it is difficult to see how MEPs can do much to imprint their stamp on those outcomes so long as the policies lack voter/public appeal and so long as the necessarily consensual support for them masks both their ideological inspiration and direction and so long as what they do is not clearly seen to be linked to policy outputs from the Commission and the Council. Two problems inhere in this: one concerns the presentational matter of the media. The other relates to inter-institutional relations in general and to the relationship in terms of policy initiation between the EP and the Commission.

The public neither identifies with MEPs as individuals nor with the EP's party groups as parties. Ideological affinities are obscure or non-existent for the most part. Accordingly, the minority, extremist groups tend to gain more than their fair share of publicity because their polarized views (and or obnoxious actions) stand out from the mainstream of political life. This detracts from the humdrum daily business both of the EP and also from that of national parliaments whose tedious business is easily obfuscated by media attention on governments, their personalities and political parties. But capturing media attention on a consistent basis will not, by itself, necessarily improve the status of MEPs in the public mind and — if a link between exposure to information

Table 13.2   Turnover in the 1994 Euro-election: new members and re-elected members

	B	DK	D	Gr	E	F	Ire	I	L	NL	P	UK	EU
New MEPs	12	10	53	17	35	56	7	66	5	15	16	33	325
Re-elected MEPs	13	6	46	8	29	31	8	21	1	16	9	54	242
Total	25	16	99	25	64	87	15	87	6	31	25	87	567

[1] The figures are calculated on the basis of MEPs actually elected and named substitutes for those elected in more than one constituency, as in Italy. Some of the 'new' MEPs were members of previous parliaments.

Source: The European Parliament, 1994.

Table 13.3   Women MEPs

	B	Dk	D	Gr	E	F	Ire	I	L	NL	P	UK	EU
1989 (518 MEPs)	4	6	25	1	9	19	1	8	2	7	3	12	97
%	17	38	31	4	15	23	7	10	33	28	13	13	18.5
1994 (567 MEPs)	8	7	35	4	21	27	4	9	2	10	2	16	145
%	32	44	35	16	33	31	26	10	33	32	8	18	25

Source: The European Parliament, 1994.

and turning out to vote does exist – will not necessarily bolster turn-out at the next elections.

In addition, the stature of MEPs affects media interest in them. Well-known national politicians and personalities enjoy immediate media recognition and can expect their activities and later their record to be reported. Younger, newer, less experienced MEPs are less able to command media attention immediately. Securing it is far from easy. The degree of continuity in the EP's make-up helps to build up an 'institutional memory' which can be exploited as necessary to capitalize on the achievements of the outgoing Parliament. A relatively high proportion of former MEPs were returned in the 1994 Euro-election to the EP from Belgium, Spain, the Netherlands and the UK (see Table 13.2). The proportion of women members – often regarded as among the most active and effective of MEPs – also rose (see Table 13.3). Confident MEPs may be expected to be well-placed to command media attention when they seek to promote a public discussion about disagreements with the Commission and Council members. But the presentation of the EP's work is not simply a product of the personalities and experience of its MEPs. Structural and procedural rules can impede and be used to inhibit effective communication. MEPs and the European Parliament's parties have a major presentational problem which is tied to the inevitable difficulties in creating effective inter-institutional legislative relations among emergent parties within an emergent polity which is itself undergoing modification in structure, membership, competence and expectations.

Inter-institutional relations

The Commission is supposed to exercise its functions in complete independence of national governments and other agencies, including the EU institutions. In practice, the individual independence of Commissioners is confirmed through the oath they swear before the ECJ. The collective independence of the Commission is assumed rather than demanded. Initiatives are supposed to reflect the common good and represent an attempt to upgrade the common good. The autonomy of the Commission is rightly prized. But the main institutions have a symbiotic relationship and their mutual dependence should be acknowledged and effectively developed. In order to do so, governments need to be clear why they are changing the parameters of the organization, how they are doing so and what the actual and intended effects are. If the EP seeks, as it is, a closer link with the Ombudsman, it must not be assumed that it does so for the simple, cynical reason of wanting to exploit its authority and power. Rather, the EP, among others, embodies a set of albeit inchoate beliefs about the nature of democratic government and the appropriate nature of links between the governed and the government. This needs to be made explicit. Arguably, that is something that the political parties within the EP should try and do, assisted by those in national parliaments.

Such a debate might help to ensure that European issues in general and Euro-election issues in particular lose their quintessentially parochial bias. The 1994 Euro-elections did not discuss the big issues of the day. This can be explained in many ways. Some would argue that the enormity of the problems posed by the changing continent elude public and national candidates' comprehension. Some would say that politics is essentially about the day-to-day management of issues: it is not about the projection of visions and ideas. If that is so, then Europe — however it is defined — will be nothing more than the expression of *ad hoc* decisions by assorted politico-economic élites.

The European Parliament: defining Europe

The European Parliament's members directly involved in the IGC preparations are keen to ensure that the IGC tackle the EU's legitimacy crisis by making it more open, transparent, effective, accountable and understandable to the public. MEPs have not wavered in this goal since the 1980s. But if headway is to be made, they need to ensure that the EU's objectives are clearly spelt out. If they are, then parties can orient themselves and their own goals to a set of principles and commitments shared by all the member states and which all accept constitute the foundations of the EU.

All the hype that surrounded the completion of the Single Market obscured the fact that behind European integration was the desire to forge and maintain a peaceful environment as a precondition of democracy and prosperity, shared endeavour and the realization of a European voice in the world. All the arguing over the definition of subsidiarity has also obscured the EU's objectives and increased public dissatisfaction with and suspicions that governments, at any level, were acting in an arbitrary, unaccountable and unresponsive manner. Some member governments seemed exceedingly reluctant on legal and political grounds to entertain the idea that the EC should accede to the European Convention on Human Rights and Fundamental Freedoms. Not surprisingly, debates about restoring or creating a civil society within the member states and at EU level seemed unconvincing. Publics fell easy prey to rhetoric as to the allegedly pernicious effects of over-centralized, European integration. The EP and its parties might confront this by trying to inject clarity into new (at Euro-level) concepts of citizenship given MEPs' avowal that they are the representatives of the people, and, if necessary, seek to re-insert the 1990 Martin declaration on human rights (put to but rejected by the Maastricht treaty negotiators) into the EU treaties. Similarly, they might capitalize on the commitment to combat racism, xenophobia (the subject of a Joint Declaration by the Parliament, Commission, Council and Member States in June 1986) and the Franco–German initiative on this advanced at the Corfu European Council in 1994. The PES suggested that they might seek amendment of Article 6 of the Treaty prohibiting discrimination on the basis of nationality by adding 'sex, age, race, colour, creed or sexual orientation'.

If MEPs are to leave a greater and positive impression on the public mind with a view to securing higher turn-out and increased legitimacy, then they must also address the issue of the electoral system. A uniform electoral procedure might be introduced for the 1999 elections or those in 2004 if MEPs secured a revision to the relevant clause in favour of a qualified majority rather than a unanimous decision on this as part of the IGC 1996 revision process. MEPs must also ensure that they not only seek a rationalized and simplified legislative procedure based on co-decision, but that their parties are fully equipped to avail themselves of the rights, obligations and responsibilities that go with co-decision. If they do not, they will inadvertently undermine themselves and exacerbate the legitimacy crisis. They have a key responsibility to realize a people's Europe.

Towards a political union?

This begs the question, what is new about integration in the 1990s? The level and scope of integration and the realization of European Union have changed. But perhaps one of the greatest changes and challenges lies in the aim of personalizing integration, of bringing the EU closer to the people; of realizing the notion of EU citizenship in a supranational system that continues to transform itself and to seek the realization of liberal democratic ideals. Article F states:

1. The Union shall respect the national identities of its Member States, whose systems of government are founded on the principles of democracy.

2. European Convention for the Protection of Human Rights and Fundamental Freedoms signed in Rome on 4 November 1950 and as they result from the constitutional traditions common to the Member States, as general principles of Community Law.

3. The Union shall provide itself with the means necessary to attain its objectives and carry through its policies.

A qualitative change in integration took place at Maastricht. Internal and external factors have propelled it into an uncertain future where even greater importance than ever attaches to its ability to maintain and enhance its capacity to act internally and externally. Institutional reforms must not only satisfy this basic imperative but accord with ideals expressed in the Common Provisions of the TEU. Article A states:

> This Treaty marks a new stage in the process of creating an ever closer union among the peoples of Europe, in which decisions are taken as closely as possible to the citizen.

While there may be an overriding imperative, it must not be assumed that there is consensus over how it should be addressed. Several competing, though not necessarily mutually incompatible images of what the EC, or EU, is or should become are under discussion. Early enthusiasm for enlargement has been replaced by a more realistic assessment of the implications for managing the EU's affairs. In 1993, the Commission boldly qualified its endorsement of enlargement to Central and Eastern Europe by stating that further expansion could not be allowed to deter deepening or to dilute the Union's capabilities and capacity to act. Equally importantly, despite the delays occasioned by the ratification of the TEU in the UK, Germany, and especially in Denmark, France and Ireland, the underlying commitment to union remained. Governments made as much political capital out of prevarication as they could but the message was clear: further integration was expected and endorsed. None of the prevaricators came up with an alternative model of future development. This confirmed the impression that they were cynically exploiting the situation to deal with domestic discontent: the TEU was a convenient scapegoat on which to vent dissatisfaction with a whole range of government policies. At the same time, the question of public consent to European integration was raised. In the past it had been implicitly assumed to exist. Opponents, some of whom pushed significant financial resources into disinformation campaigns, exploited scepticism but did little to inform the public.

A transparent Union closer to the people?

Criticism of the Commission's presentation of EC policies grew as the ratification of the TEU became increasingly fraught. The plea was for greater clarity and transparency. Yet, this contradicted governments' earlier insistence on the Commission keeping out of the public fray in the member states – and conforming, therefore, to the role of an apolitical technocracy. The Commission was and remains the wrong but an easy target: the Council, until occasionally under the Danish 1992 Presidency, met in secret. Its deliberations were, and largely remain, far from opaque and open to public scrutiny even though the Council acts as an arm of the EC's legislature, and arguably its decisive arm. Moreover, even if its sessions were all held in public, it would not be appropriate for it – if democratic practice is to be respected – to allow it to evade sharing power and responsibility for legislative outcomes equally with the people's elected representatives in the EP.

Suggesting that subsidiarity overcomes the need to create effective, democratic, open and accountable legislative procedures is disingenuous. The question of subsidiarity and of ensuring that the EU only tackle those issues that could not be better tackled by the member states at the lowest levels of responsible government complicates matters but should not be allowed to obscure the need to address the issue of universal co-decision. The check on the potential abuse of power contained in the relevant treaty article is interesting but insufficient. The TEU repeatedly stresses that the Community and its institutions shall act only within the limits conferred upon them. Article 3b states:

> In areas which do not fall within its exclusive competence, the Community shall take action, in accordance with the principle of subsidiarity, only if and in so far as the objectives of the proposed action cannot be sufficiently achieved by the Member States and can therefore, by reason of the scale or effects of the proposed action, be better achieved by the Community.

> Any action by the Community shall not go beyond what is necessary to achieve the objectives of this Treaty.

At the same time, the federal idea of exclusive and concurrent competence is recognized. This presents the Commission with the need not only for self-censorship and for stringent appraisal of its intentions. Policies cannot be simply justified in terms of their implementation of a given treaty goal. Instead, they must be justified in terms of whether supranational action is legitimate. States may therefore contest even more the purpose of EU policy on domestic political grounds rather than on the basis of their intrinsic merits or otherwise.

The Commission has been given contradictory signals. On the one hand, it is supposed to make the Union/EC more transparent and bring it closer to the people. On the other hand, the expansion of Union competence into the internal and external arenas as well as into sensitive economic and financial sectors coupled with concern over subsidiarity in practice, led the Commission to propose a classification system for confidential documents passing between the institutions and the member governments. The European Parliament's Legal Affairs Committee found the proposed classification of information 'whose unauthorised disclosure could be detrimental to the essential interests of the European Communities and of the member states and which therefore must be protected by appropriate security measures' into three categories: TOP SECRET, SECRET and CONFIDENTIAL, too vague. It argued that it left too much discretion to the authorities in deciding the classification. Moreover, it was criticized as being unlikely to bring the EC 'closer to the citizen'; and as potentially reinforcing the power of national governments in that it gave to national officials the task of vetting officials handling classified information and so could seriously compromise the independence of EC officials. The EP objected too that it had not been accompanied by a proposal for a Freedom of Information directive to safeguard citizens' rights on access to EU information. Clearly, however, the subsidiarity debate which had inspired the proposal, raises even more concerns about the relationship between national and supra-national authorities and highlights continuing suspicions that member governments are trying to evade public scrutiny. It behoves MEPs to tackle these issues. There is no longer an overwhelming need for MEPs to be overly sensitive to suggestions that if they contest what governments do or fail to do, those same governments will deprive them of further powers. They may. But the EP has come of age and is sufficiently powerful to be able to ride out any moves that patently frustrate the goal of open, democratic, effective, accountable and responsive government.

A People's Europe

During the 1980s and early 1990s, the idea of a People's Europe (as one of the tangible and not merely symbolic advantages of the Single Market phase in integration) has not been sufficiently publicized in an intelligible and relevant way or clearly enough presented to engage the public imagination. The replacement of earlier efforts to promote integration by regulations and technical norms through the mutual recognition of standards, qualifications and practices and by focusing on a limited number of sectors benefited corporate cross-border networking and the goal of realizing the Single Market. Its ramifications were felt outside the business community and outside the territory of the EC where the Community had begun to consolidate and politicize its international identity. But inside the EC, it was questionable whether people not directly engaged in EC policies and programmes were aware of the EC and its policies let alone identified themselves in any positive way with the Community. The multitude of initiatives and non-structural fund schemes designed to enhance mobility, the use of human resources and to promote mobility certainly took off but they remained visible to a small minority. Moreover, an instrumental switch in loyalty by the beneficiaries could not be assumed or demonstrated. Few saw themselves as EC citizens. As the EC inched towards realizing the goal of an ever closer union, the issues of the appropriateness, proximity, visibility, tangibility, transparency and legitimacy of the EC and its institutions had to be faced. It was no longer enough to claim that the EC rested on the direct legitimacy conferred through Euro-elections on the EP and the indirect legitimacy possessed by the Council. It was argued that popular consent was necessary to underpin the Union.

The Adonnino Committee set up by the Fontainebleau European Council in

1984 outlined measures to promote a sense of identity for people in the EC. These included proposals on rights for citizens, culture, youth exchanges, health and social security, symbols like the flag, anthem, passport, common driving licence, and educational and labour opportunities. In short, the idea was to go beyond symbolism to tangible political and social rights to consolidate the idea of common membership in a common venture. Precise obligations as a counterpart to rights have yet to be specified. A Union based on the EC in which the Four Freedoms are meaningful inevitably has to be recognized as a political union. The concept of citizenship is essentially political and highly contentious given the linking of citizenship with the issue of who is sovereign over those citizens. The notion of citizenship in the EU goes beyond the earlier idea of full-time workers enjoying labour mobility and entitlements to social security wherever they worked in the EC. It builds on the social policy (including its provisions on sexual equality and to promoting opportunities for special groups like young unemployed, disabled etc), the Social Chapter and the commitment to social and economic cohesion to embrace a concept of shared citizenship and multiple loyalty holding common to federal systems. Subsidiarity is being applied here. It remains the right of states to confer or deny a status which then automatically grants a person EC citizenship.

The rights derived from this status are mainly those of labour mobility; the right to move and reside freely within the territory of the member states; the right to vote in and contest municipal elections (in states in which citizens are resident but of which they are not nationals) and in elections to the EP. Beyond that Union citizens have the right to be protected, when in third states, by the diplomatic or consular authorities of any member state, on the same conditions as that state's nationals; the right to petition the EP; and the right to apply to the Ombudsman. The rights of minorities are not (yet) explicitly recognized but deliberations on these issues and the associated issues of the status of legal immigrants and genuine political refugees, and the development of immigration policies under the Justice and Home Affairs pillar of the TEU mean that even more delicate questions need answering. It is inconceivable that this embryonic conception of Union citizenship will not be progressively expanded during the next two decades. MEPs must play their part in this.

Towards a polity?

The next decade poses many challenges to the European Union. These are born of internal and external factors. They are also a consequence of the need for supranational, national, sub-national and regional as well as non-governmental actors in the private and public domain to adjust to the new opportunities opened by the progressive, if uneven, realization of the Four Freedoms. Perceptions as to the appropriate level of action in pursuit of or in implementing policies are compounded by the realization that supporters and rivals may lie outside traditional boundaries: mobilizing a cross–border/transnational alliance (for instance in Ireland or across the Franco–German border) may be the precondition of success whether an actor wants to block something envisaged by supranational actors (such as the Commission) or to capitalize on non-structural fund programmes which require cross-national cooperation. This change in the level and scope of actor coalitions is reflected in élite attitudinal changes towards the EU. The issue is no longer whether the EU is a 'good' or 'bad' thing, or whether disappointment would result in its disintegration. Rather, the EU is accepted as a given frame of reference and the frame within which policy must be initiated, evaluated, pursued and implemented. The overall consequence is a rapid multiplication of the potential number of actors at EU level. The management of the proliferation of actors both by those relatively new to the EU scene as well as old hands and the EU institutions themselves adds to complexity and poses additional challenges to both the member governments and the EU's institutions in terms of supranational governance.

The old issues posed during the European Parliament's deliberations on the EUT remain as valid today as they were almost a decade ago. There must be an increase in the efficiency, effectiveness, accountability, democratic responsiveness and openness of the institutions to enhance their capacity to act in a coherent manner internally and externally. This means that the questions of overload must be tackled and the autonomy of bodies within the institutions themselves safeguarded. For example, a balance must be struck between the guiding role of the EPC Secretariat and the Presidency in respect of the Common Foreign and Security Policy (CFSP) in particular and of EC/Union participation in international diplomacy in general. A psychological reorientation is necessary among decision-makers at all levels to ensure that they see themselves as engaging in the same exercise, as acting in the name of the Union. If they are unable to do so, they will not only inhibit effectiveness but undermine the credibility of their stated goals. The CFSP will not advance much beyond posturing unless some tough decisions are taken to limit the scope of EC/Union roles and to cede claims to absolute autonomy or independence when neither are logistically viable or operationally feasible: the Atlantic nexus cannot be denied. A premium must therefore be set on creating an effective working relationship with it. The same generally applies to interaction among policy-making bodies within the EU and the member states.

From integration to union?

In the past, it was somewhat glibly assumed that as attention switched (at least in part) to the supranational level, there would be a zero sum loss of power to the national government and the state would begin to wither away at a pace dictated by the increase in the scope and number of supranational functionally specific communities. Supranational integration, it was assumed, would erode national sovereignty and so trigger the demise of the nation state's supreme governing functions. The state has persisted, however. Its governments remain key players in the supranational setting. But they have to share the supranational arena not just with other supranational institutions but with other actors from the domestic milieu who are contributing to a lessening of their dominance at the centre. The cross-cutting responsibilities within the state for implementing, influencing and managing EC/EU affairs adds a further tier of complexity to decision-making. But it does not necessarily imply the imminent withering away or disintegration of the nation state's functions and role. The sources of such national disintegration as may be observed vary from state to state. They may not even be the product of a deepening of supranational integration. Instead, the seeds of disintegration may lie in the centralist tendencies of states themselves. They may be the product of a quest for local autonomy within national or regional boundaries. There does not, however, seem to be a global picture of why regional or local assertiveness arises within states. Dissatisfaction with national government for a variety of reasons may a predisposing factor. But neither it nor European integration are necessarily the primary stimuli: their confluence, however, may sharpen a questioning of the role, purpose and appropriateness of national level government.

European integration differs markedly from other attempts to create a common market or, more commonly, a free trade area. Its goal is political. Its instruments may be economic. But its essence and its *raison d'être* are cemented by the *acquis communautaire*; by the supremacy of binding supranational legislation over national legislation; and by the decision-making authority of supranational institutions and rule making. Different governments have at various times tried to move away from the full obligations that flow from EC/EU membership: some have canvassed different models for European integration. But for all their apparent tolerance of diversity in the pace at which integration is pursued by individual member states, the underlying assumption is that they are all moving towards a common and shared goal – however ill-defined – of European union. This applies even to the exceptions made in respect of functionally specific and lengthy transition periods for new members, or similar 'opt-outs' for the United Kingdom.

Integration is seen as a process rather than an end. This is both a strength and a weakness. It is a strength because it allows for flexibility, for gradualism, for adaptation and for accommodation to changing circumstances. It was at the heart of the Monnet method: supranational agencies were created to instil a sense of permanent endeavour in the process. This was coupled with the idea that each generation would lend its unique visions and imprints to the process. It was also assumed that each generation would subscribe to a set of shared core, often implicit, values such as working to preserve and further peace, to accord each member equal status, to work cooperatively in pursuit of the common good (however that was defined) and for the good of the community. The weakness of seeing integration as a process rather than an end lies in the potential to regress from as well as progress to an assumed common interest in closer, deeper cooperation. Experience denies a smooth transition or linear progression from loose inter-governmental cooperation with a minimum of commitment to elaborate and abide by common goals, actions and policies to a supranational, integrated polity (having some but not all the attributes of state authority). The vagaries of time, political and economic fortune, political and economic actors and individuals impose conflicting, sometimes contradictory and sometimes mutually reinforcing demands on the agenda of European integration.

What is the likely shape of European integration in the 1990s? Has a new phase started? Is it merely a composite of preceding phases? Is it self-contained (Pinder, 1986)? Is European integration unpredictable, random, territorially indeterminate and self-limiting? Or can it be inferred that the EC in seeking to establish itself as a European Union is making a transition from a *Gesellschaft* to the *Gemeinschaft*? In that process, has the role of the state and the nature of governance in the modern age been irrevocably altered?

The problem inherent in analysing European integration today rests with the implicit expectation that the EC/Union should 'act' whether internally or externally in an increasingly *politically* homogeneous and cohesive manner across a growing number and range of issue-areas. The institutions do not have the capacity to deliver and meet these expectations. There is a real crisis of governance within the EU. The locus of political authority has not been agreed by the member governments. Not only is the concept of a single or a central locus of political authority contested but the location of the main institutions remains disputed. Whether supranational authority is to be diffused or shared territorially, vertically or horizontally with the member governments and sub-national actors is open to conjecture and to discussion. That the absence of agreement over the parameters of supranational authority is problematic is attested to by the continuing wrangling over the political issue of the EU's democratic legitimacy. Member governments, by and large, still see supranational agencies as their rivals engaged in a zero sum game for power, authority and the loyalty of their subjects. The Maastricht and IGC 1996 processes not only show that domestic politics impinge upon the EU but that they can temporarily de-legitimize rather than legitimize reforms agreed by elected governments. It is certainly right to argue that any further treaty reforms should be subject to ratification not merely by national parliaments but by the European Parliament: that is, by a supranational *political* authority and by a supranational *political* process.

But it is precisely the question of the nature of that political authority which has to be resolved. In 1991, the member governments abandoned the logic of *unicité* (a single treaty structure) in favour of the more cautious, and ultimately untenable, gradualism implied by the three pillars. However, as MEPs insist, the TEU affirms the commitment to *unicité* and signals its attainment as a goal. Article C states:

The Union shall be served by a single institutional framework which shall ensure the consistency and the continuity of the activities carried out in order to attain its objectives while respecting and building upon the *acquis communautaire*.

The Union shall in particular ensure the consistency of its external activities as a whole in the context of its external relations, security, economic and development policies.

The IGCs and integration: beyond referendums

Since the 1980s, IGCs have become an important feature of European integration. Before then, the member states shied away from convening IGCs to reform the treaties. This was partly because it was felt that it would be impossible to attain the necessary unanimity to sanction reform. In retrospect it is assumed that when the EC was smaller in size, it was more cohesive. Paradoxically, its ability to agree fundamental reform was somewhat lower than it seems to be today. The issues of expanding the scope of integration and reforming the powers of the EC's institutions, and especially altering the inter-institutional balance of power (in effect to member governments' disadvantage) were so divisive as to deter governments from embarking on the wholesale reforms inaugurated in 1984.

It would be easy but misleading to argue that the explanation for this reticence lay in the EC's comparative youth and fragility; and/or in the compelling nature of the claims to autonomy of the more vociferous larger states. It is true that integration was still being tested and that the lead was taken from individual national governments and leaders. By contrast, from the early 1980s onwards, the EC acquired its own internal dynamic and supranational political momentum. Epitomized by the efforts of the democratically elected and legitimated European Parliament, its goals were shared by the Commission (though not necessarily for identical reasons). As before, their realization depended on the consent of national governments, but the creation of a political consensus about their desirability transcended national borders. The effect was to politicize integration; to legitimize that process and, crucially, to use the experience of integration to take it further. European union was not to be pursued for its own sake but because it enabled states to achieve goals together that they could no longer attain independently. It would be illogical, after all, for states to engage in a process that would weaken rather than enhance their capacities. (Herein lie parallels with the opening phases of European integration.) The problem was that the pursuit, management and implementation of integration across an increasing range of sectors that directly impinged on domestic politics required institutional reform. This was contentious and politically sensitive. But instead of shying away from it, political leaders grasped the nettle.

The issue could be faced at the highest political levels moreover, because inspite of its weaknesses the experience of summitry and the European Councils had conferred on the guardians of national sovereignty a visible role in promoting integration and union. The TEU entrusts the European Council with giving the Union the necessary impetus for its development and with defining its general political guidelines (Article D). National leaders, collectively, could invigorate integration and confer legitimacy on it. The IGCs are part of the process of legitimizing reform. But referendums have been hijacked for domestic political battles and have called the IGCs' legitimacy, and indeed that of national leaders and the integrative adventure, into question. There is a sense in which many of the policy initiatives broached by the TEU and IGC process simply entrench collective endeavour in new areas that have already taken root: the JHA is but one such example of this.

This experience was revealing not merely because the question of Union assumed a high profile and provoked heated debate among political élites but because it showed that even though the players interact in increasingly complex milieux and under systems of inevitably imperfect information, they are able to advance integration nonetheless. The political commitment to the goal of union is the unifying bond. The detail of its realization remains subject to the vagaries of the daily grind, institutional experience and competition, and unpredictable internal and external vacillations, pressures and developments. The next IGC cannot afford to overlook the achievement of *unicité*. The leaders need to accept the logic of empowering the EU to expand its integrative scope by matching this with adequate financial means and political authority.

A catalogue of reforms?

The context within which any changes to the European Parliament's powers (and hence also those of the Commission and the Council of Ministers) occurs will influence the IGC negotiators. The political constellation of most of the member states will change or be challenged at general elections before the end of 1998. Changes in government could have significant implications for member states' attitudes towards a number of reform proposals. It is highly likely that there would be more support for regional government and devolved administration; simplification of legislative processes; transparency; a Bill of Rights; greater power for the EP (which already has more power than the French l'Assemblée Nationale and which has seen the executive amend 50 per cent of its legislative proposals to accommodate its views – a figure unparalleled by any national parliament); a greater role for national parliaments; changed expenditure priorities; clarification over external relations and the common foreign and security policy; and a single text comprising all EC treaties. The history of institutional reform in the EC shows that minimalism and maximalism are complementary. The latter represents the high ground and a possible future vision, the former the *status quo* which inevitably changes slowly, sometimes too slowly. Constitutional and institutional reforms are inescapable. What shape might they take?

The European Union's institutional set-up is federal, heterogeneous, complex, de-centralized and diverse. A rudimentary but imperfect constitution exists. The current system is diverse and diffuse. The legislative procedures are too numerous and too varied. The division of legislative and financial responsibilities between inter-governmental and EU levels creates additional complexities. A simplified system, as sought by MEPs, would augment transparency, intelligibility, open and efficient government. The precondition of improving decision-making lies in reasserting the unitary structure (known as *unicité*) envisaged during the deliberations leading up to the adoption of the Treaty on European Union. This could entail a merging of the pillar structure of the Treaty in favour of establishing a single text to replace all existing treaties. The idea of a hierarchy of norms (constitutional, organic, and ordinary laws and regulations) was discussed during the Maastricht deliberations but not included in the resulting treaty. However, further discussion is likely as some states continue to see value in such a system.

Apart from such structural changes to constitutional documents, it is likely that the institutions will be reformed. There are numerous reasons for this but looming large is the consideration that every enlargement of the EC/EU has been preceded by a strengthening of the EC's institutions and a small increase in the powers of the EP. Refusing to sanction any further accretion of the EP's role is not a realistic option given the broad consensus in favour of some change. The EP may obtain a codification of the procedures it adopted itself in respect of the appointment of the incoming Commission and be granted a formal right to cross-examine the member governments' nominees. MEPs might express a vote of confidence on the *individual* Commission nominees before they take up office or seek a right to express a motion of no confidence in individual Commissioners. Some member states and others support the idea of enhancing the EP's role in appointing the Commission President, possibly by selecting or electing him/her from among MEPs or on the basis of a short-list of people agreed by the member governments.

The EP is seeking a greater legislative role for itself for a number of reasons designed to enhance the EU's functioning. Chief among these is the difficulty of achieving transparency, clarity and efficiency with the diversity of legislative procedures. They should be replaced by a *single* legislative procedure either derived from the co-decision, cooperation and assent procedures or applying co-decision across the board. At the very least, co-decision and assent procedures should be extended. To that end, the EP, as the elected arm of the EU's legislature should be strengthened: no proposals should be adopted that have not been approved by it.

The EP's existing powers as part of the EU's budgetary authority will continue to be explored by MEPs. The EP has important financial clout where international agreements and 'non-compulsory' spending are concerned. It is less happy with its limited role in respect of Economic and Monetary Union (EMU); and the evolution and role of the European Central Bank. There is no provision under the Treaty on European Union for co-decision in respect of EMU. How then can accountability be assured? There is likely to be continued pressure for co-decision to be expanded. The illusion that budgetary considerations and powers can be separated from legislative powers cannot be sustained. The old system of ADNs (amounts deemed necessary in the legislative process) is being replaced by a financial instrument whereby the Commission updates financial statements accompanying its proposals. The EP wants to enhance the redistributive capacity of the budget by exploiting its own powers. Article 199 of the Treaty on European Union incorporates into EC law, *inter alia*, the principles of budgetary unity and universality. However, specific articles on the common foreign and security policy and on justice and home affairs, which afford the EP very different – though limited – powers are far from clear. Disputes arise over expenditure as well as over the ambit of the EP's powers.

Given the complexity of institutional arrangements and inter-institutional relationships, four reforms are essential from the point of view of the EP:

(i)   all legislative matters should be subject to judicial review;
(ii) clarity between budgetary and legislative processes should be established. As steps towards the realization of EMU proceed, albeit possibly very slowly, the requirements of monetary policy will have to be examined and explained alongside policy and political priorities. The inseparability of budgetary and legislative matters must be recognized;
(iii) comitology should be clarified ; and
(iv) the EP's role as the conscience of the EU should be recognized. In seeking to enhance democracy, accountability and transparency in the EU, the European Parliament must be afforded an appropriate role across the board. It should not be excluded from the common foreign and security policy and Judicial and Home Affairs pillars. Such exclusion and a minimalization of its roles run contrary to the goals of transparency, openness and democratic accountability and merely exacerbate the democratic deficit.

However, one of the greatest obstacles to achieving transparency and efficiency derives from the EP's peripatetic nature. This issue may well be referred to the IGC. The EU's legislative institutions should have a **single seat**: Brussels. This would augment transparency, efficiency, intelligibility, accountability, democracy and clarity. The governments' aversion to confirming Brussels as the single seat of EU government owes something to the multi-faceted, vested financial interests of other host cities. It also owes a good deal to governments' continuing aversion to recognizing publicly that the EU does have a governing function that is embodied in a set of publicly visible institutions in a city that would inevitably come to be seen not just as the seat of EU government but as the EU's 'capital'.

It has also been suggested that democratic accountability would be better served if the EP ceded a scrutiny role to national parliaments. For reasons that will not be rehearsed here, the latter have only a minimal role in monitoring, scrutinizing and influencing the content of EU legislative proposals. It is not surprising, therefore, that the meaning of subsidiarity has been examined across the board and resulted in a number of proposals designed to insert national agencies − specifically national parliaments − formally into the EU legislative process. Should national parliaments have an official role at EU level? MEPs have never been averse to establishing mutually beneficial relations between themselves and MPs. The latter, fearful of the former's increasing power, have myopically, in many states, limited their access and role *vis-à-vis* domestic scrutiny of EC/EU proposals.

More recently, the idea of establishing a committee of national parliaments has been canvassed in some quarters as an antidote to the democratic deficit. Sir Leon Brittan suggested that such a committee might have four rights and duties:

- enforcing subsidiarity;
- challenging the legal basis on which laws are drafted;
- scrutinizing all laws taking the EU into new territory; and
- examining all laws where governments cede the right to act solely by themselves (on an intergovernmental basis) to the EU institutions.

Sensitive subjects like asylum and immigration might fall into this category. However, this is not necessarily the most appropriate way of encouraging national parliaments to exercise a responsible and effective role in respect of the EU legislative process. The EP itself originally comprised national MPs who held a dual mandate in both the European and national parliaments but who were, even then, not renowned for ensuring reciprocal influence in the European and national settings. They were certainly inhibited by the EP's extremely constrained powers but also by the youth of their institution and by national governments' and MPs' unwillingness to counter their playing a role in the domestic setting as MEPs. Adding another layer to the existing supranational institutions would not enhance efficient or open government. It would increase complexity and make it even less intelligible and transparent. National parliaments would be better engaged in redressing the democratic deficit that exists within the member states where EU policy-making is concerned. National parliaments should: enhance their scrutiny of decisions national ministers take in the Council of Ministers; support the EP's quest to strengthen its powers *vis-à-vis* the Council of Ministers; recognize that the adoption of co-decision as the predominant legislative procedure would augment parliamentary influence and democratic scrutiny; support the EP and improve co-operation with it.

National parliaments and the EP are neither rivals nor in competition with each other for power to influence and scrutinize EU legislation. A **Euro-Senate** should be resisted. Instead, a periodic Euro-assizes (of MEPs and MPs) might be convened, for example at the mid-term of the EP. This could provide not only for a public airing of priorities perceived by parliamentarians but could be linked to the issue of a state of the nation type declaration indicating future priorities. It might provide guidance on the short- to medium-term policy agenda of the EU. The national parliaments and the EP need each other. They need to work together constructively.

Another contender as a representative body at the EU level is the new Committee of the Regions. Some support the idea of its becoming a third chamber alongside the EP and of it developing its legislative ambitions. Its consultative status is unlikely to be changed radically by the IGC but it could usefully improve links with MEPs and its relevant committees as well as with local, regional and national representatives in the member states.

The overall implication is that some reforms are necessary and inevitable. They may not be radical. But any change, whether of institutions' internal procedures and inter-institutional coordination, is likely to have important constitutional implications for further reform in the medium term. Internal reforms must be effected within EU institutions to enhance efficiency, democratic legitimacy and transparency. This applies as much to the Courts of Justice, First Instance and Auditors as to the legislative institutions.

Where relations with the Council of Ministers and the Commission are concerned, the EP has some clear views on desirable – if not essential – reforms which must be addressed if only to enable the EU to act once further enlargement occurs. These include: more majority voting. This is inevitable and essential if an enlarged EU is to be capable of taking decisions within a reasonable period of time. Unanimity voting provisions might be replaced by qualified majority voting (QMV) across the board. This could be weighted – as MEPs have suggested – to ensure that the requisite majority required the support of at least one of the large member states. It might be based on a modified Spinelli-formula (the double majority of a majority of four-fifths of all member states plus a majority equal to four-fifths of the population of the EU). This would safeguard the interests of the large member states in the event of the further enlargement of the EU.

The question of reforms to ensure that the new member states cannot outvote the established members is sensitive. It is, however, imperative to find a formula that accommodates big state and small state interests and which rests on a continuation of coalition-building representing consensus and the common interest. As a result of the enlargement to Finland, Austria and Sweden, qualified majority voting rules had to be adapted to accommodate Norway's absence. Of a total of 87 votes, the qualified majority needed to adopt legislation is 62 and the blocking minority is 26. Simple majority voting is rarely used but eight votes must be mustered if a proposal is to be adopted under it. In addition, questions as to occupancy of key 'titular' roles needs to be confronted. For example, the Council Presidency is becoming cumbersome as the EU expands and small states lacking sufficient international experience or sharing the EU's history join.

MEPs have also considered the desirability of 'regionalizing' key positions. The IGC may consider whether the Presidency might be 'regionalized' and a

Table 13.4   MEPs and the IGC process

Name	Party	Nationality
Delegates to the Groupe de Reflexion		
Elmar Brok	EPP	D
Elisabeth Guigou	PES	F
Rapporteurs		
Jean-Louis Bourlanges	EPP	F
David Martin	PES	UK
Sub-rapporteurs		
Willi Rothley	PES	D
Alfonso Luigi Marra	FE	I
Francisco Antonio Lucas Pires	EPP	P
Raymond Dury	PES	B
Laurens Jan Brinkhorst	ELDR	NL
Enrico Ferri	NI	I
Anne Marie Neyts-Uyttebroeck	ELDR	B
Patrick Cox	ELDR	Ire
Alonso Jose Puer	UEL	E
Georges Berthu	EDN	F
Philippe Herzog	UEL	F
Dimitrios Tsatsos	PES	Gr
Maria Adelaide Aglietta	Greens	I
Giampaolo D'Andrea	EPP	I
Brendan Donnelly	EPP	UK
Dominque Saint-Pierre	ERA	F

parallel system (like that of the Commission) adopted of alternating big and small states. An implicit troika might be adopted for European Political Co-operation and Common Foreign and Security Policy as well as Judicial and Home affairs issues. The IGC may decide not to change current practice or to alter it in order to soften up opposition (ie among smaller states) to future streamlining in the event of further EU enlargement to even more inexperienced and small states (for example, in Central and Eastern Europe and the Southern Mediterranean). The IGC may embrace the idea of one of the Presidents of the key institutions serving for a longer period of time than is currently the practice. A President in such a position would inevitably be linked to an inter-governmental institution – probably the European Council. The EP would inevitably want to be in a position to play a role in the appointment and supervision of any such role. This in turn would require, as would all legislative procedure changes, that greater cooperation was facilitated, possibly via computer technology and the single seat, among the secretariats of the three main institutions.

It is obvious that internal reforms are needed to streamline and rationalize policy-making within the EP, Council and Commission. Given the increasing closeness of relations between the Commission and the EP, MEPs are likely to

have a particular interest in any changes to the Commission where rationaliz-
ation is on the cards. Five Commissioners currently have some responsibility
for some aspect of external affairs. Responsibilities may be divided geographi-
cally as well as functionally but overlap is inevitable. The Commission President may well be charged with ensuring overall coherence but ensuring better
coordination is not easy nor is it necessarily the most appropriate response to
the question of what role the Commission should have in respect of common
foreign and security matters which may be bound up with commercial, economic and other considerations. While streamlining of responsibilities in this
area is desirable, a case can be made for reducing the number of Commissioners
– and MEPs – overall. 'Regionalization' and hierarchy within the Commission
need to be explored before further enlargement. An enlarged EU of 20+
member states could not function efficiently if each member state had its own
Commissioner. Fewer Commissioners are needed. MEPs have already agreed
in principle that the EP's maximum size should be 700.

The IGC and the EP

A number of changes to the EP's formal role and powers are desirable. A
number of small changes would help the EU to become more transparent and
intelligible to the public. It is likely that during the negotiations various proposals will be put forward that may be dropped or postponed as part of a package
deal on reforming institutional affairs. They might include:

- recognizing Brussels as the EU's *single seat* of government because that is
  the *sine qua non* of improved efficiency;
- putting a ceiling (of 700) on the number of MEPs. This would inhibit the
  multiplicity of fragmented parties within the EP and contribute, indirectly,
  to cohesion, itself a precondition of effectiveness in the legislative process;
- endorsing *universal*, not selective, and *effective co-decision* with the Council
  across the board;
- acknowledging the EP's right to exercise its budgetary authority in line
  with recognition of the inseparability of budgetary and legislative processes;
- granting the EP the right to endorse the whole Commission and to
  'censure' individual Commissioners;
- giving MEPs a role in the appointment of the mooted Court of Review
  (entrusted with determining whether any EU institution, including the
  Court of Justice, had overreached its powers and acted *ultra vires*);
- granting MEPs a consultative role *vis-à-vis* the proposed competition
  authority (designed to be independent and to supervise the observance of
  competition laws);
- granting MEPs a consultative role in respect of CFSP and defence policy
  general principles and guidelines determined by the European Council
  (this might involve the extension of the assent procedure);

- granting MEPs a role in the examination of the reclassification of Community acts with a view to establishing legal hierarchy of norms among the different categories of acts (mooted but dropped in 1991); and
- affording MEPs the right to explore the inevitable expansion in the scope of citizen interaction with the Ombudsman, and related issues of transparency and judicial review and the EP's role *vis-à-vis* the ombudsman, when he/she is eventually appointed.

Linked to this issue is that of citizenship and a Bill of Rights. The Social Charter was originally conceived of as a social bill of rights. Over the years, the development of the concept of citizenship has been closely tied to the exercise of socio-economic rights (through freedom of movement of labour provisions – themselves limited in application to mobile workers) and the exercise of political rights inside the EU (in all sub-national and supranational elections in the state of residence but not national elections) and externally by the enjoyment of protection by other states' embassies or consular posts.

The Community treaties do not contain specific articles on fundamental human rights. The EP has consistently proposed the addition of a catalogue of such rights to them. It enumerated a number of fundamental rights in its Resolution of April 1989. This was slightly more extensive than the European Convention on Human Rights and led to some discussions as to the desirability of having two separate sets of Bills of Rights. In principle, however, the EP's position is broadly endorsed by the European Court of Justice. It has argued that fundamental rights form an integral part of the general principles of law, whose observance it ensures. It reviews the legality of all binding Community Acts and declares void those which *inter alia* infringe 'any rule of law relating to the application of the Treaty.' ECJ case law has established that this interpretation includes the general principles of law accepted in Western Europe and means that EC Acts are void if they conflict with the ECHR. In 1977, the Commission, Council and EP issued a solemn declaration in which they stressed 'the prime importance they attach to the protection of fundamental rights, as derived in particular from the constitutions of the Member States and the European Convention for the Protection of Human Rights and Fundamental Freedoms' (Schermers, 1990: 252–3). These views have informed the EP since then. Numerous declarations and resolutions of the EP and the other institutions, including the Ministers of Foreign Affairs acting under European Political Cooperation, affirm the principle of respect for human rights. (See References.)

The EP has issued declarations almost annually on human rights. In 1984 it created a sub-committee on human rights of its committee charged with examining foreign affairs and security matters. In 1992 it set up a committee which reported on public liberties. The Treaty on European Union's General Provisions affirmed the EU's respect for the ECHR. During the 1993 and 1994 deliberations in the EP on draft constitutions for the EU, MEPs noted that the existing treaties provided obligations for citizens but lacked guarantees that individual liberties would be protected. Such fundamental liberties cannot be taken for granted even in the 15 member states. The history of would-be EU members from Central and Eastern Europe indicates how necessary it is to spell them out precisely, irrespective of whether or not the Visegrad 4 and others join as full members or have a special associate status. MEPs' 1994 draft treaty contained an extensive bill of human rights and re-affirmed the European Union's adherence to basic rights under the ECHR and the basic rights set out in many – but significantly not all – member states' constitutions. They asked for a Bill of fundamental and human rights to be included in the deliberations of the next IGC. Whether they will succeed is open to debate. The issue is extremely complex and sensitive in some member states (notably the UK) partly because there is an assumption that because the ECJ can annul EC/EU legislation that infringes human rights, EU legislation will consciously be in line with accepted principles whereas national legislation may not.

There is a sharp contrast between those states which advocate the notion of the **citizen as a 'consumer'** and those that present **citizens as participants** who influence and shape policy outcomes. The two notions are not necessarily irreconcilable but they rest on opposed assumptions as to the role of citizens in a polity.

One conceives of the citizen as a passive subject, the other as an active player in the socio-economic and political processes of the EU. The former expects little from the citizen except compliance. The other expects the citizen to engage as an exponent, even challenger, of alternative ideas with a view to ful-filling the stated ideal of creating improved living and working conditions in an ever closer Union. The implication is that whereas the idea of establishing a passive citizenry may be satisfied by current treaty provisions including the right to participate in Euro-elections, the notion of an engaged citizen is far more extensive and troublesome. The disputes over positive vetting and access to the Ombudsman have highlighted this already. This is clearly an arena where MEPs might be expected to have a significant influence.

Conclusions

Any change to inter-institutional relations will significantly affect both the way in which legislation is made, adopted, passed and implemented and in the inferences drawn from them about the direction of European integration. Observers of European integration have queried whether political integration precedes or follows economic integration. Experience attests to the necessity of a political decision being taken either to initiate, authorize, consolidate or legitimize a deepening of European integration. Its realization may appear to rest on the adoption of facilitative financial and economic instruments, but these are employed by players acting in a political context (even at the micro-level within SMEs or among private and public sector players as well as at higher levels of government). The initial, and the enabling, decision is always political. So is the effect. Intra- and inter-organizational change must be facilitated in order to meet the institutional challenge of greater effectiveness, efficiency, democracy and transparency. Without this, it is unclear whether the Union will be able to consolidate itself sufficiently to attain its internal and external goals. The 1990s will be a time when the *political* face to integration has to be recognized and accommodated in its internal and external guises. The EP has a role to play in this. As a recognized and legitimate contributor to the IGC process, it cannot afford to allow the agenda to be set – and inexcusably limited perhaps – by those less mindful of the need to give effect to the quest for democratic, open and responsive government than MEPs themselves.

Moreover, politicization by itself cannot be separated from the requirements of securing consent to the way in which decisions are made, always – it is assumed – in a lawful, justifiable and justiciable way. However, whereas in the past, the EP's claims for greater legislative authority have rested almost exclusively on its assertion that direct elections conferred democratic legitimacy on it and so justified an accretion of its power, the debate has now changed qualitatively. The focus is upon the nature of the EU polity, the desirable norms, behaviour, institutional structures and participatory opportunities, rights and obligations of all involved primarily in the domestic but also in the international setting.

While there has been a shift away from an overt accent on the drafting of an EU constitution (blue-prints of which the EP has elaborated over the years), constitutional issues have not been eclipsed but have become regularized as part of *legitimate*, socio-economic and political contemporary discourse. This happened not just because the debate over the 'new European architecture' required a reappraisal of the EC/EU's structures but because there has been a significant, if almost imperceptible, switch in mutual inter-institutional interactions and expectations. The EU is beginning to be internalized and elections to the body representing the people have become normalized in the sense that they no longer are seen as the *single* most pressing reason for altering the way in which the EU legislates for the people and governs itself. However, the legitimacy of European integration will continue to be contested not just by governments and through the IGC processes but because closer links between the Commission and the EP imply a sense of joint responsibility for outcomes. The EP will have to defend the Commission's record in future along with its own. However, this does not mean that governments can duck their responsibility for EU actions, immobility or failures to act: the Council of Ministers still occupies a key role. Power-sharing with the EP is growing, but if MEPs have to defend their record and that of the Commission, they will inevitably have to be clear about the Council's decisions. This may impel them into a more confrontational position towards the Council. However, if the parties organize themselves effectively, constructive dialogue should be developed. The EP retains an interest in playing a considered, constructive and positive role in the European venture. It cannot, therefore, allow the IGC to pass without trying to ensure that it is seen to be contributing to the construction of a democratic, open, accountable European Union.

References

Casini, C *et al* (1994) 'A New Champion for Parliament', *European Brief*, 2: 32–34.

Closa, C (1992) 'The Concept of Citizenship in the Treaty on European Union', *Common Market Law Review*, 29: 1137–69.

Conseil et Etas membres, réunis au sein du Conseil, Résolution sur les Droits de l'Homme, la Démocratie et le Développement, 28 novembre 1991, *Bulletin of the European Communities*, 11–1991.

Conseil européen de Copenhague, Déclaration sur la Democratie 8 avril 1978, *Bulletin of the European Communities*, 4–1978.

Conseil européen de Dublin, Déclaration sur l'Antisémitisme, le Racisme et la Xenophobie, 25–26 juin 1990, *Bulletin of the European Communities*, 6–1990.

Conseil européen de Luxembourg, Déclaration sur les Droits de l'Homme, 28–29 juin 1991, *Bulletin of the European Communities*, 6–1991.

Conseil européen de Maastricht, Déclaration sur le Racisme et la Xénophobie, 9–10 decembre 1991, *Bulletin of the European Communities*, 12–1991.

Millar, D (1994) 'A Weak Ombudsman, a Weaker Parliament', *European Brief*, 2: 35.

Parlement Européen (1994) *Le Parlement Europeén et Les Droits de l'Homme*, Bruxelles.

— (1989) Déclaration sur les Droits et Libertés Fondamentaux, 12 avril, *Journal Officiel*, C120, 16 mai 1989.

— Conseil et Commission (1977) Déclaration Commune sur les Droits Fondamentaux, *Journal Officiel*, C103, 27 April.

Pinder, J (1986) 'European Community and nation-state: a case for a neo-federalism?' *International Affairs*, 41–54.

Schermers, H G (1990) 'The European Communities Bound by Fundamental Human Rights', *Common Market Law Review*, 27: 249–58.

Appendix
The New Members: Sweden, Austria and Finland[1]

Lee Miles & Andreas Kintis

The purpose of the appendix is to examine the role of the EP and European direct elections in the three new member states of the EU – namely Sweden, Austria and Finland. The first part analyses the Swedish European parliamentary election held on 17 September 1995 as this country represents the only one of the three in which direct elections have taken place since their accession in January 1995. The second part examines the role of Austrian and Finnish representation in the EP during the first year of full EU membership.

Sweden

The Swedish European parliamentary election was symbolic for both Sweden and the EU. From the Swedish perspective, this election was important for several reasons. It was the first direct election to the EP to take place in Sweden since it became a full EU member in January 1995. The elections, therefore provided the first official test of Swedish public opinion regarding EU membership since accession some nine months earlier and to a lesser extent, Swedish awareness of the role of the EP itself. To a limited degree, this election also attracted interest as Sweden had only narrowly approved full EU membership in its referendum by 52.2 per cent on 13 November 1994 and it was hoped by the pro-EU forces that there would be a significant increase in support for the EU now that the country was a full EU member.

Secondly, this election represented the first national election in which a new electoral procedure had been comprehensively used in Sweden. In other words, the Swedish European parliamentary election was also used as a constitutional experiment. Thirdly, this election was being conducted almost exactly twelve months after the minority Social Democratic government of Ingvar Carlsson had been elected to power in September 1994 and provided a timely opportunity for the Swedish people to voice their opinions on its performance.

For the EU, the Swedish election was also of significance. In one sense it was unusual as it did not take place at the same time as other European parliamentary elections in other member states. The Swedish experience is atypical in that it represents one of the few times when a direct election to the EP has not run concurrently with those in other member states since 1979. The Swedish direct election could provide a useful occasion to consider the potential for 'opinion transfers' between member states and whether, there are any implications for public opinion formation due to external influences of direct elections in other member states. Whether, for example, the 1995 result of the Swedish European parliamentary election will have any effects on the forthcoming Finnish direct election on 20 October 1996.

In addition, and in symbolic terms, the election also represented the first of the three direct elections to take place in the new member states since the enlargement of the Union to fifteen. It was argued that these elections may provide some rather tentative indicators of both the success of EU membership and to a lesser extent, the EP in these new member states. From this perspective, the Swedish example seemed to be the most relevant given the fact that Swedish public opinion had been consistently the least enthusiastic about the merits of EU membership and had according to opinion polls turned solidly against full membership since the referendum in November 1994. In theory, the Swedish European parliamentary election should have attracted substantial interest from both within Sweden and from outside EU observers.

Certainly, for the Swedes, the European parliamentary election was the first time that a personal vote system had been used in Sweden. The new electoral system had been tried previously in the 1994 local elections (although only to a limited extent) and would be used, if successful, for the forthcoming national elections in 1998. The electoral procedure used was in fact, based largely upon the party list system which had traditionally operated in Sweden. The country, was for example, treated as one large electoral district. However, the Swedish electorate was permitted in this election to also express a preference for particular candidates on the party list on their voting forms. The electoral rules for this election dictated that if any candidates gained a 'personal vote' of more than five per cent of that party's overall national vote, then these candidates would rank above all those on the national party lists. They would also rank in descending order of popularity according to the share of their personal vote.

This new electoral procedure did introduce some interesting, at least for the Swedes, new aspects to elections. Personal as well as party campaigns became more apparent as candidates sought to raise public awareness of their personal attributes in order to differentiate themselves more from other party candidates. For example, Cecilia Mälmstrom, a Liberal ran a personal campaign in Goteborg. Indeed, this new option seemed to be popular with Swedish voters as 55 per cent of those who voted in the EP election indicated a preference for individual candidates, even though this was not compulsory. However, at the same time, the new procedure may have also deterred some voters from voting, although this remains still to be proven.

However, despite all the symbolism associated with this Swedish election, the actual event was rather low-profile and low-key. To some extent, it can be argued that the Swedish voters were suffering from electoral fatigue as regards the EU. The Swedish government had only completed the rather long process of negotiating and ratifying full EU accession a year earlier and, for the most part of 1994 full EU membership had been a dominant political issue in Sweden. Indeed, the November 1994 referendum had proved to be the culmination of a rather divisive debate on the merits of EU membership and had only narrowly approved EU membership. Furthermore, public opinion polls during 1995 had already indicated rising disillusionment with both the EU debate and the EU itself. In July 1995 for example, 61 per cent of Swedes stated that they would vote 'No' if the referendum on approving EU membership had been conducted eight months later. The Swedish public believed that there have been few initial and apparent benefits to EU membership. Food prices, for instance, have not dramatically fallen in Sweden as they have done in Finland as Swedish agriculture was more closely adjusted before accession.

In particular, the party campaigns were rather lack-lustre. The campaigns can be roughly split into two types – those of the pro - and anti-EU membership parties. For the most part, the pro-EU parties tended to concentrate on themes which centred on how they intended to influence the future development of Europe. One of the main campaign slogans of the Social Democrats was *Sätt Europa i arbete* (Put Europe to Work), while the Liberals' (People's Party) main party slogan was *Se möjligheterna* (See the Opportunities). However, the pro-EU parties did not refrain from criticising each other's positions even though they all followed a pro-EU membership line. The Moderates, for example, led their campaign with the slogan *Man måste veta vad man vill* (One Must Know What One Wants), which was primarily targeted at the governing Social Democrats and alluded to both their limited success in revitalising Swedish public finances and took a swipe at their internal party division over the merits of EU membership.

In contrast, the two main anti-EU parties, the Greens and the Left Party tended to emphasise that they were pro-Europe, but against Swedish EU membership. In particular, the Greens focused on the theme of *Mot Europa* (which in Swedish is actually a pun as 'Mot' can mean 'against', yet also 'towards'). The Left Party also tended to follow this line and with the Greens, stressed the threats of EU membership to Swedish social and environmental policy, women's rights, the welfare state and Swedish democracy under the banner *Mer demokrati – mindre union* (More Democracy – Less Union).

Perhaps the most interesting campaign though and certainly the one that attracted both the most attention and criticism came from the Swedish Centre Party. The Centre Party based its campaign around the slogan, *Nja till Europa* (which actually translates in English as both 'Yes' and 'No' to Europe at the same time) and argued that it provided the most honest campaign of all the Swedish parties by taking a moderate stand. In theory, the Centre Party claimed that there were both positive and negative benefits to Europe and that this should be seen as the most pragmatic and realistic approach. However, in practice, this campaign was tailored to cater for intraparty opposition, especially within the rural heartland of Sweden where the Party is especially popular and for the most part, the Centre Party was criticised as being indecisive and vague.

The outcome of the Swedish European parliamentary election produced some quite striking results (Table 1). In general, the pro-EU parties did badly and the anti-EU parties benefited. Ingvar Carlsson's, Social Democratic Party (SAP) was the main loser, having gained only 28.1 per cent of the votes, compared to 45.3 per cent in the 1994 general election some twelve months earlier. However, this disastrous result for the Social Democrats cannot be entirely attributed to their pro-EU stance but did also reflect their open division on the issue and that they are presently in government. Although the pro-EU Liberals also suffered (seeing their share of the vote reduced to 4.8 per cent in 1995 from 7.2 per cent in 1994), the Moderate party of former Prime Minister Carl Bildt (which is widely regarded as the most solidly pro-EU party in Swedish politics) actually slightly improved its share of the vote to 23.1 per cent in 1995 from 22.4 per cent in 1994).

However, in contrast, the clearly anti-EU parties, the Greens and Left Party did exceedingly well. The Greens, for instance, more than trebled their share of the votes (17.2 per cent compared to 5 per cent in 1994), while the Left Party also doubled its share (12.9 per cent instead of 6.2 per cent). In sum, the electoral results seem to indicate that the Swedish electorate is far from enthusiastic about either EU membership or the role of the EP.

Table 1 Swedish European Parliamentary election results

	Votes	Per cent	Seats
Moderate Party	621,568	23.2	5
People's Party Liberals	129,376	4.8	1
Centre Party	192,077	7.2	2
Social Democrats	752,817	28.1	7
Left Party	346,764	12.9	3
Green Party	462,092	17.2	4
Christian Democrats	105,173	3.9	0
New Democracy	2,841	0.1	0
Others	70,443	2.6	0
Valid votes	2,683,151		
Blank and invalid votes	44,166		
Total votes	2,727,317		
Electorate	6,551,591		

Turnout, including invalid votes, 41.63 per cent.

Indeed, probably the most indicative variable in the Swedish election result was not the levels of party support but the very poor turnout amongst Swedish voters. The overall turnout, including invalid votes amounted to a mere 41.63 per cent and thus represented less than half of the entire Swedish electorate. In Swedish terms, this turnout figure was highly unusual as Sweden has a tradition of very high turnouts in elections and high participation rates; for example, the turnout for the previous September 1994 general election was 83.3 per cent.

Thus, in many ways, the first Swedish European parliamentary election displayed similar characteristics to those in other member states. The fact that these were secondary elections to a mostly unpopular European institution in Sweden had a dual effect. On the one hand, the electorate was suffering from the problems of electoral fatigue and growing disillusionment regarding the EU membership issue. Moreover, the fact that a new electoral procedure was also introduced could have also deterred voters. On the other hand, the elections also provided a chance for the electorate to register a 'protest' vote at the progress of the minority Social Democratic government, especially as the government had introduced numerous cost-saving reforms aimed at cutting the large budgetary deficits and high levels of national debt. To some extent, the very poor performance of the Social Democrats was exaggerated by the fact that they were in government and cutting public expenditure and trimming welfare state provision, which were unpopular among their traditional voters.

Similarly, the exceedingly good performance of the Left Party and the Greens can in part be explained by the transfer of disillusioned Social Democratic voters to these parties. Yet, it is also fair to say that success of the Greens and the Left Party must also be due to the fact that these two parties were the two main anti-EU parties. In particular, as the Social Democrats were internally divided on the issue, these parties acted not only as a reservoir for disillusioned voters protesting at the national performance of the Social Democratic government, but also for traditional voters across the political spectrum who vehemently oppose EU membership. In sum, the Greens and the Left Party benefited from both 'protest' votes aimed at the national government and from those focused at EU membership.

Nevertheless, the outcome of the Swedish European parliamentary election does have ramifications for both the Swedish political scene and the EP. As regards Swedish politics, both the Left Party and the Greens were quick to call for a national referendum on whether Sweden should stay in the EU and for the wider principle of using referenda to approve any further extensions of EU competencies. Although the former demand is unlikely and Sweden will continue to remain an EU member, the principle of using further referenda to approve any future TEU-based reforms will probably be heeded.

The result of the election will also have implications for the composition of the European Parliament[2]. Prior to the September 1995 election, all of the twenty-two Swedish MEPs were appointed by the Riksdag, based on the proportion of seats each party held in the national legislature. However, since the direct election, Swedish Social Democratic representation in the EP has been reduced from eleven to only seven MEPs, which will severely inhibit its influence on the Socialist Group in the EP. In particular, Pauline Green, leader of the EP's Socialist Group, claimed that the poor Social Democratic performance in Sweden illustrated that 'Europe has to deal with issues that affect people's lives. We need to take action on issues, like the Employment Union which the Swedish Social Democrats have been trying to pursue in the Council of Ministers. When the Swedish people see the result of that sort of policy, they will reassess the way they vote.' (Agence Europe 19 Sep 1994:3)

The Moderates retained their five seats, the Centre Party its two and the Liberals their single seat, although the Christian Democrats lost their only seat as a result of a fall in their vote to below the 4 per cent threshold for seats (their vote fell from 4.1 per cent in 1994 to 3.9 per cent in 1995). All these parties will retain their limited influence on their various party groups in the EP.

Nonetheless, whereas the Greens and the Left Party only had one Euro-MP (from the Left Party), the Greens now have four and the Left Party three. This will have two effects. First, roughly half of the twenty-two Swedish MEPs have been elected on anti-EU platforms and could be seen as comparable to Danish 'anti-marketeers'. Secondly, the inclusion of four anti-EU Swedish Greens will create some tension with the EP's Green Group as the Swedish Greens will now be joining a Group that is by no means anti-European. The effect of the incoming and directly-elected MEPs into the Parliament will have mixed results – in some cases, even damaging the homogeneity of the existing political groups. Yet, the small number of Swedish MEPs numerically will mean that the overall impact on the EP workings will be relatively small.

Austria

Austria intends to directly elect its MEPs within two years of the day of its accession to the EU. Therefore, although European parliamentary elections in Austria have not yet been conducted, it is possible to infer likely political preoccupations from an overview of the referendum to decide Austria's accession to the EU held on 12 June, 1994. The latter date was chosen to coincide with that of European elections in most countries of the Union.

Three months before the referendum, opinion polls suggested that 54 per cent of those eligible to vote were in favour of accession to the EU with 30 per cent against and 16 per cent undecided (Agence Europe 8 April 1994:3). According to Austria's Vice Chancellor, Mr Busek, in a statement made in Strasbourg on 19 April 1994, Austria was prepared to participate in the construction of a new European order.

Austria, he said, is 'for a reinforcement of the democratic and parliament structures, for further integration and deepening', and he noted that Austrian public opinion was generally favourable to membership in the EU. Mr Busek cited also the stability and security of Europe as a powerful reason in favour of enlargement of the EU.

Following the EP's assent to the accession of Austria, Sweden, Norway and Finland to the EU, the Austrian parliament on 5 May 1994 approved the accession agreement by 140 votes – the Social Democrats (SPÖ) and the People's Party (ÖVP), which made up the government coalition and the Liberal Forum (LF) – to 35 – the national right-wing Liberals (FPÖ) and the Greens, except for one member. Eight MPs were absent.

In a speech three weeks before the referendum Chancellor Franz Vranitzky claimed that his country's accession would 'in no way serve to create a Germanic bloc within the Community or to polarise the Union between North and South'. According to Mr Vranitzky in order to 'secure and expand the efficiency profile of the Union' the principle of majority voting would have to be extended 'to give the institutions of the Union the flexibility to establish the flanking policies to prevent distortions of the internal market and broaden the scope of quick common action in a variety of fields'. The Chancellor went on to underline three areas in which Austria would be 'particularly interested and prepared to contribute to the formation of future Union strategies'. These were the environment, social policy and the Union's relations with Central and Eastern Europe. Moreover, he called for 'new models for the flow of information and participation without hampering quick concerted decision-making and implementation'. (European Report 21 May 1994, I:3)

One week before the referendum a poll conducted by the institute IFES showed that 80 per cent thought that the 'Yes' vote would win, whereas 35 per cent said they would vote 'certainly' for accession, 20 per cent 'quite' in favour, as against 15 per cent 'certainly' against. Four days before the Austrians had to cast their votes in the referendum on accession pro – and anti – were finely balanced at 32-30 per cent, with the remaining 38 per cent still undecided. This was due to the 'No' campaign which brought together right-wingers, Greens, intellectuals and artists. At the forefront of the 'No' campaign was Jörg Haider, the populist leader of the right-wing Freedom Party. 'Austria First' was his slogan, suggesting that Austria in the EU would be overrun by a tide of foreign penetration and immigration and EU membership would lead to Mafia-style crime and 'square tomatoes' being foisted on the Austrian people. According to him, accession to the Union would also result in Austrian Alpine water be piped to Brussels in return for which, Austrians should expect to receive Spanish yoghurt containing lice and chocolate made from blood. Another leader of the anti-EU drive, the painter and architect Friedensreich Hundertwasser, had designed campaign artwork saying membership would be treason and likened the EU to Nazi Germany which annexed Austria in 1938.

Such statements served to stimulate the 'Yes' campaign into being more assertive. Ferdinand Lacina, the finance minister, warned Austrians that a 'No' vote would mean tax increases and higher unemployment whereas the economic minister, Wolfgang Schüssel, predicted a currency crisis, devaluation, slump and real wage cuts if EU membership was rejected.

Despite a strong indication by the polls that the vote would be close the 12 June referendum had as a result a resounding 'Yes' vote – 66,36 per cent against 33,61 per cent of 'Nos'. The overall turnout was 81,27 per cent. Foreign Minister Alois Mock, proclaimed that the result gave 'grounds for great optimism in Austria's future. This will undoubtedly strengthen our political standing in the world, particularly within Europe'.

Following the signing ceremony of the Accession Treaty the President of the Austrian Republic Thomas Klestil expressed the hope that Austria 'would contribute to the development of the EU through its affirmation of federalism and subsidiarity'. According to Mr Klestil Austrians 'were interested in the construction of a 'pan-European order and planned to contribute to this'. Moreover he cited 'the scepticism shown by his fellow citizens towards nationalism and intolerance and their particular openness towards broader European structures'.(Agence Europe 6-7 June 1994:4)

Following the accession to the EU on 1 January 1995, twenty-one Austrian MEPs were appointed. Eight of them are members of the Sozialdemokratische Partei Österreichs (SPÖ), six are from the Österreichische Volkspartei (ÖVP), five from the Freiheitliche Partei Österreichs (FPÖ), one from the Liberales Forum (LF), and one MEP is from the Grüne. Nine MEPs out of the twenty-one have joined the PSE, five the PPE, one the ELDR, one the V, and one is non-attached. Austrian MEPs are involved in all the main parliamentary committees of the EP with the exception of the subcommittee on Security and Disarmament and the subcommittee on Human Rights (Table 2). They are also active members of the various EP delegations responsible for relations with non-EU member countries (Table 3).

Finland

The Finnish European parliamentary election will be held on October 20, 1996, in conjuction with Finnish municipal elections.

On 16 October 1994 the Finnish referendum on accession to the EU was conducted. Finland was the first to vote for membership since it was the most likely of the three Nordic countries to decide in favour. The assumption was that a Finnish 'Yes' could help to produce 'Yes' votes in Sweden and Norway on the grounds that the four Scandinavian countries, including Denmark, could then form a strong Nordic block in Brussels.

One week before Finland's referendum, 49 per cent of the electorate planned to vote 'Yes' to membership, while 26 per cent were actively opposed to accession. The 'Yes' campaign was emphasising the economic and strategic advantages of EU membership, claiming that it will bring investment, long-term growth and a fall in unemployment. Most importantly Finland, traditionally not at ease with its powerful neighbour Russia felt that it would be more secure within the EU.

Those advocating a 'No' vote however were arguing that as an EU member, Finland would have to identify with Western security and defence policy, which would be provocative to Moscow. Moreover, Finnish farmers were reluctant to sign away their current national subsidies under a new streamlined EU agricultural system and they were afraid that they would be worse off under the CAP. In addition, Finnish women were sceptical about their future within the EU since they were anxious to avoid a diminishing of the benefits they received under high-level Nordic social security systems.

On 16 October on a turnout of 74 per cent, 57 per cent of those who voted favoured accession to the EU, while 43 per cent were against. Regionally the highest 'Yes' vote came from the southern part of the country, including the capital of Helsinki. By way of contrast the biggest 'No' vote came from the north of Finland. This was largely due to the stark division in the Finnish population over agriculture and fisheries.

The Finnish representation in the EP consists of sixteen MEPs. Five come from the Suomen Keskusta (KESK), four from the Kansallinen Kokoomus (KOK), four from the Suomen Sosiaali Demokraattinen Puolue (SDP), one from the Vihreat (VIHR), one from the Vasemmistolitto (VAS), ,and one from the Svenska Folksparti (SFP). Four Finnish MEPs have joined the PSE, four the PPE, six the ELDR, one the GUE/NGL and one the V. Finnish MEPs participate in the EP's parliamentary committees as well as in its parliamentary delegations (Tables 2 and 3).

Table 2

Committees	Austrian MEPs	Finnish MEPs
C1: Committee on Foreign Affairs, Security and Defence Policy	4 (including 3 substitutes)	4
SC1A: Subcommittee on Security and Disarmament	-	1 (substitute)
SC1B: Subcommittee on Human Rights	-	-
C2: Committee on Agriculture and Rural Development	4 (including 2 substitutes)	2 (including 1 substitute)
C3: Committee on Budgets	3	2 (including 1 substitute)
C4: Committee on Economic and Monetary Affairs and Industrial Policy	4 (including 2 substitutes)	5 (including 3 substitutes)
SC4: Subcommittee on Monetary Affairs	-	-
C5: Committee on Research, Technological Development and Energy	2 (substitutes)	2 (including 1 substitute)
C6: Committee on External Economic Relations	4 (including 2 substitutes)	2 (including 1 substitute)
C7: Committee on Legal Affairs and Citizen's Rights	1	1
C8: Committee on Social Affairs and Employment	2 (including 1 substitute)	1
C9: Committee on Regional Policy	3 (substitutes)	2
C10: Committee on Transport and Tourism	2 (including 1 substitute)	3 (including 2 substitutes)
C11: Committee on the Environment, Public Health and Consumer Protection	5 (including 2 substitutes)	3 (substitutes)
C12: Committee on Culture, Youth, Education and the Media	1	2 (including 1 substitute)

Table 2 (continued)

Committees	Austrian MEPs	Finnish MEPs
C13: Committee on Development and Cooperation	–	1
C14: Committee on Civil Liberties and Internal Affairs	2 (including 1 substitute)	1 (substitute)
C15: Committee on Budgetary Control	2 (including 1 substitute)	2 (including 1 substitute)
C16: Committee on Institutional Affairs	3	2 (substitutes)
C17: Committee on Fisheries	–	1 (substitute)
C18: Committee on the Rules of Procedure, the Verification of Credentials and Immunities	2 (including 1 substitute)	2 (substitutes)
C19: Committee on Women's Rights	2 (substitutes)	2 (including 1 substitute)
C20: Committee on Petitions	1	2
CT: Temporary committee on employment	2 (including 1 substitute)	1 (substitute)

Table 3

Delegations	Austrian MEPs	Finnish MEPs
D1: Delegation for relations with the Czech Republic, the Slovak Republic and Slovenia	2	1
D2: Delegation for relations with the Bulgaria and Romania	1	–
D3: Delegation for relations with Russia	–	2
D6: Delegation for relations with Estonia, Lithuania and Latvia	1	3
D7: Delegation for relations with Switzerland, Iceland and Norway	3	–
D8: Delegation for relations with South-East Europe	1	2

Table 3 (continued)

Delegations	Austrian MEPs	Finnish MEPs
D9: Delegation for relations with the Maghreb countries and the Arab Maghreb Union	1	–
D10: Delegation for relations with the Mashreq countries and the Gulf States	–	1
D12: Delegation for relations with the United States	4	–
D13: Delegation for relations with Canada	2	–
D16: Delegation for relations with Japan	–	1
D17: Delegation for relations with the People's Republic of China	1	–
D20: Delegation for relations with the Member States of ASEAN, South-East Asia and the Republic of Korea	1	–
D21: Delegation for relations with Australia and New Zealand	–	2
D22: Delegation for relations with South Africa	–	1
DM4: Delegation to the EU-Poland Joint Parliamentary Committee	1	–
DM5: Delegation to the EU-Hungary Joint Parliamentary Committee	2	1

Notes

1. The authors would like to thank Anders Widfelt, University of Goteborg and Amanda Smith, University of Humberside for their help in the production of this appendix.
2. Due to the fact that this appendix was completed shortly after the Swedish European parliamentary election, Swedish representation in the Committees of the EP was not finalised.

Index

Note: Page numbers in **bold** type refer to **figures**
Page numbers in *italic* type refer to *tables*
Page numbers followed by 'N' refer to notes eg 122N
To avoid confusion political parties are listed under individual countries